DR. B.R. AMBEDKAR : MAN OF MILLENNIUM FOR SOCIAL JUSTICE

DR. B.R. AMBEDKAR : MAN OF MILLENNIUM FOR SOCIAL JUSTICE

S.L. DHANI

PUBLICATIONS

KALPAZ PUBLICATIONS

DELHI-110052

Dr. B.R. Ambedkar: Man of Millennium for Social Justice

ISBN: 978-81-7835-565-8

Price: ₹ 990

Reprinted in 2014 in India by
Kalpaz Publications,
C-30, Satyawati Nagar,
Delhi-110 052
E-mail: kalpaz@hotmail.com
Phone: 9212142040

Printed at: G. Print Process, Delhi

Contents

PART IV
MEDIA REACTION FOR AND AGAINST VILIFICATION

PART V
AMBEDKAR-HATERS IN DOCK

PART VI
AMBEDKAR SEARCH FOR ALTERNATIVES

PART VII
AMBEDKAR AND HINDU TRADITIONALISTS

PART VIII
AMBEDKAR AND SOCIAL JUSTICE

PART IX
DR. B.R. AMBEDKAR MAN OF MILLENNIUM FOR SOCIAL JUSTICE

PART X

Preface

We know that the bug of the Man of Millennium has bitten almost every one on earth. There are many people who are engaged in finding out the man millennium for every walk of life. Dr. SL Dhani suspects that many of those engaged in the search for the Man of Millennium in any particular field start with a conscious or unconscious prejudice based on considerations of colour, creed, region, race or economic and social standing of the community to which their preferred candidate might have belonged.

The present work of Dr. Dhani titled *Dr. B R Ambedkar Man of the Millennium for Social Justice,* is sequel to his webs site *www.sldhani.com* which resulted in the publication of his book *Indian Freedom Struggle: New Insight* in 2003, which was released by well-known Hindi Scholar, Kamleshwar, in a function held in the Constitution Club, which was presided by Ramdas Asthwale MP, National President, Republican Party of India.

The Foreword to the Website in question had been given by Nanak Chand Rattu, who had served for 17 long years as Honorary Secretary to Babasaheb Dr. BR Ambedkar. In that capacity Rattu had typed practically all the manuscripts of the works of Babasaheb. The sense of devotion of Rattu to Babasaheb and to the cause for which Babasaheb himself stood is unprecedented. Rattu wrote about Dr. Dhani in 2001 as follows:

> *"The discerning readers may like to have a better idea about the background of Dr. Dhani's work and recognition from the opinions available in the concerned Web Site. The said opinions have emanated from numerous scholars and scientists, statesmen and administrators, the University teachers and generalists, the orthodox Hindus and the liberal ones.*

"The information that has been put on the said Web Site is the outcome of his hard labour put in by him in order to vindicate the position of Dr. Babasaheb Ambedkar, which has been unnecessarily undermined by Arun Shourie, obviously for monetary gain and for the purpose of strengthening of Hindu fundamentalism against the most exploited sections of Indian population, the hapless Dalits.

"It is obvious that by presenting the result of his labours for the information of the whole world, through the concerned Web Site, Dr. Dhani does not hope for any monetary reward or official recognition. He has done so only for the sake of his inner satisfaction and in larger public interest.

"The case of undue vilification of Dr. Ambedkar has unfortunately tended to widen the gulf between the Upper Castes and the Dalits, through the machinations of Hindu fundamentalists like Arun Shourie. They have been unfortunately turned into warring parties of unequal strength and resources. The Upper Castes have practically every thing and the Dalits have practically nothing. Still, Dr. Dhani has endeavoured to help the voice of the weak rise to a pitch, which can be heard even by their adversaries only if their conscience somehow gets pricked.

"This Web site is meant more for the Hindu Fundamentalists, who are suffering from an incurable disease of prejudice inclined to do injustice to those who have deserved nothing but justice for the ages. It is designed to shake their conscience not only in the interest of the Dalits and other weaker sections but also in their own interest."

Whatever was said by Nanak Chand Rattu in respect of concerned Website, which has died an unnatural death because of lack of funds, is true about the book in hand, since it is in continuation of the same old thrust, although this time with a view to finding India's man of millennium for social justice. Dr. Dhani is of the view that since thousands of individuals are engaged in the activity of finding the man of millennium in the fields of their choice, there is need to introduce some sort of objectivity and a sense of purpose in such a pursuit. Therefore, he raises the question as to what the Man of Millennium is about.

Dr. Dhani then illustrates as to how men of different disciplines and religions or other Isms have shown keenness to put forward the claim of one of their own men from what they call past history but which is in many cases not more than a myth. He has produced specimen of quite a few sites on the Internet, which have already invited millions of persons to respond to them. Some of the persons called upon to respond have given their comments, quite a few of which are far from being trustworthy. Dr. Dhani, then, underlines the preferences for the already expressed for Man of Millennium.

Dr. Dhani points out that most of the Indians do derive great satisfaction from the fact that one of them, Mahatma Gandhi, Father of Nation, continues to invite imagination of many notable persons of the world. The competitors of Gandhi in this behalf include Albert Einstein [according to Frederic Golden], Franklin Delano Roosevelt [according to Doris Kearns Goodwin], Hitler [?], [according to Nancy Gibbs]. Similarly, the Times magazine had also offered its own choice under the caption *"Who Mattered—and Why"*, under the pen of Walter Isaacson. William Shakespeare was picked up as Britain's Man of Millennium.

Dr. Dhani fondly hopes that we the Indians will derive similar satisfaction from the present endeavour also, since another illustrious Indian, Babasaheb Dr. BR Ambedkar, reputed to be the Father of Constitution of India, is being projected to be India's Man of Millennium for social justice. It is important to note that Dr. Ambedkar is not being projected to occupy the top slot through a non-serious question on the Internet but in the light of a serious research, which in itself might be received as being unprecedented.

In relation to the declaration of Shakespeare, Dr. Dhani points out that Urdu knowing people might like to opt for Ghalib, the eighteenth century Urdu poet and that the Hindus might like to consider the poet Tulsidas, author of *Ramacharita-manasa* [Popularly known as Ramayana] for this honour. Further, Pakistanis might like to confer this honour on Jinnah or Mohammed Iqbal, the poet. Similarly, he says that the division can be seen on the lines of mutually opposed philosophies of capitalism and communism. Even the freedom fighters of different countries can be made to stand in an independent queue. Thus he concludes that the list could be endless, depending on the emphasis one might decide to lay on particular parameters. He seems to be perturbed over the fact that some authors of web pages on the NeT have made the mockery of the question of finding the Man of Millennium, and asked the Net surfers to vote for certain people who according to him are not at all widely known in the world.

Dr. Dhani confesses that there cannot be any unanimity about any one being declared as the Man of Millennium, irrespective of the fact whether the man chosen is a living person or a dead entity. In spite of all this even Dr. Dhani has joined the fray of those obsessed with the question of finding the Man of Millennium. He has done so particularly for the reason that under the prevailing circumstances the millennium bug is not likely to stop agitating the mind of the people all round the world for quite a few years. Dr. Dhani admits that it is not easy to find the real man or women of the millennium in view of various difficulties. He suggests that prior to evolution of printing process, there could be no reliable research on any subject. Apart from prejudices of race, religion and regions, no comparable data could be collected from all over the world. Among other difficulties, existence of so many languages posed problems. These difficulties are obviously illustrative.

It is obvious that Dr. Dhani is keen to address the question of finding the Man of Millennium, if it has to be raised in any case, to the specially targeted group of readers. Such readers should be reasonably expected to have comparatively more reliable information about the man who is sought to be declared as the Man of Millennium. Being an Indian, Dr. Dhani has shown preference for discussing only the Indians and mainly in Indian context and that too in the sense of changing the course of history of India in a very significant manner.

Then, Dr. Dhani has chosen the issue of social justice, since it has been traditionally denied to the masses by the clergy, the rulers and their stooges in all times, all climes and in all regions of the world. Still, the question of social justice has been the favourite subject of discussion of all the religions, philosophies and the states, the world over. Further, the question of social justice has been ushering revolutionary changes in history since the subject directly affects the lives of the entire population of a country. In India, most of the religions have arisen by way of providing alternative to *Vedic* religion which according to the followers of those other religions has been oppressive to and exploitative of the common man because of the clever machinations of the religious preachers.

In Indian context, the Hindus have always remained obsessed with their social divisions, according to them, ordained by their religion, known as Hinduism but which they prefer to call it as the *Vedic* religion. They also like to compare it with the class system of the western conception, with a view to make their caste system appear to be natural and scientific. India claims to be the land of the *Rishis* or sages and the saints. But most of the saints and sages of India, with the exception of those of the medieval times, have supported and propagated the *Varna* or caste system which binds the people to the privileges or the disabilities with reference to their birth in a family tied to a traditional occupation. Thus, the system has been denying the normal opportunities of rising in life to common man in accordance with his own choice, capabilities and propensities.

In modern times, only Mahatma Gandhi got the reputation of caring for the most lowly people, through his declared policy of removal of untouchability, condemned in ancient times as untouchables, un-seeables and un-approachables. Mahatma Gandhi's main emphasis had been in solving all the problems of human beings through peaceful means, which has been appreciated all over the world. Most people do attribute the winning of freedom of India to Mahatma's philosophy of peace or *ahimsa*, although there are others who question this hypothesis.

Birth of Gandhism and Ambedkarism

The emergence of Babasaheb Dr. B R Ambedkar on the political scene in India turned the scales against the Mahatma and in his own favour by propagating the cause of the Untouchables, who are today generally referred to as Dalits. Separate Isms have come to take birth with reference to the philosophies of both, Mahatma Gandhi and Babasaheb Dr. B R Ambedkar. These Isms, known as Gandhism and Ambedkarism, are known to assume special significance at the time of elections to the Lok Sabha (Indian Parliament), the Vidhan Sabhas (State Legislatures) and local bodies.

Both Gandhism and Ambedkarism are poles apart so far as their objectives are concerned. Gandhism favours veiled reverence to Hindu social organisation or Varna system or caste system, whereas Ambedkarism is totally opposed to them, since the problems of the masses are directly traceable to the same Varna System.

Since Mahatma Gandhi has already been named as the Man of Millennium for non-violence, his example gives rise to an assumption of truth to whatever he did or wrote. If so, Ambedkar's philosophy gets automatically hit in view of the propaganda of his adversaries that he was opposed to Gandhi and Gandhism. Further, analytically speaking, Gandhism does not keep the overall development of the masses in social, religious, political and economic senses, and in Ambedkarism, the over all interests of the masses are central to its philosophy, a question naturally arises as to whether Ambedkarism becomes totally irrelevant in that behalf.

Dr. Dhani has successfully shown through his analysis in the book in hand that it Ambedkarism rather than Gandhism is going to stay in India. Mahatma Gandhi has been placed at the top slot of the Man of Millennium with reference to non-violence. But Dhani believes that the question of providing social justice to the common man is equally, rather, more important. He holds that social justice can be ensured only through Ambedkarism and not at all through Gandhism. Dhani has endeavoured to find India's Man of Millennium for social justice, and has come to the conclusion that Baba Saheb Dr. BR Ambedkar is the only person who deserves to be named as India's Man of Millennium for Social Justice.

Transparency of Dhani's Pesrsonality

An interesting feature of Dr. Dhani's personality has been that it has been quite transparent. He has been questioning many of the fundamentals and yet he has been regularly exhibiting a queer courage in the sense that he has been presenting his views and findings to the very dignitaries who have been among the best defenders of the prevalent theories and philosophies. He has been putting up his views before them with a view to having their immediate response to his presentations.

Opinion of Expert of Public Administration

For example, when he evolved the *Philosophy of Administration* in 1987, he requested a scholar to write a *Foreword*, who, in addition to being an enlightened Brahmin, was the Chairman and the Head of Department of Public Administration in one of the most prestigious universities, namely, Panjab University. He was Professor SK Sharma who, *inter alia*, observed as under:

> *"The present work is a sequel to Mr. S.L. Dhani's earlier thought -provoking interpretation of the most fascinating Indian Mythological Story, "Samudra Manthan" in his book "Politics of Gods; Churning of the Ocean", which had, inter alia, highlighted 50 ancient principles of gaining and retaining political power but having eternal relevance. The said book had evolved the indigenous 'Philosophy of Politics' by re-interpreting Hindu social system and religious philosophy. The present Volume evolves the 'philosophy of administration".*

About the book *Philosophy of Administration: Mythological interpretation,* Professor Sharma wrote:

> *"The book forcefully inspires the reader to think on unfamiliar lines and yet it remains simply absorbing up to the end. By questioning the very fundamentals of the established facts of the society, it points out to alternative fundamental truths of life, which have been ultimately found to be undoubtedly stark naked, to the astonishment of any theorist or practitioner in the field of public administration. Perhaps, it needed the astute eye of a sensitive*

brain, well-steeped into the ancient scriptures, duly equipped with the knowledge of the theory of public administration and the laws of the land and, finally, the decades of experience as practical administrator, coupled with a human heart, to unravel the truth behind the art of administration. And, undoubtedly, the author has at his command everything needed for such a delicate and yet most effective offensive against the prevailing massive ignorance about the ways of the society and it so-called saviours".

Opinion of Expert of Department of Philosophy

The Foreword to *Politics of Gods* had been written by Professor Dharmender Goel, the then Chairman and the Head of Department of Philosophy, Panjab University. The following observations of Professor Goel are significant in the matter of providing a peep into the scholarship and his sense of objectivity:

"This study of the most fascinating Indian mythological story "Churning of the Ocean" is a sequel to Mr. S.L. Dhani's earlier pioneering Indological work on the theory of cosmogony in Hindi - Srishti Vikas Ka Manvantara Siddhanta (Manvantara Theory of Evolution of Universe) which was well-received in scholarly and scientific circles within India and abroad and an appreciative notice of the Press, Radio and Television including B. B. C. in the late seventies.

"Mr. S.L. Dhani, as an author, has well shown here his wide scholarship in presenting his ideas regarding "Churning of the Ocean". Besides, his well-equipped semantic skills in unpacking some of the most intriguing and cryptic linguistic terms, he has a rich and fertile interpretative mind that enlightens, in an extremely delicate manner, some of the otherwise fortuitous mythical juxtapositions of seemingly arbitrary motifs in Pauranic Traditions.

"He applies his thoughts not for the sake of scholarly luxuriance for its own sake, but wishes to provide a fully articulated frame-work of analysis and appreciation of life, society and ideology of Aryan or Brahminic culture that assimilated non-Aryan culture while the Aryans subjugated non-Aryans and condemned them as Shudras and Asuras in ancient periods of Indian history. How far Mr. S. L. Dhani would be able to carry conviction with authorities in the field of scientific analysis of folklore and ethno-methodology is open to question, but I certainly feel pleased that the present work is again a pioneering effort and, as such, merits open-minded careful consideration."

Dhani had joined the Punjab Civil Service in 1959 only with educational qualification of an ordinary graduate. But by the time of his retirement, he had acquired *Master's Diploma in Public Administration* (1964) from the Indian Institute of Public Administration, New Delhi, *Degree of Bachelor of Laws* (1971) from Panjab University, Ist Class *Master's degree in Ancient Indian History, Culture and Archaeology* (1974) from Kurukshetra University. Finally, he secured the Degree of Doctorate of Philosophy (PhD) in 1989, again from Kurukshetra University.

Earlier, he had also obtained Certificate in *Promotion of Small Enterprises in Developing Countries* from Cranfield School of Management, Cranfield, United Kingdom, in 1979.

Dr. Dhani had shot into international prominence with reference to the *Manvantara Theory of Evolution of Universe*, based upon the Hindu Vedas and the Puranas in 1975, that is, 14 years prior to his acquiring the Doctorate of Philosophy. His doctoral thesis was *Solar System and Its Evolution: A Study Based upon the Puranas.*

Between 1980 and 1987, Dhani published a number of books all devoted to the re-interpretation of Hindu philosophy. Such books soon established him as an "Indological Genius".

Incidentally, he became a member of the premier service of Government of India, namely, the Indian Administrative Service (IAS), to which he was admitted with effect from 1970. Dr. Dhani is one of rare examples of a person, who has been commanding respect both in government and in public, because of his qualities of head and heart. He set an example in the IAS in 1989 by sacrificing his service for high public values after giving a tough fight to the government, he had been serving, by starting a tirade of exposing the organised corruption in government, which was continued for a number of years. When threatened with humiliation and reprisals, he chose to opt out of the service in a bid to establish high ideals of service.

Shooting into International Prominence

Dr. Dhani had propounded the Manvantara Theory of Evolution of Universe, based on the *Vedas* and the *Puranas* in *1975*, as already stated above. He had first of all presented his theory on invitation before the Theosophical Society, Chandigarh, on 26 June 1975, the day on which Mrs. Indira Gandhi had clamped Emergency on the Country. The story regarding the presentation of the theory was released by UNI. It made appearance in many of the national papers on 28 June 1975, including *The Hindustan Times, The Indian Express and The Patriot*. On the basis of newspaper reports, the Editor of *The World of Science* programme of All India Radio, New Delhi, interviewed Dr. Dhani. The interview was broadcast in the first week of July 1975 along with those of the reputed scientists including Dr. D S Kothari and two scientists from National Physical Laboratory. Dr. Dhani was then interviewed by many of the national newspapers over a period of quite a few years. Such interview reports soon caught the attention of the prestigious organisations like the World Theosophical Society and the Indian National Science Academy.

Invitations for Participation in International Seminars

The World Theosophical Society was going to hold the International Seminar on *Theosophy and Science* in December 1975 at its international headquarters, Adyar. Similarly, the Indian National Science Academy was going to organise *International Seminar on Aryabhata,* at its headquarters in New Delhi, to commemorate the 1500th birth anniversary of Aryabhata, the 5th century astronomer of India.

Both the organisations invited Dr. Dhani, by establishing his identity apparently on the basis of the newspaper reports, to present his findings on his *Manvantara Theory of Evolution* in their respective international seminars. In response to the invitations, he did present his findings in both the seminars in December 1975 and November 1976.

Incidentally, his paper was prominently reported in the official bulletin of the World Theosophical Society. The news about the Centenary celebrations had been covered, *inter alia,* in *The Mail* of Madras, which had mentioned just three names - John SBS Coats, the International President of the World Theosophical Society, the famous scientist Dr. R. Ramanna, and SL Dhani.

Astounding Feat

Moreover, Dr. Dhani's paper became the only paper out of those presented in the National Science Academy, to be reported in the national papers. The report appearing in the Times of India was four-column-captioned, covering about 1500 words. The fact that

- Dr. Dhani had never been a science student;
- He was at the relevant time, an administrator, who is normally unwelcome among scholars, the scientists and the University teachers; and
- His presentation pertained to the field of Vedic studies and

modern disciplines of science like Astronomy, Geology, Anthropology and Biology etc., must bear some testimony to the status of the relevant papers, presented by him, on invitation.

Later on, the BBC featured Dr. Dhani for its Overseas Programme about his theory in October 1979, when he happened to be undergoing a training course in *Promotion of Small Enterprises in Developing Countries at Cranfield* in UK.

On his return from UK in November 1979, Dr. Dhani published a book on his theory in question in Hindi for the simple reason that the theory had used lot of Sanskrit terminology, which could be best appreciated by the scholars of Hindi, the spoken language of the Hindus. The book was titled *Pracheen Bharat mein Vijnaana: Srishti Vikaas kaa Manvantara Siddhaanta* (*Science in Ancient India, Manvantara Theory of Evolution of Universe*). The book was reviewed in quite a few national papers and prestigious Magazines. Vishuddhananda Shastri, Kulapati (Chancellor) of *Gurukula Vishva Vidyalaya, Vrindavan* was among the long list of scholars to offer wholehearted appreciation.

Special Audience Granted by Mrs. Indira Gandhi

A copy of the book was sent to the then Prime Minister of India, Mrs. Indira Gandhi. She had been good enough to have it examined by her own secretariat and on its recommendation to invite him to personally present a copy of the book in a special presentation ceremony in her office on 21st June 1980.

Thereafter, Satellite Television had also carried a 20-minute programme when Dr. Dhani had explained the salient features of the theory on the Television, with the help of artistic visuals. The concerned producer of the Television was one Gopal Gupta.

Interest Taken by Prestigious Institutions

In 1983, Bharatiya Vidya Bhavan, Bombay, invited him for a lecture on the same subject. Earlier in 1977, he had lectured in Yogic Research Institute, Lonavala, Maharashtra. The occasion was incidentally reported in a section of Poona Press.

After some years, as already mentioned, Dr. Dhani made his theory a subject of regular research as a "Thesis for Doctorate of Philosophy", in the Department of *Ancient Indian History, Culture and Archaeology,* under the guidance of Prof. U V Singh, the then Chairman of the Department. Consequently, the Kurukshetra University awarded him a regular Degree of PhD in 1989, in the year of his seeking premature retirement at the age of 56.

Challenging Government on Institutionalised Corruption

Dr. Dhani continued to challenge his own government on the question of institutionalised corruption in government for a period of more than two years at a stretch. The print media kept on continuously cheering him up for his unprecedented fight for values. Mr. Rajiv Gandhi, the then Prime Minister of India, came to know of his struggle and volunteered to ask his secretariat through a demi-official letter to get details in that connection. That was the time when he had already served three month-notice on the government to seek premature retirement. Incidentally, he had written the notice on Christmas of 1988, and served on the government the next morning.

Stint in Politics

After retirement, Dr. Dhani was invited by Rajiv Gandhi to join the Congress, by offering the chairmanship of one of the Cells under the Haryana Pradesh Congress Committee (HPCC) as also membership of the said HPCC. Dhani joined as such in middle of 1989 but the state stalwarts like Bhajan Lal, did not relish his joining the party through direct intervention of the Congress High Command, headed by Rajiv Gandhi. Dhani thought it proper to part company with the Congress leadership, especially in view of growing nearness between the then Chief Minister of Haryana, who had been challenged by Dr. Dhani, and Mr. Rajiv Gandhi. Soon after, a national level registered political party, known as *All India Kisan Mazdoor Sabha* made him its Working President. In order to give him a free hand, it also made him its national president towards the end of 1991. Partly on account of lack of financial resources, and partly on that of his obsession with higher values, he belied the expectations of the Party, which had been established as back as 1936.

Literary Pursuits

Although Dr. Dhani is basically a researcher, yet his life is not entirely devoid of emotions. His literary activities have already earned him *Babasaheb Dr. Ambedkar National Award* in 1985 and Sahitya Shromani Award, in 1991. He remained National Vice President of Bharatiya Dallit Sahitya Academy for a period of five years. Presently, he is the patron of *Haryana Dalit Sahitya Academy, Pradesh Haryana*, which is functioning under RS Sirohiya, as president. He is also the guest columnist of *World Reflections, An International Magazine,* being issued from New Delhi.

He has already fed about 100 manuscripts into the computer, which are awaiting publication. He has also written a book on personality development titled *Opportunity Well-Caught, Hands You Out Jackpot,* under the joint authorship with Captain JS Bishnoi.

Poetic Flights

He is equally proficient in Hindi, Urdu and English. He has published books only in English and Hindi. He has composed more than three thousand verses in Urdu and Hindi. Some of his collections are titled as *Srimad Bhagavadgita Tark ki Kasauti Par, Prasna Shatak, Swagat Shatak, Apne-paraye Shatak, Manvantaracharya Shatak, Vidambana Shatak, Uljhan Shatak, Vyavastha Shatak, Rajtantra Shatak, Itihas Shatak, Jeevan-Rahasya Shatak, Dharma-Prayog Shatak,* and *Agadon ke Naam. Shatak* signifies a 'century' or collection of 100 verses. All of them are likely to be sent to press in due course.

Overcoming Worst Adversities

He has been able to accomplish all that in spite of very serious handicaps, hardships and adversities. Since he was born in pre-independent India, and in the month and year, which saw the signing of Poona Pact, namely 1932, conferring the first installment of human rights on the Dalits, he naturally came to have a much larger share of adversities, from the first day of his emergence in the world, which he had inherited from his parents, under an unholy tradition. And, he did not have either money or woman to save himself from adversities in order to take the advantage of Chanakya's advice contained in Chanakya-Niti. Further, he did not have means suggested by Chanakya to protect himself, yet he has been steadily rising in life with reference to his career, prosperity, intellect, education, and scholarship, of course, in the light of his own dreams and the objectives set before himself. Some of the readers might feel inspired to emulate his example and draw inspiration to the extent possible for them. Some of the adversities that came his way are illustrated as under:

1. He was born in one of the poorest and the traditionally most hated families of Indian society who were claimed by the Hindu leadership as Hindus for demographic reasons but were not given a treatment of equality by the so-called Hindu fraternity.
2. The members of his community had been condemned to work as landless labourers, whose wages were limited to unwholesome cooked food served only once a day.

3. Not only they could not purchase any land for construction of houses for themselves, they were also not in a position to demand any cash wages or accumulate any kind of wealth.
4. If they happened to get some wealth from somewhere, the so-called higher-class people were free to loot that under religious and state sanction.
5. They were considered community slaves, who could be ill-treated by any higher caste man in his discretion and yet they had no forum to which they could go for redress of their grievances.
6. They were not entitled to dress well, wear any ornaments or discuss their problems even among themselves. They had to lead a forced life of poverty, drudgery, humiliation, forced ignorance and an organised exploitation.
7. They were required to live on the outskirts of villages. They had been forced to exist on a sub-human level, which was worse than that of the domesticated animals.
8. No medical facilities were available to them since the tradition did not permit them to be touched by others and they could not touch others and,
9. They were not permitted to draw water from public wells and the doors of public schools and hospitals had remained closed to them since times immemorial.

I am quite sure the book in hand will set new standards of thinking and inspire better sense of objectivity among the authors and the readers. Sense of objectivity deserves to be used by everyone engaged in the pursuit of excellence in any particular field. I do believe that any kind of pursuit aiming at promoting the best human welfare shall be guided by a proper sense of social justice, without which even spirituality will remain a barren slogan.

Ambedkar's Role in Granting Human Rights to Masses

History of India available till today seems to highlight the role of mainly Mahatma Gandhi to the exclusion of many other stalwarts of freedom movement. Mahatma Gandhi is the Father of Nation whereas Babasaheb Dr. B R Ambedkar stands acknowledged as the Chief Architect of Constitution of India. Mahatma Gandhi has already been rightly declared Man of Millennium for Non-Violence. Babasaheb Dr. B R Ambedkar had led the tirade against the caste system, which was incidentally not supported by Mahatma Gandhi. These two stalwarts had come into clash in connection with Dr. Ambedkar's masterpiece *Annihilation of Caste.*

Both of them had participated in the Round Table Conferences convened by the British rulers over the question of transfer of power to the Indians, during the period between 1930 and 1932.

Dr. Ambedkar had forcefully argued there for granting separate electorates to the Depressed Classes or erstwhile untouchables or modern Dalits. Consequently, the British Government had announced the Communal Award, granting the said separate electorates to such classes. Mahatma Gandhi had opposed such electorates by resorting to fast unto death. Ultimately, the said award had been modified as a consequence of which Poona Pact of 1932 came into being between the representatives of the Hindus on one hand, and Dr. Ambedkar, as a representative of the Depressed Classes, on the other.

Dr. Dhani has described Poona Pact as the Magna Carta of Dalit rights. It was the first formal government act conferring, *inter alia*, human rights to the Dalits, that laid the foundation of social justice initially for 15 per cent population of India, thus far condemned as untouchables. Later on, the principle came to be extended to Other Backward Classes also, who had been condemned as Sudras, a class that had been denied all kinds of rights under the Hindu scriptures and hence by the state.

The book in hand has a bearing on the history of freedom movement of India, in connection with which both Dr. Ambedkar and Mahatma Gandhi had endeavoured hard in their own particular ways. In that connection also, there is an independent book of Dr, Dhani published only in 2003, which chiefly dwells on the roles of these two great personalities. The said book is titled *Indian Freedom Struggle: New Insight*, mentioned above in which he questioned the veracity of the story of freedom movement that is still being taught in schools and colleges.

Ambedkar Role in Confering Social Justice on Masses

Dr. S L Dhani's book in hand, examines the role of Babasaheb Dr. B R Ambedkar in the matter of conferring social justice to the masses of India. He did so first by questioning the very fundamentals of the exploitative social system known as caste system, then by securing human rights for Dalits under Poona Pact and finally as the Chief Architect of Constitution of India. The book also brings us face to face with many new insights into the freedom struggle, which is bound to baffle some serious students of history of the movement, particularly, in the background of socio-politico-religious analysis of some of the more important events concerning the movement.

A Word About Dr. Dhani's Credibility

In spite of very serious hardships and adversities, Dhani has not only survived in life but has always been registering stupendous progress in so many fields that he has come to be known as multifaceted personalities. For an ordinary person, it would have been impossible to cope with the demands of realities of life. His formal educational qualifications, progress and evolution of his writings make it evident, that before he picks up his pen on any subject, he first acquires the requisite formal qualifications and then comes out every time with a pioneering work. The experience has shown that his every coming work has always caused a stir among the intellectuals and scholars of the relevant fields. The first formal shock of the type was expressed by *The Statesman,* in 1975, with reference to his *Manvantara Theory of Evolution of Universe,* which was based on the Vedas and Puranas, and which had endeavoured to establish a synthesis between, science and religion, between ancient and modern, and between the orient and the occident.

Dr. Dhani has been in the habit of presenting his manuscripts for evaluation to the established scholars of the concerned field, some of whom could be naturally considered even as his natural adversaries, judged from the angle of Indian social and religious realities. Then, most of his books were reviewed in prestigious newspapers and magazines. Further, his knowledge and understanding was consciously or unconsciously tested by shell-shocked scholars by inviting him to lectures in reputed academic and scientific organisations.

Nature has been both kind and unkind to him. Some of the adversities that he had to face have already been listed. But that is only one side of the coin. In spite of them all he has been surpassing his fellow students and colleagues in some sense or the other. In spite of his birth in the erstwhile family of untouchables, he was able to become a Sanskrit graduate, even when study of Sanskrit had been practically denied to every non-Brahmin. After joining civil service, he became the first officer from his State, the erstwhile Punjab, to secure formal training and qualifications in Public Administration, from the distinguished Institution known as Indian Institute of Public Administration, New Delhi.

Presenting Example of Deserving before Desiring

When circumstances required him to perform legal duties as Head of Law Department in Municipal Corporation, Delhi, in 1968, he became a Law Graduate (LL B) as a private candidate from Panjab University, in 1971. When academic circles felt challenged by his strange facts and logic and presentations and when they refused to take his logic and scholarship seriously, on the ostensible ground that he could not be regarded as expert or specialist in any subject in the absence of formal master's degree in the relevant subject, he secured first class Master's Degree in Ancient Indian, *History, Culture and Archaeology* from one of the most prestigious universities, Kurukshetra University again as a private candidate, in 1974.

Faced with a challenge from his senior colleagues in senior bureaucracy, he wrote a treatise known as *"Philosophy of Administration: Mythological Interpretation"*. Professor S K Sharma, the then Chairman and Head of Department of Public Administration in Panjab University, had hailed the work in the following superlative terms :

> *"The prevailing administrative theories made popular by Management School led by F. W. Taylor and Human Relations Management propounded by Elton Mayo have touched only limited aspects of administrative system. Herbert Simon, Donald Mc. Gregor, Peter Drucker, Dwight Waldo and Spencer have directed their attention only to specific operational problems, but till today there is no comprehensive theory, which can take care of all the intricacies of the working of the administrative institutions and organisations and of their impact on the society. Mr. Dhani's comprehension is all-pervasive and includes the salient features of all the leading thinking in this area and makes a useful addition by breaking new grounds and bringing out salient features of the new foundations".*

Since he was challenged by the unsympathetic Hindu religious Pundits, he came out with pioneering analysis of Hindu mythology and wrote something which was titled by him as the "Politics of Gods" after analysing the story of *Samudra-Manthana*, the mother of Hindu mythology, with reference to which, he was described in reviews as an iconoclast. When he was challenged with reference to the so-called divine origin of the Varna theory, he subjected *Manu-Smriti* to serious analysis. The concerned book titled *Hindu Scheme of Things: Socio-Political Analysis of Manu-Smriti,* was debated in the most prestigious daily of North India, namely, The Tribune, for a long period of four months between April 1988 and July 1988. He came out unscathed in that debate and created a history. The then Editor-in-Chief of The Tribune Group of Papers, V N Narayanan, while praising the scholarship of Dr. Dhani wrote as under:

> *"This book points to a basic fact about every Hindu – who synthesises opposites. Mr. Dhani's analysis may sound shockingly outrageous, but Hinduism has perhaps the oldest tradition of atheism."*

He went on to declare, 'For those filled with illusions and myths, Mr. Dhani provides a brilliant de-mystifier. Are we ready to countenance so much reality about ourselves?"

Some of the readers may like to repeat the same question about the book in hand. Either on account of ignorance or our own prejudices for or against particular personalities or values, some of us tend to overlook some incongruities prevailing in our thinking about the nature of certain thoughts being injected into our minds about some simple matters. It must be the duty of some of us to set such thinking right to the best of our abilities. Dr. Dhani has ventured to perform that duty and according to my assessment he has been successful in his mission. I wish him all success and pray that he continues playing such a role for many more years.

I am sure those believing in sense of objectivity and rationality, will find the book in hand, not only readable but really informative. The book incidentally highlights the dangers of fundamentalism of all sorts. It also underlines the great need for a real secular approach, which is one of the most important factors in the matter of ensuring a place of honour and dignity to all the citizens of India, irrespective of their caste and creed.

D S Ranga

Acknowledgements

The theme of the book in hand was conceived immediately after deliberate campaigns of vilification of the two most important Icons of modern India, Mahatma Gandhi, Father of Nation, and Bharat Ratna Babasaheb Dr. B R Ambedkar, Father of Constitution of India, were launched, almost simultaneously, in Maharashtra, when India was busy celebrating the Golden Jubilee Celebrations of Indian Freedom.

Mahatma Gandhi, was maligned through a street corner play titled Ami Nathuram Godse Boltoi, in which the role of Bapu's assassin was played by Gopal Godse, the brother of the assassin, who had returned after serving a life term of imprisonment for being the accomplice of the assassin. **Babasaheb** was vilified through a book titled Worshipping False Gods, Ambedkar and the facts which have been erased. It seems by unsuccessfully trying to erase the memory of Dr. Ambedkar, its author had volunteered to be remembered after his death, on the analogy of Nathuram Godse.

At that time, this author had launched his Website sldhani.com, by way of a rejoinder that carried a Foreword by his great friend Late Shri Nanak Chand Rattu, who had acted as Honorary Secretary to Dr. Ambedkar for full seventeen years, who in that capacity had typed almost all the manuscripts of the books of the latter.

From that Website, the idea of publishing this author's **Indian Freedom Struggle: New Insight** took birth, which got translated into reality, four years ago. The said book was released by the top Hindi Playwright of his time, Kamleshwar, in an impressive function held in Constitution Club, New Delhi, that was presided over by Ramdas Athwale, National President, Republican Party of India. The said book is now being serialized in a monthly magazine of Chandigarh, titled The Consumer Censor, which is being edited by the veteran journalist, U K Bhanot.

After the publication of that book, many friends and admirers urged this author to write another book, highlighting the role of Babasaheb in the matter of restoring Social Justice to the masses of India, who had stood condemned in Hindu scriptures as Sudras and Ati-Sudras. In this connection, obviously, this author feels greatly indebted to all those who have beem mentioned above.

Captain J S Bishnoi deserves a special mention, who has been to this auithor a pillar of strength and proving the saying true that a friend in need is a friend indeed.

The author feels a special sense of gratitude to D S Ranga, a scholar and a social activist connected with an organization known as **Lakshya**, who agreed to write the Preface to the book in hand.

The book in hand would not have seen the light of the day, without the encouragement of RK Verma, Advocate, Punjab and Haryana High Court. M G Bhagat assisted this author by revising the whole manuscript and providing important inputs. The help of G S Thind of Canada, through long discussions has been commendable.

Credit in this behalf also goes to the industrialist-cum-philanthropist T L Verma and his son Mohit Verma who voluntarily offered luxurious comforts to this author in their well-furnished guest houses, which fact made the work of finalising the manuscript of the book in hand, really enjoyable.

Thus, the encouragement and help, provided to this author by all concerned in different ways, at a time, when he stands disowned by his own kith and kin, has been wonderful in many ways.

S L Dhani

Part I
Preliminary

1. Bug of Man of Millennium

1

Bug of Man of Millennium

The bug of the Man of Millennium has bitten almost every one on earth. There are people who are engaged in not very fruitful effort to find out the man millennium for every walk of life, in every discipline of the university, in every art form and the like. If they had engaged in the search for such a man in any particular field in a dispassionate manner, the so-called search might have led to some workable conclusion.

But those engaged in the said exercise unfortunately start with a conscious or unconscious prejudice for someone based on considerations of colour, creed, region, race or economic and social standing of the community to which their preferred candidate might have belonged. The problem becomes more serious when a person is sought to be declared a Man of Millennium out of all the disciplines.

Man of Millennium: What is he about?

Still, the question must arise behind *The Man of the Millennium* as to what is the Man of Millennium all about? The following facts might suggest an answer to the above-said question.

The Christians of the world seem to have established an exclusive Web Site on the NeT, obviously to influence the world opinion in this behalf, which has been named as —http://homepages.enterprise.net/bcfgoodnews/screenshow/mi....

Accordingly, many men and women started posting replies and comments in this connection. In that case, it becomes a question, which can be debated only among the extra rich who can afford an Internet connection and plenty of time and energy to spend on the topic.

If so, the poorer people and those standing for the poor might stand already defeated in the race, even before they could think of joining the one.

Incidentally, the search is already on for *Man of Music for Millennium.* Entries therefor are being invited at the Internet at the site —http://millman.co.uk/. And Shakespeare is already being sought to be voted as the Man of Millennium at the Web Site —http://www.dawn.com/daily/19990103/int10.htm. He has already been declared as being Great Britain's Man of Millennium.

Some Web Sites in Search of Man of Millennium

In this behalf, the Microsoft Corporation may not like to do this honour to any one else but to its own man being one of the greatest inventors in the history of the world. In this connection one might like to visit the Web Site — http://2000.tvspielfilm.de/date/date.htmland the Site — http://countdown2000.com/The_Millennium_Fun_Page/Millenni...

Other sites, which might be of interest in this behalf, include the following:

—http://www.edfman.com/y2k/mm2a.htm

—http://www.angelfire.com/wi/hitman3000/

—http://www.mtv.com/news/headlines/981016/story3.html

—http://www.fidm.com/Features/Fclub/fclububag.html

—http://www.gov.im/tourism/activities/walkwild/walk1.html

andhttp://www.maintenanceresources.com/ReferenceLibrary/Main...

Interestingly, in the Battle of the Millennium - HyperMart Dollar Auctions, hi-tech office equipment, bidding starts at $1 with no reserve. ONE MAN.. ONE YEAR.. ONE CHAMPION.. It's been one thousand years since mankind has last experienced the dawn of a new era. In this connection, the site —http://vwr.hypermart.net/botm.htm can be visited. These examples are only illustrative.

Significantly, the importance of the bug of the millennium can be judged from the fact that today the number of Web pages on the Internet runs into humnreds of thousands.

Man of Millennium

Help - Personalize

Search Result Found 98769 web pages for man of millennium

The Millennium - the man behind it all! - The man behind the Millennnium - what is the millennium all about?

—http://homepages.enterprise.net/bcfgoodnews/screenshow/mi...

Re: Man/Woman of the Millennium - Re: Man/Woman of the Millennium Posted by Nima Iranpour In Reply to: Man/ Woman of the Millennium posted by on January 10, 1999 at 05:18:04 PM EST Posting:Ferdowsi is a good choice, he is definitely a great national hero of Iran. Hafez, also...

—http://www.ait-cec.com/Jebhe2mesg/773.html

Millennium Man - Millennium Man Music for The Millennium Enter site here

—http://millman.co.uk/

Shakespeare voted Man of Millennium -DAWN - International; 03 January, 1999 - 03 January 1999 Sunday 14 Ramazan 1419 Click Here to Visit our Sponsor Shakespeare voted Man of Millennium LONDON, Jan 2: William Shakespeare, picked as Britain's man of the millennium, was hailed on Saturday as an international superstar - but...

—http://www.dawn.com/daily/19990103/int10.htm

Man of the millennium, invention of the millennium, event of the millennium and more! -

The very latest y2k news and millennium news

—http://countdown2000.com/The_Millennium_Fun_Page/Millenni...

Man Millennium - December 31, 1998 Contact Information Group Y2K Committee

Name Committee/Div. Phone Richard Askew Legal/Corporate 44-171-285-3149 Mark

Brinkman Systems/Brokerage 1-312-663-7991 Sheila Dunsire Finance/Corporate

44-171-285-3157 Mick Elliott Status...

—http://www.edfman.com/y2k/mm2a.htm

THE MAN OF THE MILLENNIUM - Status Bar Text Wiper

—http://www.angelfire.com/wi/hitman3000/

Walking and Wildlife on the Isle of Man-Millennium way - Return to map The Millennium Way was the first long distance footpath in the Isle of Man, established to coincide with the Millennium Year of Tynwald, the Parliament of the Island, in 1979. The route of the footpath is based on the 'Regia Via', the.

—http://www.gov.im/tourism/activities/walkwild/walk1.html

Method Man Goes To the end of The Millennium For New Album - 10.16.98 10:00

EDT Method Man Goes To the end of The Millennium For New Album Wu-Tang

Clan's Method Man 28.8 RealVideo It's been four years since Wu-Tang Clan rapper

Method Man released his solo debut, "Tical," and it's taken the impending end of...

—http://www.mtv.com/news/headlines/981016/story3.html

Fashion Club Monthly Trend Report - Millennium Man - No Summary

—http://www.fidm.com/Features/Fclub/fclububag.html

Preferences Already Expressed

The Indians might derive great satisfaction from the fact that one of them, Mahatma Gandhi, continues to invite imagination of many notable persons of the world. It will be pertinent to have an idea thereof.

There are features existing on the NeT under the title *Test Your Knowledge: How much do you know about Mohandas Gandhi?* There is another poll being conducted on the Net under the title Poll, *Do you believe Mohandas Gandhi should be Person of the Century?* Then, there is a debate started by the interested parties about a number of persons, one of whom could be named the person of the Century. Those who have been made to join this debate include Nelson Mandela and Johanna McGeary. The Competitors of Gandhi in this behalf include Albert Einstein [according to Frederic Golden], Franklin Delano Roosevelt [according to Doris Kearns Goodwin], Hitler [?], [according to Nancy Gibbs]. Similarly the *Times* magazine had also offered its on choice under the caption *Who Mattered—and Why,* under the pen of Walter Isaacson.

Bill Clinton considered F D Roosevelt and Churchill as the most important individuals in the first half of the 20th century who, according to him, had reawakened the West to its core values: freedom, civility, common decency in the face of evil, destructive forces of hate. They had been credited with battling the great diseases of the century: nihilism and defeatism. Churchill's apostles argue for him as the century's titan on these grounds, observed Clinton.

There are the sites on the NeT suggesting that "The Mahatma, the Great Soul, endures in the best part of our minds, where our ideals are kept: the embodiment of human right and the creed of non-violence. Mohandas Karamchand Gandhi is something else, an eccentric of complex, contradictory and exhausting character most of us hardly know. It is fashionable at this *fin de siècle* to use the man to tear down the hero, to expose human pathologies at the expense of larger-than-life achievements. No myth raking can rob Gandhi of his moral force or diminish the remarkable importance of this scrawny little man. For the 20th century — and surely for the ones to follow — it is the towering myth of the Mahatma that matters. There are others like "Read the full story by Johanna McGeary; Appreciation: Nelson Mandela writes on Gandhi; Photo Essay: A photographic tour of the life and times of Mohandas Gandhi. There are Web Resources like Mahatma Gandhi Album; A detailed site offering everything from quotes and cartoons to book excerpts and an Ask Gandhi section.

Still others have already expressed themselves in favour of Shakespeare being declared the man of the millennium for the whole world. The Indians and Pakistanis, in line with the thinking of Shakespeareans, might like to opt for Ghalib, the eighteenth century Urdu poet. The Hindus might like to consider the poet Tulsidas, author of *Ramacharita-manasa* [popularly known as Ramayana] for this honour. The Pakistanis might like to confer this honour on Jinnah or Mohammed Iqbal, the poet.

The Communists of the World might like to confer this honour on Marx or Lenin. The South Africans might decide in favour of Nelson Mandela. Similarly, Khomeini of Iran cannot be left behind according to some hard core Muslims. Likewise, Some Americans might regard George Washington to be the fittest person to hold that honour. The list could be endless, depending on the emphasis one might decide to lay on particular parameters. There are votaries for Hitler also, in this behalf.

Totally Unknown Persons in the Run

Will the readers feel amused to know that some authors of web pages on the NeT have made the mockery of the question of finding the Man of the Millennium? One such person has given on the Net a very long list of names, out of whom, the Net surfers have been asked to vote and also to give reasons why. This author must confess his total ignorance about all these so-called great men. Each one of them must have achieved some kind of greatness, but we because of geographical distance or other reasons, may not have heard about any of them. Such a situation might be a pointer to the need for finding a man of the millennium etc. from out of those belonging to a reasonably limited geographical unit. In any case, let us be informed about the great men about whom all the Net users all over the world have been asked to choose from. They are Ray Sibul, Doug Reese, Nic McPhee, Billy Beckwith, Roland Guyotte, Mark Fohl, Abe Welle, Dennis Seyer, Dennis Dahl, Robbie Bahr, Matt Knakmuhs, Eric Volk, Bobby Noonan, Jim Severson, Von Myart, Loren Vaughn, Terrance Robinson, 30 Point Buck, Todd Neuharth, and Jim Gremmels.

Incidentally, the debate that was started in respect of *The Person of the Century* can now be naturally taken to the question of finding *The Man of the Millennium.* From the above, it would be appreciated that there cannot be unanimity about any one being declared as the man of the millennium, irrespective of the fact whether the man chosen is a living person or a dead entity. Still, it is true that since someone has posed the question, the millennium bug is not likely to stop agitating the mind of the people all round the world for quite a few years. It is in the light of this possible certainty that this author has also decided to join the race of those out to declare someone of their choice as the man of the millennium.

Futility of Exercise

However, it is a futile exercise to find or name a man or woman of the millennium for the whole world. For example, in one case, the nominator, an Iranian, has not been able to imagine anyone out of Iran although those outside Iran might not have heard the name of the man or woman sponsored to be the one of the millennium.

Besides, it would be reasonable to first determine the qualifications for such a man or woman. I am an Indian and, as such, I am more likely to be better informed about the great men in Indian context. Here also, it would be worthwhile to suggest particular discipline out of which man or woman of the millennium is sought to be chosen or voted for.

One Changing Course of History Has Better Claim

To my mind only such a person should be considered for the top slot, who has played the most outstanding role in changing the course of history, and that too in relation to restoration or conferring of social justice. Such persons have so far been coming out of the field of religion, with the exception of Karl Marx, who did not seem to believe in any religion or in any God.

In Indian context, only such a person, who has endeavoured to confer social rights and social justice to the vast masses, who have been denied such rights through the ages, under the impact of the social stratification sanctioned by the unjust Varna system, should be considered for such an honour. Likewise anyone, who has been supporting such an exploitative social, religious, political and economic system, should be debarred from such a contest.

In that sense, even Mahatma Gandhi would stand disqualified from the contest, in spite of the fact that he is commonly believed to have played significant role in gaining freedom for India. Judged in this light the only name which comes to my mind is that of Bharat Ratna Babsaheb Dr. B R Ambedkar, who is remembered as the Father of Indian Constitution and as the modern law-giver, after superseding the mythological Manu, who is declared by the Hindus as being the first law-giver. Manu's law had deprived the bulk of population of all kinds of rights. Ambedkar was not only the most original thinker and crusader for restoration of social rights and justice to vast sections of Indian humanity, but he was also successful in his objective.

Coming to Mahatma Gandhi, he was no original thinker and he was only a prisoner and a follower of tradition. Any follower cannot deserve any special respect in connection with the question that is being considered at present. Dr. Ambedkar was one man in India, who had broken new paths for the masses, and he had himself treaded thereon. In view of this, my man of the millennium is Dr. B R Ambedkar. I would like to suggest a note of caution in connection with the consideration of the question concerned. All the living personalities of the world must be kept out of such a contest.

Now, let us have a look at the manner in which man of millennium or century is sought to be voted for. Here ia an extract from Internet about Mahatma Gandhi :

Man of the century

International Opinion Poll

The first of its kind on internet where people of this globe voted with reason and personal details.

Who is the person of 20th century?

Yes

"Mohandas Karamchand Gandhi"

Mahatma Gandhi

Survey Result

Survey held on Internet

Website Address

http://www.geocities.com/CapitolHill/Lobby/9727/

Date of Commencement

15th March 1998

Date of Conclusion

5th December 1999

Total Number of Voters

92480

Yes Votes

87866

No Votes

3691

Don't Know votes

923

Result

Mohandas Karamchand Gandhi

is

"The Person of 20th Century"

The visitors' Views and the complete report are compiled in a book by name

"The Man of Millennium"

This work will soon be submitted to various organisations working in the direction of Non-violence.

You may help me by submitting this book to the dignitaries and personalities of the world for their considerations.

You may help me by publishing this work in different medias like newspapers, TV or on Internet or in magazines.

I personally need help from all the people who may share their valuable time and submit this work to the mayor of their city, chief of the country, chief of the organisation.

Please email me your name, address and number of copies of the book. You will receive it.

Then visit dignitaries or chief of your city may be mayor, if possible submit it to the chief of your country. Publish report in the media if possible or just send me the photographs. I will make the complete album of the global submission of this report.

Thank you very much for your tremendous responses.

I love you all.

Sunil Ganatra

Lecturer in Chemistry,

Institute of Science, Civil Lines,
Nagpur - 440001, India.
Email : ganatra@nagpur.dot.net.in

Since the bug of man of millennium has already bitten many of the writers, since around the same time, when many stalwarts and others are in the run for being put on the top slot, and since a great man like Ambedkar has been vilified by a man known as Arun Shourie, by dishonestly comparing with him with the measuruing rod of Mahatma Gandhi, it is considered by this author not only to vindicate the position of Ambedkar, but also to consider him for the top position of India's Man of Millennium for Social Justice, since social justice is the most important issue the world over, but particularly in India.

In India, at one satge, before coming of Ambedkar on the political scene of India, more than 75 % of Indian population, known as Sudras, who are today referred to as OBCs, had been denied the human rights under the Hindu social organisation known as Varna-vyavastha. In addition, not less than 15 % of population was regarded as untouchable, un-seeable an un-approachable, which stood condemend as Ati-Sudras, or worse than the Sudras.

Ambedkar was the only man in India who had by taking up the cause of lowliest of the lowly, the untouchables, had shocked the Haves of India and embarrassed the British rulers in Round Table Conferences that had been convened by the then British Prime Minister, during the period between 1930 and 1932, and when he had been able to secure a communal award for the concerned section of population. But strangely, the same man was vilified without any justification and by a man, known as Arun Shourie, who had no locus standii to do so, barely two years before the close of the last millennium, in the year 2000

Relevance of Recent Controversy On Vilification Campaign against Ambedkar

Not oly this, in the Golden Jubilee year of India's independence, the same Shourie condemned Babasaheb as a false god in *his book Worshipping False Gods, Ambedkar and the Facts that have been Erased*. The purpose of that endeavour was to suggest that the latter should not be worshipped or idolised in the manner it is being done today. But, the same Shourie came to be idolised for his "feat" of vilifying Babasaheb Dr. B R Ambedkar for the fault of the latter's unprecedanted endeavour to demolish the Varna system on account of its being totally inhuman and the biggest obstacle in the progress of not only the individual, but also that of the whole nation.

Failure of Mission of Vilification

Shourie had, of course, failed in his book under reference to state as to what he meant by false God or by true God. Throughout that longish book, Shourie, by measuring Dr. Ambedkar against the measuring rod of Mahatma Gandhi, has tried to prove that Ambedkar was Gandhi-hater, that the former never supported the latter in the struggle for freedom of India, and that Ambedkar brought shame upon Hindus by criticising the sacred Hindu scriptures. Moreover, by arrogating to himself the position of giving a judgement on both Gandhi and Ambedkar, the author of the above-said book of vilification, Shourie, has tried to prove himself as also Mahatma Gandhi as true gods, while projecting Babasaheb Ambedkar as a false god. In view of that event being very recent, It will be important to throw more light on that issue, in the next chapter, since the hype that was experienced in 1997 is likely to attack the sense of objectivity of this author with reference to the assumption being examined in the book in hand.

Part II
Search for Greatest of the Great

2. Search for Greatest of the Great
3. Test of Greatness
4. Test of Vilification :Tie between Gandhi and Ambedkar
5. Difference Between Vilification of Gandhi and Ambedkar

2

Search for Greatest of the Great

Some of the celebrities, who are being considered for the top slot of the Man of the Millennium, have been mentioned in Chapter 2 There are some others who deserve mention in this behalf. All these persons are surely going to set our minds to the way one must approach the question of finding *The Man of the Millennium.*

Some Celebrities Under Consideration

According to a site on the Internet, **Albert Einstein** (1879-1955) was the pre-eminent scientist in a century dominated by science. 'The touchstones of the era—the Bomb, the Big Bang, quantum physics and electronics—all bear his imprint', so was said by Frederic Golden. Thus, Albert Einstein is the choice of Frederic Golden. He seems to be supported by Stephen Hawking, Madeleine Nash and Roger Rosenblatt. Franklin Delano Roosevelt is the runner up for the Man of the Century as Goodwin.

In this context, Churchill and Roosevelt had been described to have reawakened the West to its core values: freedom, civility, common decency in the face of evil, destructive forces of hate. The challenge that Hitler presented became the occasion for Churchill and Roosevelt and the lovers of freedom to battle 'the great diseases of the century: nihilism and defeatism.' Churchill's apostles argue for him as the century's titan on these grounds.

Bill Clinton in his *Captain Courageous* is full of praise for one of the past presidents of United States of America, F.D.R. and Winston Churchill. Bill Clinton says, "In the century's struggle for freedom, Roosevelt won two decisive victories: first over economic depression and then over fascism ... Roosevelt's leadership steered not only America but also the world through the roughest seas of the century."

Roosevelt had been President of the United States for 12 of the most tumultuous years in the life of the United States. He had guided his nation through democracy's two monumental crises—the Great Depression and World War II. Twice in mid-century, capitalism and democracy were in the gravest peril, rescued by the enormous efforts of countless people summoned to struggle by their peerless leader—Franklin Delano Roosevelt.

Mohandas Gandhi [Mahatma Gandhi] is the runner-up for this slot as per Johanna McGeary. Nelson Mandela's choice is the same as expressed in his article The *Sacred Warrior*. **Mahatma Gandhi has already been mentioned, in respect of whom the responses are being invited on the NeT on more than one site. There is an official Web Site on the Internet, which, *inter alia*, discusses 'Mohandas Gandhi' as the possible man of the century. In an age of empire and military might, he is believed by Johanna Mcgeary to have proved that the powerless had power and that force of arms would not forever prevail against force of spirit. He is also believed to have been *'the embodiment of human rights and the creed of non-violence.***

All these endeavours are pointing out to the need for certain good through the actions or the illustrations of the respective choices of the individuals or groups, making such endeavours. Naturally, they are against the evil. This must lead us to the question of knowing what the evil is.

The Web Site continues: "No myth raking can rob Gandhi of his moral force or diminish the remarkable importance of this scrawny little man. For the 20th century—and surely for the ones to follow—it is the towering myth of the Mahatma that matters.

"His work and his spirit awakened the 20th century to ideas that serve as a moral beacon for all epochs." The idea behind quoting these references is not to express a total agreement to the opinions noted, but it is to emphasise that the number of those being made to compete for being declared as the Man of the Century or the Millennium is quite large. It must, of course, be realised that it depends in certain cases on the mere whim of those who can afford to indulge in the game of keeping the debates alive, by spending lot of time, money and energy on such questions. Still, the importance of those who have played an effective role in changing the shape of the world or the course of history, in a particular region, cannot be minimised. This cannot be so because it lies definitely within the power of such people to inspire many others of coming generations to emulate their examples.

Unlikely Names

Apart from those already mentioned earlier, the number of those being considered as the person of the century or millennium as per the Internet is fairly large. Some of the names will appear to some of the readers quite unlikely. For example, Nancy Gibbs had asked in his article *The Necessary Evil?* "Why not Hitler?" The specific question, apparently put not very seriously, was "Why all Adolf Hitler's destructiveness is not enough to make him Person of the Century?"

According to the said site, there has been a long modern conversation over the nature of evil. The debate goes back to Socrates. It was argued that anyone who was acquainted with good could not intentionally choose evil instead. But according to many modern thinkers, Hitler, is claimed to have demanded a whole rethinking about good, evil, God and man. And thus, his contribution deserves a special merit, since he actually not only shook the whole world, but he also set us to rethink about the manner this world should be governed.

Ron Rosenbaum, author of "Explaining Hitler" says, "He [Hitler] showed how much lower we could go, and that's what was so horrifying. It gets us wondering not just at the depths he showed us but whether there is worse to come."

Are persons like Hitler entirely irrelevant? "It is a fundamental tenet to many religions that evil, while mysterious, may clear the way for good, that the soul is perfected only in battle, that pain and ecstasy are somehow twins, that only a soul ... that has truly suffered can truly realise joy."

Before Hitler, it has been said, the West was ruled mainly by thin-blooded despots, with the exception of the more entrenched democracies of England and the U.S. Hitler did not believe the Western democracies capable of defending the principles they espoused—and as "they wavered and appeased and betrayed in the face of his expansion, Hitler appeared to be right."

Danger of Subjectivity

It is evident from the above that each one participating in the strange debate to find out the man of the Century or the Millennium has talked from his own angle, which cannot be easily divorced from his sense of subjectivity. Moreover, each one has talked on the basis of one's own knowledge limited by the limits of his own horizon. Naturally, every author has targeted a particular kind of readership or audience, which is sought to be informed about the specific point of view of the concerned author.

The world is very vast. It is divided into many regions and countries. Many of the countries like India have complex and composite culture, influenced by many religions and languages. Some of the countries may have single culture and a single language. Besides, a period of millennium or 1000 years is very long period for the world as a whole to allow a comparable data being available for the correct selection of the man of the millennium. This difficulty will be experienced even in case of a single country even if it has had a single culture and single religion.

In Absence of Universally Accepted Comparable Data

In the centuries prior to the time when the printing process started, there was no systematic method of collecting universally accepted comparable data for any particular subject or individual. Comparable data can be said to be available mainly after invention of printing machines a few centuries ago. Prior to that there were of course written records in the form of the hand-written biographies of some kings or emperors or in that of edicts engraved on stone. Such records could be said to be suffering from various kinds of prejudices. Particularly the biographies could have been written in respect of the contemporary rulers by those hoping for rewards for presenting the best piece, which could please the ruler with the best form of sycophancy.

Prior to the evolution of printing process, there could be no reliable research methods to take care of objectivity and fair-mindedness. Besides, there could be no takers for the laudatory references to the heroes of earlier ages, unless such heroes happened to be claimed to be the forefathers of such takers. Obviously, such pieces of writings cannot be considered as being the reliable evidence in favour of this or that conclusion.

Considerations of sycophancy and the hopes of getting suitable rewards, directly or indirectly, can be surely said to play a significant part in case any living person is put for selection for this kind of slot. The result can be further vitiated if such a person happens to wield vast political or money power. If so, this author hopes to be excused for his insistence that any living person, must not be considered for such a top slot.

Importance of Exemplary Mission and Character

Although Christ cannot be considered for the top slot of Man of the last Millennium, yet his life mission, character and suffering for humanity, according to an internet site, provides an apt example for considering why one should be understood to be great. Christ split time between AD and BC. His example and teaching have inspired millions of followers all around the world to this day. Christians consider Him to be the Son of God. He is recognised everywhere as a good man and a great teacher. His example remains as a standard for spiritual and religious people all over the world. Even those who have lost faith in organized religion admire Jesus as one worthy of respect and reverence.

According to one opinion. Jesus hid His divinity. It was for others to discover it but Jesus asked them not to tell anyone. Jesus' greatest mission was to identify with humanity. He let them discover that He is rightly called the Son of God. He allured people to follow him not in the hope of securing the kingdom of this earth. Rather, he promised the Kingdom of God to them.

By and large, the people have failed to follow His example. They tend to do the opposite. His followers get caught up in the revelation of Jesus as the Son of God. By doing so, they minimize His humanity. They flaunt their spirituality and hide their humanity. They proclaim His revelation to the world that reacts to its insistence by resisting the real message.

In spite of these difficulties, a modern rationalist would expect that only such a person should deserve the title of the Man of the Century or the Millennium, who had influenced the course of history for the benefit of the majority of humanity.

Basically man feels more concerned with his own surroundings, his own circumstances and his own problems. A sense of history can take him to the history of his own country, his own religion and in certain cases his own racial or ethnic group, in his endeavour to appreciate origin of his own circumstances and problems. He can think of the outside world only after understanding himself and his own circumstances. It is in view of this that the most of the examples of those considered for the slot of the Man of the Century pertain to the people who are comparatively stranger to us. Similarly, the persons who may deserve better treatment in our estimation may appear foreign to some of the foreign readers.

3

Test of Greatness

Both Mahatma Gandhi and Babasaheb Dr. Ambedkar had already been acknowledged as the great men of their time. Mr. Arun Shourie (Mr. 'S') grudges the greatness of Dr. Ambedkar, obviously on account of some deep-rooted prejudice against the latter. In this onnection, we should like to start with the measure of greatness as determined by disinterested luminaries. Madhu Limaye[1] has quoted G.W.F. Hegel [from ***Philosophy of Right***] to show who is the great man of the age. According to Hegel:

> *"The great man of the age is one who can put into words the will of the age, tell his age what its will is, and accomplish it. What he does is the heart and essence of the age; he actualises it.*
>
> *"A world-historic individual is not so unwise as to indulge in a variety of wishes to divide his regards. He is devoted to One Aim, regardless of all else. It is even possible that such men may treat other great, even sacred interests, inconsiderably... But so mighty a force must trample down many an innocent flower ; and crush to pieces many an object in its path."*

In the light of the above, this author is going to endeavour to show as to who out of Mahatma Gandhi and Dr. Ambedkar approaches the exact standards of greatness for the really disinterested minds.

Truth had been an obsession with Mahatma Gandhi. It should be natural with some one who is seeking greatness since it has been said that "if any one seeks greatness let him forget greatness and ask for truth, and he will find both."[2] But then the question arises as to 'what is truth?' There is an anonymous saying, which says that who ever tells the truth will be chased out of nine villages.[3] Such a thing never happened with the Mahatma except when he was assassinated. Perhaps at that time he was telling the truth about the need for Hindu-Muslim unity.

Had the Mahatma always been telling the truth, he would have met with his end long back. In fact, the art of achieving the true is very little practised. It is not even known, because there is no personal humility or even love of the true. We desire as a matter of course, the kind of knowledge that strengthens our hand or tongue and serves our vanity or our desire for power; but the criticism of ourselves, of our prejudices and inclination, is antipathetic to us.[4] The Mahatma had no independent definition of truth. He regarded the message of Gita as truth but we wonder he had also the correct idea of what Gita actually stood for.

Truths for New Year

The language of truth is unadorned and always simple. Mahatma Gandhi regarded the **Varnasrama** as the Law and as truth, which will be seen, from his own quotations in the followings pages. The truths for a new year stand mentioned in Great Quotations as listed by Baha 'U' Llah, Which are reproduced below:

1. The oneness of mankind.
2. Independent investigation of truth.
3. The foundation of all religions is one.
4. Religion must be the cause of unity.
5. Religion must be in accord with science and reason.
6. Equality between men and women.
7. Prejudice of all kinds must be forgotten.
8. Universal peace.
9. Universal education.
10. Spiritual solution of the economic problem.
11. A universal language.
12. An international tibunal.

Truths Propagated by Mahatma

Gandhi as per his own description was a *varnasrami* Hindu or the one who believed in the religion of *Varnas* and *asramas* or the four departments of life, namely, *brahmacharya* (celibacy), *grihastha* (householder), *vanaprastha* (going to forest) and *sanyas* (recluse). These *asramas* are also to be regulated as per the status of a Varna, which now stands converted to many thousand castes.. *Varna dharma* is another name of Hinduism, which divides the society into four *Varnas* having unequal duties. In so far as rights are concerned, Brahmanas have all of them. Kshatriyas can be said to have the right of bearing arms, and vaisyas that of being traders, producers and distributors of all kinds of wealth, but of course, in the pleasure of the Brahmanas. Gandhi believed in this *dharma* or religion. Those interested in detailed analysis of this dharma, may like to consult this author's *Hindu Scheme of Things: Socio-Political Analysis of Manu-Smriti,* published by D D Books, Panchkula in 1987, which had been debated in *The Tribune* for four months in the letters to Editor Column between April 1988 and July 1988. Thus, his truths are to be understood in the background of the traditional approach of this religion, as under:

1. If truth must consist in the oneness of mankind, Hinduism does not stand for such oneness ;
2. If truth must consist in independent investigation of truth, then Hinduism does not consider that as truth which runs counter to ther Varnasrama Dharma. It does not believe in independent investigation of truth since its authority is the Veda which in turn is believed to be authority in itself;
3. If truth must consist in the foundation of all religions being one, Hinduism does not subscribe to this view point;
4. If truth must consist in that the religion must be the cause of unity, Hinduism believes in graded inequality, which must be enforced by the state, since according to it state is a tool of religion.
5. If truth must consist in religion being in accord with science and reason, then Hinduism believes in Vedas being proof in themselves or being not subject to debate, which means that there cannot be any place for reason therein. The Sankracharyas do not tire saying that ultimately religion shall prevail and science will lose.
6. If truth must consist in equality between men and women, the Varna Dharma does not treat them as equal.
7. If truth must consist in forgetting all kinds of prejudices, Hinduism believes in perpetrating the prejudices for some castes and varnas and against some others, sanctioned by it.
8. If truth must consist in universal peace, Hinduism believes in peace which comes with the total submission of man to the religion of inequality of sexes, rights, duties and prejudices.
9. If truth must consist in giving universal education to all, Hinduism grants monopoly rights over education only to Brahmanas. It permits Kshatriyas and Vaisyas to have

education pertaining to their religious duties. Further, it has closed the doors of all kinds of knowledge to Sudras and Ati-Sudars, who form about 90% of the total Hindu population.

10. If truth must consist in seeking spiritual solution of the economic problem, then Hinduism promises spiritual knowledge only to those who are born into Brahmana Varna, and others have to wait for their "turn" to be born as Brahmanas in some future birth of theirs.Thus, solution to their economic problems stands totally barred.

That nation is proudest and noblest and most exalted which has the greatest number of really great men.[5] Judged in this background also, Hindu religion has hardly produced any great men who are revered and respected all over the world. The Mahatma himself is one of the exceptions but he is respected not for reason of his being a staunch follower of Hinduism, but for being supposed to bring freedom of India through non-violent means.

Why Someone Is Great?

A great man is great not because his personal qualities give individual feature to great historical events, but because he possesses qualities which make him most capable of serving the great social needs of his time, needs which arose as a result of general and particular cause.[6] The Mahatma's great contribution as already pointed out, can be said, if at all, to be in the field of winning freedom for India. To that extent, he can be said to be a good claimant to greatness but that claim also has been questioned by many. Apart from that, he might have served the interest of the Hindus. If so, the interest of Hindus cannot be said to be qualifying for general interest. Judged between Ambedkar and the Mahatma, Ambedkar served much larger interest, and if so, the Mahatma loses in the game.

"The great are great only because we are on our knees. Let us rise!"[7] So had been said by Max Stirner. In the light of this saying, the Mahatma was great because other of his contemporary countrymen were pigmies even in the matter of fighting for freedom of India. Eugene V. Debs had said:

"The truth has always been dangerous to the rule of the rogue, the exploiter, the robber. So the truth must be suppressed.[8]

The Mahatma, interestingly, never put forward any analytical argument in support of the *Varnasrama,* although Dr. Ambedkar had written volumes condemning the said pernicious system, which had kept millions of the weaker sections at sub-human level for thousands of years. Any one supporting the *Varnasrama* has to be regarded as the supporter of organised exploitation of the weak and the meek by the strong and crafty. If so, the Mahatma cannot be said to deserve a place in the queue of great men in the special sense of term.

By supporting the *Varnasrama*, he had been trying to please the progeny of the propounders of a dangerous system. In this behalf the following quotation appears to be very apt:[9]

Some truth there was, but
Dash'd and brew'd with lies
To please the fools and puzzle wise.[10]

Condition for Understanding Truth

No man thoroughly understands a truth until he has contended against it.[11] The Mahatma holds that the *varnasrama* or the Gita or the Veda or the Hindu Saastras are based on or are the repositories of truth. But he never contended with any of them. In the present context, it is only Dr. Ambedkar who had contended all of them and written extensively to expose the fraud played in the name of the said sources or systems. As such, the real claim to greatness lies with Dr. Ambedkar rather than with the Mahatma.

Becoming Subservient to Authority

The greatest danger against which men have warned us is that which comes from communicating intellectual secrets to minds become subservient to the authority of an inveterate habit, for such is the power of a long-lasting observance, that most men prefer death to giving up their way of life.[12] Mahatma Gandhi also suffered from this sort of habit, which was the culmination of orthodox practices continued for generations in his family. Another name for such habits is tradition.

The Mahatma was obviously the prisoner of tradition, which was found very useful by the then rulers and exploited by them to their best advantage. Being a prisoner of tradition, the Mahatma, at best could have felt no harm in co-operating with the British so that the latter could enjoy the fruits of their Empire, comparatively uninterruptedly. The British rulers in view of their better strategy and having adequate means, sought to counter such moves of the revolutionaries in a thoroughly organised manner, through the agencies of the orthodox elements.

Swami Vivekananda had once said that the reason is the helper and the reason is the bar. The same can be said about the Hindu tradition. The country had slipped into a long spell of slavery because of sticking to the same tradition. There came to be reaction against the rulers because of the same tradition. The same tradition was exploited by the Imperialists and yet the same tradition was utilised by those who ultimately rose as the beneficiaries of the so-called freedom movement which was no better than trading into the slavery. The Mahatma belonged to the same category of traders or of Vaisyas, who had traded into the slavery of the country, for the limited advantages of their class. He represented the classes, which allowed him the benefit of masquerading as a saint, although he was out and out a politician, with all the normal failings of one. The upper three castes or *Varnas* of Hindu social organisation constitute that class. There is a quotation:

> *"God offers to every mind its choice between truth and repose. Take which you please; you can never have both. Between these, as a pendulum, man oscillates. He in whom the love of repose predominates will accept the first creed, the first philosophy, the first political party he meets —most likely his father's. He gets rest, commodity, and reputation; but he shuts the door of truth. He in whom the love of truth predominates will keep himself aloof from the moorings, and afloat. He will abstain from dogmatism, and recognise all the opposite negations between which, as walls, his being is swung. He submits to the inconveniences of suspense and imperfect opinion, but he is a candidate for truth, as the other is not, and respects the highest law of being."*[13]

Mahatma Gandhi belonged to the category that opted for repose and ignored the truth but by pretending that he was following the truth as enunciated in some remote and out-dated scriptures, which had been repeatedly rejected by the earlier generations.

Respecting Rejected Tradition

The tradition based on a earlier Vedic sources had been rejected by the Kshatriyas who had created their own scriptures known as *Upanishads* which were later on appropriated by Brahmanism or the erstwhile *Vedic* religion. Kshatriyas and the Sudras under the banner of Buddhism had rejected it. The Vaisyas who had once propounded their own independent and anti-*Vedic* religion known as Jainism had rejected it. Practically, all the medieval saints, who had ultimately helped the emergence of Sikhism and other unorthodox sects, had rejected it. It had been able to keep alive by extensively borrowing from the heterodox sources with a view to appear an accommodating religion, accommodating of the secular principles.

Dr. Ambedkar, on the other hand, chose the path of real truth and, therefore, he was obliged to question all the fundamentals of the same religion. He had not hesitated to criticise and expose the philosophy of Gandhi himself. The latter had never chosen to directly contradict Ambedkar, simply because he had no satisfactory argument to counter the criticism.

Violation of Truth

Mahatma Gandhi under the guise of upholding the truth had been in fact violating the truth, and as such he tried to harm the society as much as he could. The harm was lessened by the conspiracy of circumstances, which threw up men like Dr. Ambedkar and Netaji Subhash Chandra Bose to oppose him. Even a man like Jawaharlal Nehru, by working as the trusted lieutenant of the Mahatma, and by seemingly sympathising with the said pursuer of truth, conveniently and surreptitiously, chose to undo the loss caused and proposed to have been caused by the Mahatma for whatever reasons, by setting the ideal of socialistic pattern of society, which negated much of *Varna-vyvastha*. Here, the following words of Ralph dc apply and are very pertinent:

> *Every violation truth is not only a sort of suicide in the liar, but is a stab at the health of human society.*[14]

The Mahatma does not seem to be a votary of truth. Ratherheappears to actually fear truth and, as such, he was lesser than an ordinary man, judged in the light of the following quotation:

> *We are afraid of truth, afraid of fortune, afraid of death and afraid of each other.*[15]

The Mahatma was perhaps not aware of the pleasure he could seek from pursuing and discovering the real truth. Or perhaps his own prejudices were dearer to him, which held him up from the better path than he had adopted. He is not the only Hindu failing in this matter. It is the lot off all the obscurantists and, therefore, no Hindu has ever achieved the real heights. The Hindus have been taking great pride in their now owned up *Upanishads* and the philosophy of non-violence. But they know too well that the Upanishads had risen as a revolt against the Vedic religion and the non-violence also had never been the creed of the Vedic religionists.

Creed of Non-Violence and Gandhi

The creed of non-violence had been evolved out of the revolt against the Vedic religion and on the foundation of Non-violence, the

Buddhism and Jainism had risen as great scientific religions. The propounders of the said two religions had first tried to reform the ancient Hinduism by purging it of all the deep-rooted prejudices. When it continued to stick to the age-old prejudices and refused to change in keeping with the demands of the changing times, the propounders of the philosophy of reason and non-violence had no option but to raise their own independent flag and establish an alternative religion. This alternative religion was opposed to the Vedic religion. Still, the Mahatma never tired of proclaiming that Hinduism was the repository of the greatness truth. The new religion based on truth and non-violence, later, on got bifurcated into two – Buddhism and Jainism – perhaps due to the question of leadership. In this connection, the following quotation deserves notice:

> *The greatest and the noblest pleasure, which we have in this world, is to discover new truths, and the next is to shake off old prejudices*[16]

Test of Being False or True God

Shourie has unnecessarily introduced the concept of gods in order to hit Ambedkar. In this sense, he has done disservice to Ambedkar, to the latter's new faith, Buddhism, and to Gandhi. Comparison should have been kept confined to humans. Actually, Shourie was comparing only two humans with reference to their human actions. But only in order to denigrate Ambedkar, he raised Gandhi to the level of Hindu gods, and projected them to be true gods. To the believer of one religion, the gods of his religion will always appear to be true gods as compared to those of others.

However, true and false god can be distinguished also in the light of various parametres. One of them can be whether they differentiate between the sexes on the basis of their gender. For example, Hindu God is known as *Purusha* [male] as distinguished from *Nari* [female]. The entire Hindu religious literature, is heavily prejudiced in favour of males as against the females. Ambedkar did not discriminate between the sexes like this. Considered from this point of view, Ambedkar was much more superior to the gods of Shourie's imagination.

Hindu Gods also discriminate between the different social divisions based on the accident of birth. Ambedkar, through his philosophy culminating in the Constitution of India, gave equal opportunity to all the persons of rising to any height and their flight was not checked by the accident of birth. In this sense also Ambedkar was much better than the mythological gods. Thus, even when compared to such gods, Ambedkar was the only true god, but in a different sense, the absolute sense, instead of being so in a relative sense.

This can be said in spite of the fact that Ambedkar himself did not believe in God in the sense of belief of an ordinary person and in that of Buddhism to which Dr. Ambedkar converted towards the end of his life, which also does not believe in the concept of God of layman's understanding.

A rationalist of today cannot afford to believe in a sectarian God devoid of a scientific character. In that sense, Dr. Ambedkar cannot be accepted as or compared with God of scientific description either. And, it is the case of none of Ambedkar's declared devotees also.

God, which means, in scientific terms, only The Ultimate Reality or the law of cause and effect, which sustains everything in this Cosmos, should be realised through the knowledge of correct relationship of things and men in this Universe. With the dawn of that realisation, none can try to rule over others for any material gain in exchange for loss of the real spirit, the soul, *atman* [self] within himself or herself or just self. Realisation of God, then, would mean engaging in service of humanity, nay, all the creatures or objects in the universe for bringing a supreme sense of balance. The whole humanity is the sum total of all the souls of human beings or *atman* and, therefore, all constitute *Paramaatman*, the Great Soul, the God, both in the religious and the scientific senses. Since women of modern world have come to be regarded as deserving all kinds of equality with men the name of God need not continue to be *Purusha* [male]. Let it now be only the *Paramaatman*, the great Soul] or any other name of neuter gender.

References

1. Madhu Limaye; The *Prime Movers; Role of Individual in History;* Sangam Books, London; 1987' Quoted before introducing the book in question.
2. Horace Mann; *On Achieving Greatness.*
3. Quoted in *Great Quotations.*
4. Ibid. The quotation is attributed to Henri Fredric Amiel.
5. Sinclair Lewis; *This week*, August 5, 1956.
6. George Plekhanov; quoted in *Great Quotations.*

7. Max Sterner; Der Einzige and sein Eigentum —*The Ego and his Own*; Ibid. p. 485.
8. Quoted in Great Quotations at pp. 919-920.
9. Ralph Waldo Emerson; Compensation; Quoted in Great Quotations, p. 920.

   Mary Baker Eddy; *Science and Health with key to the Scriptures*; Quoted in *Great Quotations* at p. 920.
10. Mary Baker Eddy; *Science and Health with key to the Scriptures*; p. 920.
11. Ralph Waldo Emerson; *Compensation*; *Ibid.*
12. Nichloas of Cusa; *De Docta Ignorantia* [Learned Ignorance]; Quoted in *Great Quotations*
13. Ralph Waldo Emerson; *Intellect;* Quoted in *Great Question;* p. 921.
14. Ralph Waldo Emerson; *Prudence; Ibid.*
15. Ralph Waldo Emerson; Self-Reliance; *Ibid.*

4

Test of Vilification Tie Between Gandhi and Ambedkar

For finding Man of Millennium for Social Justice, it is important to assume certain reliable criteria. One such criterion has been suggested in a book authored by Madhu Limaye, *The Prime Movers: The Role of Individual in History*. Obviously, the suggestion is that the honour of being declared to be the Man of the Millennium should go to a man, who played a decisive role in history. If so, the next question can be as to the field in which such a role has been played. Justice and fair play have been the most wanting things in this world, since it has been generally controlled and managed so far by the forces of injustice and exploitation.

Madhu Limaye's book had been published at a time, when the Millennium Bug had not yet bitten the world. Naturally, Limaye had only the last two centuries in his mind. Only a few years ago, the search had been on for the greatest man of the 20th century. That kind of search appeared to be more exact and more manageable, in view of reliable comparative data being available, within the scope of the frame-work to be determined by particular opinions.

On Question of Personal Preference

Many of the Indians are inclined in favour of Mahatma Gandhi for occupying the pride of place. But that is in connection with the field of non-violence. He has already been named to be *The Man of the Century* for Non-violence, as per the so-called survey conducted on Internet. The verdict has many serious flaws, which will be discussed later in proper context. There are many others who are inclined to put him as a contestant for the honour of being *The Man of the Millennium.* There are still others who have been still inviting postings through suggestive hints as to whether the internet users regard Gandhi as the man of the century.

As already stated, apart from the Indians, there are others counted among the top intellectuals, who have been debating about particular individuals for placing this or that person on the top slot. The futility of naming someone as the Man of the Century has already been noted. We have found greater advantage for finding a man of the millennium for a particular geographical region of the world, in which the author has lived for most part of the time and about whose personalities he can have comparatively a deeper knowledge. In such a case, many readers are like to be from the same region, and to share some of the first hand knowledge, about such personalities under examination.

Similarly, they may have common expectations from the great men, who may be the competitors in the concerned field. They are further expected to be in a better position to understand the particular ethos of the region as also the genuineness of the expectations from the great men in the areas that have remained neglected so far. It is not to undermine the importance of the views of the foreigners in such matters. But in case of famous people, particularly those, who may have been conferred the titles like the Father of the Nation, there has to be a compulsion on the foreign dignitaries visiting the concerned countries, to say some thing only positively about such a father figure. And, if so, that something has to be perforce in laudatory terms. Others, who might have been the contemporaries of the same Father of the Nation and had occasions to play similarly important role to play, have not only to remain behind but they have to be totally kept out of such discussions. Such inevitabilities cannot be made the sound basis for dispassionate evidence in such matters.

Possibility of Opposite Viewpoints

Normally, there are tendencies to cash on the name and importance of such father figures. Opposition parties also do not like to lag behind in this respect. They remain at pains to sometimes exaggerate the positive qualities of such a father figure, only with a view to put the ruling party at a particular point of time on the mat, on the ground that it has failed to fully appreciate the worth of the great man.

This author found it quite tempting to endeavour an answer to the question about the Man of Millennium, in the background of the attempts of certain groups to efface the memories of two great men of India from the pages of history. Such attempts obviously started in Maharashtra. The concerned great men were Gandhi and Ambedkar.

Attempts at Effacing Memory of Great Men

The memory of Mahatma Gandhi was sought to be effaced with the help of staging a street corner Marathi play titled *Me Nathuram Godse Boltoy*, which reportedly became suddenly extremely popular among the roaming audience. The said fact seemed to suggest that the real hero was not the Mahatma but his assassin Nathuram Godse.

The second attempt was on Dr. Ambedkar, which also started in Maharashtra, but found culmination in the said book of Shourie, published from Noida in the state Uttar Pradesh, but a suburb of New Delhi, in July 1997. Such attempts can be made obviously with a view to killing the memory of those who are very much living in public memory. It can be said as a corollary that in regard to those, whose memory is not sought to be effaced, they are not considered as living, comparatively speaking, in public memory.

Effacing Memory: Tie between Gandhi and Ambedkar

In the light of this argument, there can be a tie between Gandhi and Ambedkar only over the question of being the Man of the Millennium. If Mahatma Gandhi is claimed to be given the honour of being the Man of the Millennium, then naturally, Ambedkar's name should come forward to challenge the Mahatma on that account also and vice versa. To borrow the idea from Madhu Limaye's book mentioned above, there could be some more claimants to the honour, who will find mention at another place.

There was no survey in respect of Ambedkar, of the type that has been shown to have been made in respect of Gandhi. The reasons therefor are to be best imagined rather than explained. Still, some of them might be found in the fact of the higher financial status of the sponsors and the existence of a definite regard, which could even be termed as prejudice for Gandhi in the mind of those conducting such a survey. There is no denying the fact that Gandhi is believed to be a Hindu Mahatma and, therefore, to be naturally dear to the upper castes.

There is also no denying the fact that Ambedkar has been the greatest critic of the inhuman exploitative character of Hindu scriptures, of Hinduism and therefore of Gandhi.

On Attempts at Exploitation

From the day man started thinking, a debate began between reason and faith. Coming to reason, the debate began between the reason of the exploiters and that of the exploited. The exploiters had an upper hand, since they began the game of exploitation before the exploited could even imagine that someone had already started the game of their exploitation.

The game of exploitation was started by those who were in minority as compared to the vast majority, initially on the basis of racial or ethnic considerations. The minority in numerical sense, had to perforce adopt craft in the matter of dealing with the majority which was regarded by it as its adversary, even though the majority had no inkling so far that someone had started considering it as an adversary.

The crafty, after his initial success over the adversary, had to employ the force against the majority to keep the latter under permanent control. Simultaneously, the majority had to be broken in artificial segments so that each segment had to regard itself as a minority, against all others. This process resulted in the policy of divide and rule.

The reason of the exploiters gave rise to the concept of private property, which started the practice of competition. The exploiter sometimes assumed the role of a politician and at other times that of a religious leader. The religion and politics, though posing to stand for different principles, tended to collectively work against the interests of the common masses, although each of them left no stone unturned to falsely pose to be concerned with the welfare of the masses themselves.

Initial Tussle: On Basis Of Race And Colour

In India, initial tussle started between the groups of fairer complexion and those of the darker complexion. Those of darker complexion, were generally the original inhabitants of the Indian sub-continent, the aborigines, the forefathers of the Dalits and the like. And those of the fairer complexion had come from the colder regions of Asia and Europe, who were the fore-fathers of firstly the Brahmanas, and to some extent of some of the other upper caste people. Although it has to be admitted that through the process of sanskritisation, a sizeable portion of the natives and other non-Aryans had been made to join the Aryans or Brahmanas and to be called by different names, which are today said to qualify for being the upper castes.

The Dalits and the Sudras were relegated to the position of the community slaves. Slavery did not involve necessarily untouchability. Therefore, the Sudras were kept as touchable slaves. The exploitation all over the world, at one stage took the form of slavery, which was being practised, all over the world, till the 19th century AD. In India, in addition to slavery, untouchability also took birth, with the result that at the time of the dawn of independence in 1947 AD, about a quarter of the population was constituted of the so-called Untouchables.

On Fight for Amelioration of Dalits

Ambedkar had led a valiant fight for the amelioration of the Dalits. He had been able to make the British agreeable to granting to the Dalits separate electorates. The question of separate electorates had been opposed tooth and nail by the Mahatma. So much so, he had staked his own life. Ambedkar, with a view to saving the life of the Mahatma had agreed to the modification of that formula, which had resulted in what is known as Poona Pact of 1932, which accepted the principle of joint eelectorates in place of separate electorates.

The said pact had highlighted the character of the Mahatma as the Hindu leader and that of Babasaheb as the leader of the Dalits. Since then the two leaders had been understood to be representing different and opposing interests within Hinduism. The fact of Ambedkar's fight for the rights of the Dalits had been projected for public consumption by the interested parties as being against Hinduism and against Gandhi.

On Hindu Leadership

The Hindu leadership continues to be in the hands of the Brahmanas, who had named Gandhiji as the Mahatma. The Upper caste Hindus have been traditionally the *haves* and the Dalits and the Sudras have been the *have-nots*. Ambedkar had applied these words to the exploited sections of Hinduism, including the women. The orthodox Hindus received this fact as a challenge to the Hinduism. Mahatma Gandhi and his Congress could not check the flow of ideas supporting justice for the exploited sections and therefore, invited Dr. Ambedkar himself to be the first Law Minister of independent India and the Chairman of the drafting Committee of the Constitution of India.

In those capacities, it became easier for Ambedkar to introduce the provisions of the Government of India Act of 1935 [which had incorporated the spirit behind the Poona Pact], in the Constitution of India. The Congress being already bound by the pact, could not oppose the relevant provisions of the draft Constitution, but the orthodox Hindus, including those within the Congress, sympathised with and supported other orthodox sections within Hinduism in their criticism of the relevant provisions of the Constitution.

On Hindus Choosing Political Platform Separate from That of Hindu Fundamentalists

Soon, the orthodox Hindus chose to make their own political platform that declared itself as the defender of Hinduism in its ancient form. During the course of the so-called fight for freedom, the orthodox Hindus had continued to have full faith in the leadership of the Congress and that of the Mahatma. Therefore, instead of having an independent platform of theirs, the orthodox Hindus had been providing leadership to the Congress from its own ranks of Hindu Mahasabha and the RSS.

In the light of the above, during their lifetime, the real fight had been between Mahatma Gandhi and Dr. Ambedkar, during the currency of the so-called fight for freedom. It follows that after their leaving this world the fight has to continue only between them or over them.

Ambedkar was being sought to be killed a second time by the orthodox Hindu leadership occupying political offices in this or that party, by being ignored mainly till 1990. Dr. Ambedkar was resurrected by the political compulsions of V P Singh, the then Prime Minister of India. Meanwhile, the orthodox character of Mahatma Gandhi came to be made prominent by the fundamentalist party Jan Sangh and its present avatar, BJP. A stage came when the fundamentalist party chose to erase the memories of both Dr. Ambedkar and Mahatma Gandhi. Such efforts became actually pronounced in the 50th year of Independence, in the hope of capturing power from its opponents, during 1996.

On Consequences of Organised Exploitation

The organised exploitation at one stage had resulted in establishment of many slave colonies in different countries and also that of establishment of vast empires. Mutual imperial and colonial rivalries had resulted in wars for freedom of the colonies from the clutches of the colonial powers. Such rivalries also ended in two World Wars. One of the consequences of the First World War was the end of Imperialism in Russia and establishment of the USSR, or that of communist regime, as opposed to capitalism.

The expansion of the idea of communism, was the cause of establishment of Communist International [Comintern]. For quite a few decades, there remained an atmosphere of Cold War between the forces of Capitalism and those of Communism. The cold war ended only with the disintegration of USSR, bringing an end to communism in the country of its birth, only a few years back.

Meanwhile, communist parties had been established in many countries. Communism was established on the basis of Marxism. Then, it was bifurcated between Marxism and Leninism. In China, it took the shape of Maoism. In India, Communist Party of India was divided between the CPM and CPI. The communism had taken some roots mainly in West Bengal and Kerala.

But Indian communism is much different from what had been aimed at by its founders. The longest rule of communists has been in West Bengal, which has seen no harm in perpetrating the caste and social stratification ordained in Hindu scriptures, which very much negate all the basic principles of communistic philosophy and doctrines.

Democracy and Hopes of Untouchables

The democracy had given rise to some hopes in the mind of the Untouchables and other weaker sections of Indian population. But the democratic form of government has allowed the continuation of the same sort of exploitation of man by man, of caste by caste and of class by class, almost on the lines sanctioned by *Varnasrama Dharma* or Casteism of Hindu society. Thus, the Untouchables and others placed in circumstances like those of the Untouchables have not only failed to improve their lot to the desired extent, but also to join the so-called mainstream of Hindu society.

5

Difference Between Vilification of Gandhi and Ambedkar

Every society has its icons of honour. India is country of many sections having self-contradictory vested interests and philosophies. Each section may have its own icon. Gandhi is the icon of the upper caste Hindus, (but according to some, that of all sections of Indian population), whereas Ambedkar is that of the weaker sections, particularly, the Dalits. Both the groups have been living together since time immemorial. They are bound to live forever on account of being needed by each other for different reasons. Therefore, the followers of one cannot wish away the existence of the other. If Gandhi as an icon is hurt, the Gandhian society is hurt. If Ambedkar as an icon is hurt, all the Ambedkarites are hurt. Analytically speaking, the ancient Hindus have been hurting the ancient icons of the Dalits by referring to them as *Asuras* and *Raakshasas*.

The process is continuing till today. Ancient Vedics had added another icon in the category of those to be so hurt. He was Lord Buddha. Modern Hindus have added Dr. Ambedkar to the list of such ancient Icons of weaker sections meant to be hurt at the slightest excuse. Buddha had been chosen for attack because he had been instrumental in wiping out the Vedic religion from the face of earth. The same danger now lurks for Hinduism at the hands of Dr. Ambedkar, since he also has attacked *Varna* system of the Hindus, which is claimed to have originated in the Vedas. Moreover, he had lured about 5 lacs of untouchable Hindus to Buddhism in 1956. The story has been repeated in May 2007, in Bombay under the stewardshipp of Ramdas Athwale, National President of Republican Party of India, who led more than a hundred thousand Dalits to embrace Buddhism.

Therefore, Ambedkar has beem hit by Arun Shourie, with a view to having his memory erased from the minds of the public. In the matter of maligning Dr. Ambedkar, Arun Shourie has committed a similar mistake, which had been committed by Nathuram Godse in killing Mahatma Gandhi. Milind Thatte in one of his articles dated 24 July 1998, made an interesting observation, which he applied to Godse, but which applies with equal vigour to Shourie also:

> *This reminds me of Albert Einstein's childhood memoirs: One day his teacher in the school told the children that "Jesus Christ was crucified" and then looking at Albert, she said "by Jews". Then the whole class looked at little Albert with such disgust as Christ's murderer. Brahmins have suffered similar disgust in every field of social life, simply because one of them murdered Gandhi. This has had a bounce-back effect on Brahmins. A lay Brahmin hates Gandhi and preaches Godse.*

Rule of Apaddharma
And Temporary Acceptance of Other's Icon

This fact points out to another disturbing factor in Hinduism. Brahmanas may accept the icons from other communities as measure of rule of adversity. They had done so in case of Kshatriya Rama and Sudra Krishna. In independent India, they adopted a Bania Gandhi for the time being as one of their working icons.

But soon they reverted to a Brahmin, Jawahar Lal Nehru, just as they had never forgotten their own Ravana and Para*sura*ma. They haven't forsaken their Brahma and are keeping him alive for all the Hindus under a rule according to which all the pilgrimages will be fruitless unless at the end one does obeisance to Lord Brahma at Pushkara, Ajmer (Rajasthan). But they cannot get reconciled to Ambedkar, unless he also becomes or is made the author of an epic, like the *Mahabharata* or the *Ramayana* on the analogy of Vyasa and Valmiki, aimed at perpetuation of slavery of the *Sudras* and excommunication of Dalits. The Brahmanas would have accepted Ambedkar also but his writings and speeches in this electronic age are presenting the greatest hurdle in this behalf, since they cannot be interpolated beyond recognition, on the pattern of the Ramayana and the Mahabharata now being attributed to Sage Valmiki and Sage Vyasa. Hence, there has to be a parallel impact of Brahminism and anti-Brahminism, to the inevitable dismay of the orthodox Hindus, like Arun Shourie.

Immunity from Attacks on Icons

Any icon, which may be in any form, namely, 'a book, a statue, or a living person' is protected against all attacks. As such, Ambedkar having become an icon in more than one sense must be protected by its own intrinsic worth. He cannot be killed by hundreds of Shouries. There was a stage when Atal Behari Vajpayee, had strategically declared as the chief guest of Dalit Sahitya Academy function a few years ago that "Ambedkar was modern Manu, and he himself was Manuvaadi." The same Vajpayee as Prime Minister, in changed circumstances said on 14 April 2000, that he was not a believer in Manu-*Smriti*, but a believer in the Constitution of India, which is in effect a Bheema-*Smriti*. Judged in the light of this statement, Mr. 'S' is not being defended by his own Prime Minister. While speaking for Ambedkar, the Prime Minister was denouncing what Mr. 'S' had done to Ambedkar. In this connection, the words of Milind Thatte deserve to be quoted:

> *The society, that cherishes the icon revolts when there is attack. Take the instance of Ambedkar. Ambedkar is an icon for a section of the society. Even if a statue of him is molested, that society revolts.*

Difference between Vilification of Two Icons

There is a difference between the vilification of Gandhi and Ambedkar. Nathuram Godse belonged to the Brahmin community of Maharashtra. In the event of Mahatma Gandhi's assassination, Brahmins were believed to have been killed, looted, raped, and their properties were believed to have been burnt. It was done after it became known that Gandhi's assassin was a Brahmin. But nothing like that has happened to Brahmanas, when one of them Arun Shourie has tried to efface the memory of Dr. Ambedkar. Only his own face was reportedly blackened by some Ambedkarites as per own admission of Shourie made in his own book of vilification.

There is another difference. Godse had to die but Mr. 'S' was made suddenly to climb the political staircase so that he first became a spokesman and a celebrity of the Sangh Parivar and then, after becoming a Union Minister of State, he came to be counted as a key to the then Prime Minister, Atal Behari Vajpayee. This difference is explainable in the fact that at the time of murder of Gandhi, the Congress was in power but at the time of Shourie's trying to efface the memory of Ambedkar, the Sangh Parivar was in ascendance.

There is Hindi saying *Sanyiyaa bhaye kotwaal ab dar kaahe kaa?* **That is, now my master has become the head of the police station, so whom I have to fear?** In this sense, the feat of Mr. 'S' must appear less spectacular. It is true that on the day the book was released, BJP was not in power at the Centre, but it was so in Maharashtra all right. But the day BJP came to power at the Centre, Mr. 'S' received his 'well-deserved' award for "killing" the memory of Dr. Ambedkar and through that for trying to make the Dalits irrelevant in Indian Politics.

In case of Gandhi, the problem is that his own men disown him, and, they are the people, for whom he worked and for whom he died. On the other hand, the people for whom Ambedkar is being projected to have worked for all his life are worshipping Ambedkar. Dr. Ambedkar is being accepted by more and more sections of people, who are learning from the example of his followers, and who are increasingly realising, through his literature, the reality of their own existence, which is actually threatened by the forces of exploitation. The latest example in this behalf is of Ms. Mayawati of Bahujan Samaj Party, becoming Chief Minister of Uttar Pradesh with the active support of Brahmins, Banyas and Rajputs.

Attraction of Ambedkarism

Ambedkarism is silently attracting the newer and newer sections every day. This process is naturally eating into the vitals of the exploitative system and the exploitative society. Thus, the Hindu fundamentalism is in danger of extinction. Gandhism is also threatened with such extinction to the extent it tends to favour the forces of exploitation. But Gandhism in so far as it stands for feelings of tolerance and mutual understanding must remain alive forever. More and more people of the world are also accepting Gandhi only on that account. **But it is not the Gandhism of the description of Hindu fundamentalism; it is Gandhism of non-violence and of passive resistance against tyranny, which is destined to stay.**

According to Thatte, "when logic dies, a leader degenerates into an icon." These words can be made justifiably applicable to Hindu fundamentalism in one sense and to Gandhism in another sense. The logic of Hindu fundamentalists and that of Gandhi as a defender of orthodox brand of Hinduism has already died. It seems alive because of the violent groups of RSS, using organised force against their adversaries. Any idea, which needs the support of organised force, must be considered as already dead. Christ had said: "Those who live by sword, are killed by sword."

Hope for Freedom from Exploitation

The present day logic is in favour of those who give to all concerned a hope for freedom from exploitation of all sorts. Therefore, the balance of convenience lies overwhelmingly in favour of Ambedkarism as against Gandhism, so far as the latter issues from *Varnas*rami Gandhi. Even in India, Gandhi was not revered on account of his being a *Varnas*rami Hindu, but because he was able to pose as the uplifter of the lowliest of the lowly and as the treader of middle path of the description paved by Buddhism. Ambedkarism is alive because of its natural attraction to the exploited masses and women, who comprise 95% population of India.

Gandhism did not leave any message for the exploited masses. He asked them to be merely passive and to hope for sympathy of their tyrants. His message of non-violence does not help the exploited but it makes the exploiters safe in the game of the suppression of the exploited. Thus, Gandhism is alive to some extent not because of its own intrinsic value but because of the fact that it is made to wrongly pose as the sympathiser of the weak, the poor and the exploited. Gandhi being a mere icon of an unspecified section of population, which have been traditionally perpetrators of injustice is destined to lose public respect. But he can be remembered for administering some saner advice of political nature to his political followers. But then Thatte also regards Gandhi as a dead icon:

> His [Gandhi's] advice to dissolve Congress was never followed by Congressmen. His teachings of "building the nation from below" were turned upside down by Nehru. His idea of *Graam-Swaraj* (self-reliant village) lost its sway to globalisation. His teaching of peaceful resistance (*Satyagraha*) became futile in independent India. Peaceful movement often died without success. All movements became prone to violence and their voice reached the Government only through the barrel. Gandhi is nowhere in practice; he is a dead icon.

Gandhi Steadily Losing Following

Neither Congressmen nor anyone else has followed Gandhi. And hence, they have no stature, no authority to stand by Gandhi, says Thatte. If so, Gandhism has no legs to stand on. On the other hand, his words about Ambedkar are worth quoting:

> *India has witnessed and accepted - though unwillingly - criticism against many of its icons. Even gods like Rama and Krishna were not spared. "Riddles of Hinduism" by Ambedkar criticised the gods, and rocked the society. "Worshipping false gods" by Shourie targeted and maligned Ambedkar. Rama and Ambedkar have not lost their cherished place because of these works.*

Referring to the street play against Mahatma Gandhi, Thatte had asked, "Is Gandhi so weak an idol that he will be broken by a stage-play?" He himself replied, "I do not think so. Gandhi had and has his own glory, which cannot be molested by small people. Someone has a desire to spit at Sun, let him spit. In democracy, it is his right!"

On Defending of Two Icons

One rarely comes across a real dispassionate defence of one's icons. But Thatte has to be considered among the exceptions, who allots better importance to Ambedkar than Gandhi at least in the sense of reaction to their respective vilification. Then, he also seems to give better credit to the followers of Ambedkar than to those of Gandhi. Here is an illustration:

> Let Gandhi face what Ambedkar faced. If he was great, he was. Trust in him, nothing will happen to him; the row over the play shows that they do not have trust in him. When Shourie's book on Ambedkar was published, a similar hullabaloo was launched by some people. A ban on the book was demanded, but Ambedkarite intellectuals gathered and proclaimed that let the book be in the open. We will face it. The self-proclaimed Gandhiites neither have these guts nor do they think Gandhi as capable of facing attacks.

Genesis of Attack of Vilification

India was preparing to celebrate the Golden Jubilee of her independence, in view of completing 50 years of independence on 15 August 1997. At the same time, attempts were on for denigrating, the most important personalities of the century, who had played the most decisive role in winning India her freedom from foreign yoke and in shaping the destiny of Independent India. Mahatma Gandhi had been the lifetime dictator of Indian National Congress, which is believed to have been the only party working in the field of winning the freedom and which ultimately got away with the maximum credit for winning such freedom.

Bringing Status-Quo-Ante Regarding Varna System?

Mahatma Gandhi had been working for winning the political freedom for the country. So far as Hinduism is concerned, it had been the endeavour of Gandhi, being a Hindu Mahatma, to work for restoration of status quo ante, in the matter of inter-caste and inter-*Varna* relationships. Dr. Ambedkar had been endeavouring to put a better social sense in the efforts for winning the freedom as also for restoration of human rights, generally for all the disadvantaged sections but particularly for the Depressed Classes or the present day Dalits. He had been trying to convince those engaged in the so-called fight for freedom to give safeguards for political rights of all the elements in the Indian population divided on considerations of caste, creed, and gender as also on racial, cultural and economic considerations. In view of these facts, he had been urging the Mahatma and his Congress, to include the consideration of social reforms in the political agenda of the party. The Congress had been resisting for a long time the efforts of Dr. Ambedkar, but ultimately it had to relent and agree to give political rights to the Depressed Classes, through what is now known as the Poona Pact.

After transfer of power from the British rulers to the Indians, the Mahatma came to be regarded as the Father of the Nation. Dr. Ambedkar was entrusted with the task of ensuring the social justice and fundamental rights to all the sections of population, through the Constitution. Therefore, as we know, he had been invited to become the first Law Minister of India and the Chairman of the Drafting Committee of the Constitution of India. Having performed the onerous task of Constitution-making most creditably, Dr. Ambedkar came to be regarded as the Father of Constitution of India. He also came to be known as the Babasaheb, or the Grandfather [of India?]. In 1990, after 34 years of his leaving body, Ambedkar was resurrected into new life on the national scene, by being conferred the highest civil award, the *Bharat Ratna Award*, posthumously.

Congress Posing as Secular Political Party

Congress Party had been propagating itself to be a secular political party, as against being a fundamentalist party. Therefore, those having an eye at the reaping the best fruit of independence on traditional lines found themselves at a great loss either to satisfy the Upper Caste Hindus or the others including the Minorities and the weaker sections of the society. But they did see their selfish advantage in forming into a declaredly fundamentalist party under any name. It is in the light of this reality that the fundamentalist party has been steadily changing its name, with a view to having better appeal with the majority of the people, so that it comes to hold the reins of political power. Upto 1934, the Congress, Hindu Mahasabha and RSS were sharing the same political platform. Present day situation has also tended to dim the line of demarcation between the above said groups. The Hindu fundamentalists are trying to appear to be less dogmatic and the Congress Party, claiming to be a believer in secularism has been tending to be leaning towards fundamentalism. And, in the process, it might feel forced to sing with Ghalib :

Na khuda hi milaa na visaal-i-sanam,
Na idhar ke raha, na udhar ke rahe.

That is, we could neither realise God nor get united with the sweet-heart. We have come to be in such a predicament so that we are neither here, nor there.

Part III
Planning Strategy Against Ambedkar

6. Vicariously Hitting Real Targets

7. When Reason Has to Face the Unreasonable

8. Choosing Time of Attack on Ambedkar

9. One Adversary Made Measuring Rod for Another

6

Vicariously Hitting Real Targets

Fundamentalists found in the nineties of Twentieth Century the greatest and the most solid road blocks in the matter of serving their own vested interests, in the shape of Mahatma Gandhi and Dr. Ambedkar and in that of their respective ideologies, having appeal to different groups of people, sitting on either side of the fence. It is in this background that such people decided to bring a bad name to both of them. Mahatma Gandhi and Babasaheb Dr. B R Ambedkar had come to be considered as the ideals by different sections of population, divided on traditional lines. Both of them finally came to be the founders of two different sets of thoughts, Gandhism and Ambedkarism.

Popularity of Gandhism

Gandhism, in view of the Congress emphasis on secularism, came to be popular among certain sections of the Minorities. Similarly, Ambedkarism had its own attraction for such minorities. So far as the weaker sections were concerned, their hearts were with Ambedkarism but at times, their selfish interests, forced them to put themselves into the lap of the so-called secularists who were themselves neck-deep into their respective fundamentalisms. Since, secularism had come to have its own appeal, more parties came to be formed in addition to the Congress, with secular agenda, with a view to enticing both the minorities and the weaker sections. The crux of the policies of the secularists as also that of the Ambedkarites was to oppose the fundamentalists, the Hindu fundamentalists. Thus, those following both the ideologies were found at times soft towards both Gandhism and Ambedkarism.

Both Gandhi and Ambedkar Earmarked for Attacks

Now, the question was of launching the attacks on each of them. Half a century is an important landmark in any long term planning. Any programme that is highlighted with reference to divisions of time into century or half a century is normally expected to engage the attention of the population for an equally long period. As such, the fundamentalists found it expedient to tarnish the fair names of Gandhi and Ambedkar, on the occasion of the Golden Jubilee celebrations of India's independence.

Each Party's Own Components of Fundamentalists

All the political parties had their own components of fundamentalists. Such fundamentalists had only one point programme of seeing both the sides of their bread buttered, irrespective of the names or the declared programmes of the respective parties. Thus, there were the followers of all the parties to sympathise with the nefarious programmes of the declared fundamentalists, having grouped into a particular political party. Even the Congress party had its own hidden agenda to appeal to the fundamentalists, without declaring itself as the Hindu fundamentalistic party. The Congress party had started feeling aggrieved with the weaker sections and the minorities, for giving up the party, when the latter found that their interests were not safe in its hands, in the latter half of the seventies of the 20th century.

Effort to Vicariously Hit Contemporaries

Since Dr. Ambedkar was not the contemporary of Mr. 'S', the former cannot be believed to have provoked the latter to make such a senseless attack on him. The sheer volume of his book suggests that it has kept its author engaged for a number of years [not less than two years] according to Mr, 'S' himself. Surely, the book in question is the outcome of some serious reaction to the actions, if not of Dr. Ambedkar himself then at least of some of the devotees of Dr. Ambedkar, namely, the Dalits. Some of such Dalits have been mentioned by Mr. 'S' himself, who include Kanshi Ram, Ms. Mayawati, V T Rajshekar and Athavale.

Surely, such Dalits are the devotees of Dr. Ambedkar and they are also the contemporaries and the targets of Mr. 'S'.

In the light of the above, the book in question had been apparently sought to hit, *inter alia*, the above-named followers and devotees of Dr. Ambedkar and through them all the Dalits, who are largely constituted by the erstwhile Untouchables. This objective has been sought o be achieved through a clumsy condemnation of their singular source of inspiration, Dr. Ambedkar, their Messiah. But the political situation, prevailing at the time Mr. 'S' had undertaken to write the book in question, would go to suggest that the actual targets of his are all the Dalits. This impression is further confirmed by the antecedents of Mr. 'S', and by the reward he has obtained for the labours of his, at the hands of the Hindu fundamentalists, through his nomination to the Rajya Sabha, soon after.

Did Shourie Criminally Hit National Icons?

Mr. 'S' has engaged himself in false and arrogant campaign of mud slinging on the personality of one of the most illustrious luminaries of this great country, and a national hero, Dr. B. R. Ambedkar. It is hereby reiterated that Mr. 'S' has done so without any apparent justification or provocation. If he claims to have done so as a matter of retaliation, the book does not indicate any specific action of Dr. Ambedkar, which might have deserved so much of anger in the mind of Mr. 'S', who has brought out his book in 1997, while Dr. Ambedkar had left his physical existence more than 41 years ago.

Moreover, Mr. 'S' has not informed the serious readers about the specific need for such a hard-hitting attack on Dr. Ambedkar, which, as already stressed, is virtually an attack on the dignity of the Dalits. Therefore, someone has to take pains to delve deep into the recesses of his mind. The answer can legitimately be found in relation to the happenings in or around the time he had undertaken to write the book in question.

Shourie Errs on Time Taken to Plan Attacks?

Mr. 'S' replied to a question by Pritish Nandy that he had been working on the book in question for only one and a half year before publication thereof in July 1997. Mere loading of the vast, though not entirely relevant information in 663 pages of the book in question, must take much longer even for a writer, whose hands are not full with so many pressing jobs, at a time, unlike Mr. 'S'.

Immediate Cause for Sudden Attack: Conferment of Bharat Ratna Award on Ambedkar

In so far as the cause of grouse of Mr. 'S' against Dr. Ambedkar is concerned it can be legitimately traced with reference to the most important writings and actions of Dr. Ambedkar against the Hindus or Hindu religion much before the dawn of independence of India in 1947. In this connection, the act of Dr. Ambedkar in the matter of his denouncing the Hindu religion accompanied by his conversion to Buddhism can not be lost sight of, so far as its impact on Sangh Parivar ideologue like Mr. 'S' is concerned. Surely, such actions can be said to have been sufficient to constantly irk a fundamentalist Hindu.

It appears more probable that the mind of the fundamentalists like Mr. 'S' could have been agitated at the time of resurrection of Dr. Ambedkar in 1989, when the latter was suddenly remembered again so that he was conferred the highest civilian award of Bharat Ratna. Their sense of discomfiture can be said to have further multiplied manifold, when the country decided to celebrate the birth Centenary of Dr. Ambedkar in 1991. The sense of shock of the fundamentalists was further aggravated by the fact that the celebrations were arrogantly extended by another year, by VP Singh, the then Prime Minister who was continuing in office with the support of the Hindu fundamentalists themselves.

Other Tragets : V P Singh and Kanshi Ram?

VP Singh had not been caring to consult the Hindu fundamentalists in most of the crucial matters and the one regarding the conferment of the highest civilian honour to Ambedkar was one of such matters. That Mr. 'S' begins the first page of his book in question with expressing his grievance against Ambedkar about his idolisation can be cited as sufficient proof in support of the suggestion. The after-effects of these events were bound to be shocking for the intellectuals of Sangh Parivar. Naturally, they had been burning their midnight oil in order to hit back both VP Singh and Dr. Ambedkar. As such, the answer of Mr. 'S' regarding spending of the time on the book in question also smacks of intellectual dishonesty. But this aspect harms him alone and, therefore, let him be left free to inflict the harm to himself, if so advised.

Attacking New Dalit Identity

Understandably, some of the Dalit leaders were successful in giving a new sense of identity to Dalits as a class. Consequently, a party declaredly headed by one of the Dalits, Kanshi Ram, gave an unprecedented call to unify to the majority of the Indian population, under the new name of Bahujan Samaj Party. *Bahujana*, literally means, the majority. The said party called upon the masses to unite against the Upper Caste minority, constituted by the Brahmanas, Kshatriyas and Vaisyas, and to snatch power from such a minority.

The slogan proved to be catchy enough so that the party in question came to capture the office of Chief Minister for one of its lady members, the well-known Ms. Mayawati, in spite of the fact that it had only 20 percent members in the legislature. More astounding was the fact that such a revolution took place in Uttar Pradesh, the largest state of India which has claimed to be the seat of the Hindu religion, having the assumed birth places of the latest Vishnu-re-incarnates, Lord Rama and Lord Krishna.

Demolition of Babri Masjid on Ambedkar Jayanti

There was another significant development. The Hindu fundamentalists had been able to demolish the Babri Masjid at Ayodhya on the 6th December 1992, which "happened" to be the day of the death anniversary of Dr. Ambedkar. By that time the idea of the unity between the Dalits, OBCs and the religious minorities, particularly, the Muslims, which had taken birth in the late sixties of the present century, had started being translated into a reality. In the event of such a reality, being established, the Hindu fundamentalism could have received a very serious set back.

In 1992, the Congress was the ruling party at the Centre with Nrisimha Rao being the Prime Minister and SB Chavan being the Union Home minister. BJP was the ruling party in UP, with Kalyan Singh as the Chief Minister. The political pundits know that the Congress and the BJP are the two sides of the same coin so far as the real concern for Hindu fundamentalism is concerned.

What the BJP had been trying to do openly, the Congress has been trying to achieve the same results in a clandestine manner, with an eye on the money of the Hindu fundamentalists and the votes of the OBCs, the Dalits and the minorities. The Congress has, however, been extending lip sympathy to the Muslims, in the name of secularism. The BJP and its previous incarnates had almost politically given up the above mentioned classes and, therefore, they had been concentrating on the upper caste Hindus by trying to prove the Congress to be against the Caste Hindus.

Rift between AJGR and Brahmin-Bania Combine

A significant fact in this behalf is that the conferment of the said honour on Ambedkar had been made in the V P Singh regime, which was the one of the AJGR castes, indicated by the Hindi alphabets 'A' for Ahirs, 'J' for Jats, 'G' for Gujars and 'R' for Rajputs. These castes claim to represent the Kshatriya forces, and their rise to supremacy reminds the students of History and Hindu Mythology, of the game of hide and seek between the Brahmanas and the Kshatriyas throughout the history. The Hindi pronunciation of the combination of the above said four letters is *Ajagara*, meaning python. The *Ajagar* was and is fundamentally opposed to the idea of the Hindutva and the Brahmanical supremacy in social, political and religious life of the Hindus, and the Brahmin- Bania nexus in India.

The new nomenclature, which is believed to have been coined in the first decade of the twentieth century by a revolutionary, Raja Mahindra Pratap Singh, gave rise to a rare unity among the Kshatriya castes. The said dominant Kshatriya castes had been able to also forge another equally rare unity between the Dalits, the OBÇs (Other Backward Classes), and the religious minorities, especially the Muslims and the Sikhs. This unity was used by the Kshatriya leadership to their own advantage and against the Brahmana-Bania combine. The said combine had been reigning supreme in all spheres of Indian life since the birth of the Indian National Congress, in 1885, and particularly after Mahatma Gandhi's becoming the formal Dictator thereof in 1921.

Incidentally, Dr. Ambedkar had been the first important political leader to point out the strength and the menace of the Brahmin-Bania Combine, which has been repeatedly mentioned by Mr. 'S' as being one of the most important charges against him (Dr. Ambedkar). The AJGR castes found a ready-made slogan to topple the *Brahmin-Bania Combine* as also to enlist the support of the Dalits and OBCs and, of course, the minorities. Thus, Vilification of Ambedkar was sought to be used as a multi-pronged arrow to hit the enemies of Hindu fundamentalism, namely, the contemporary Dalit leadership, AGCR Castes, Minorities and secularism, at a time when the nation's mood could be expected to be very receptive.

7

When Reason Has to Face the Unreasonable

Response to the said book of vilification against Ambedkar, authored by Arun Shourie had remained divided on caste lines in the sense that Upper castes generally welcomed the book, through print media, which is almost entirely in their own hands. The reviews had almost fully supported Shourie in the matter of denigrating Ambedkar, where a Dalit writers and speakers found every fault with Shourie and his assumptions. Some of the rejoinders also appeared, which condemned the book questioning the assumptions of Shourie but all of them were from Dalit writers.

Dalit Writers Supported by OBC Intellectuals

Dalit writers were supported by some of the writers from OBCs also but the latter generally decided to keep away from the controversy for reasons best known to them. Non-Hindu and minority writers ignored the book and the reviews about it, apparently by wrongly treating the matter as being internal to the Hindus.

This attitude was similar to that exhibited in 1932, on the question of Communal Award, and Mahatma Gandhi's fast unto death. That matter was resolved only through a pact between the Hindu leadership on one hand, and Dr. Ambedkar, in his capacity of being the sole representative of the Dalits, then known as Depressed Classes. Interestingly, the Upper Caste Hindus had sent Mahatma Gandhi to the Round Table Conference as their sole representative. Thus, he was the common representative of Indian National Congress and the Upper caste Hindus. By opposing the Communal Award as above the Mahatma confirmed his position of representing the upper caste interests as against the weaker sections.

Old Prejudices Continuing

That sort of division was apparently holding true even in 1997, after 50 years of independence. The same appears to be so today in 2007, after a lapse of 10 years. In view of the situation as it stands, this author does not expect a different sort of response to the book in hand. But still, he has ventured to rehabilitate Babasaheb Ambedkar to the elevated position, he deserves. Since the controversy regarding the vilification of Babasaheb Dr. B R Ambedkar had been generated in the very recent past, which must be fresh in the minds of some of the readers and lay masses, it is considered imperative to keep the same in the background while proceeding with the thesis, this author is going to work upon.

Book in Hand Being Addressed to Indians and Hindus

Since, this author is going to prove the assumption that Babasaheb Dr. B R Ambedkar is India's Man of Millennium for Social Justice, it might be assumed that the book is largely being addressed to Indians. Since the injustice that has been meted out to the deprived sections is directly attributable to the Hindu social organisation or Hindu Varna system, which continued to be fought by Babasaheb throughout his life in his capacity as both a Hindu and a Buddhist, the book can also be said to be addressed to Hindus. The system had originated in the Hindu scriptures, and codified in Smritis, particularly, *Manu-Smriti*. It was called *Varna-vyavastha* or *Chaturvarnyam* or the system of four Varnas. The special characteristic of this system is that it creates in the society a graded system of inequality, injustice, exploitation and tyranny. The higher the Varna, the lower is the injustice etc. meted out to it and the lower the *Varna*, greater is the degree of injustice and exploitation etc.

Reaction to Varna Determined by Vested Interests

This Varna has been interpreted by its beneficiaries, as an ideal system of social organisation, aimed at eliminating social strife through determination of occupations for an individual at his very birth. This system has been preached as such by Hindu religious leaders known

Swamis, Mahatmas, Rajrshis, Brahmarshis and Paramhamsas depending on the level of so-called spiritual advancement determined in the light of one's birth in a particular Varna.

The beneficiaries of the system have been finding justification for it, on the flimsy ground that inequalities exist in all societies and religions. After emergence of class system in the world, the Hindu brains like Swami Vivekananda have been taking pains to prove that Brahmanas represent the priestly class, Kshatriyas stand for warriors, Vaisyas stand for trading class and the Sudras stand for labour class. But the Swami failed to inform his readers that in Hindu social organisation, there are Brahmins, who are not priests, that there are Kshatriyas, who are not warriors, there are Vaisyas, who are not traders and that there are Sudras, who are not labourers. He failed to disclose that vice versa was also true. He also failed to tell that that Varna system exists even among priests, warriors, traders and the labourers.

Shifting of Arguments for Varna Justification

Finding that determination of Varnas by birth is not entirely logical, some so-called reform organisations like Arya Samaj tried to argue that the Varnas are to be determined not with reference to the birth of man, but with reference to his *guna* (qualities), *karma* (actions) and *svabhaava* (disposition). But, it is true that no Hindu has ever been formally downgraded or upgraded on the basis of *guna, karma or svabhaava*. Thus, net result is that the exploitative and unjust system of Varnas has been arbitrarily and permanently imposed on the weaker sections. Mahatma Gandhi continued to subscribe to the same Varna system throughout his life, which fact resulted in making him and Dr. Ambedkar stand opposite each other. While appreciating the discussion about both of them and the Hindu social organisation, these facts ought to be borne in mind.

In the light of the above, the thesis that Ambedkar was the Man of Millennium ending the year 2000, for Social Justice, is not expected to have smooth sailing for the simple reason that both Dr. Ambedkar and this writer suffer from the same stigma of not volunteering to accept an unjust, inhuman, exploitative and tyrannical social organisation, and that they have questioned the divine origin of such a pernicious system. But this sort of fight has continued at least from the time of advent of Jainism and Buddhism more than 2500 years ago as a righteous reaction against the same *Varna* system, which has been kept alive by its beneficiaries with the avowed purpose of continuing the game of suppression and exploitation of the *Sudras* and *Ati-Sudras* or the modern masses.

Gandhi's Close Association with Hindu Celebrities

Mahatma Gandhi had been a close associate of the celebrities of the orthodox Hindus, like Madan Mohan Malaviya and Hedgewar. They had been for a long time heading their respective fundamentalist organisations like Hindu Mahasabha and Rashtriya Svayam Sewak Sangh and still, they had remained Congressmen as supporters of the Mahatma and the Congress at least till 1934. They had separated from him on the question of Poona Pact and his establishing Harijan Sewak Sangh in 1933 for the welfare of the Untouchables.

On Hindu Mahasabha and Congress Sharing Paltform

To begin with, Congress rode on the shoulders of Hindu fundamentalists like B. G. Tilak, the author of well-known *Arctic Home of the Vedas* and the man credited with making popular the worship of Ganapati in Maharashtra and the stalwarts of Hindu Mahasabha like Pandit Madanmohan Malviya and partly on those of RSS founder Hedgewar, as also those of Arya Samajists. The Congress firstly shed the weight of Arya Samaj, Hindu reform organisation suggesting thereby that Gandhi supported Pauranic Hinduism. The said organisation had come into prominence for opposing the rituals of Pauranic Hinduism and was interested in taking Hindus back to the Vedas, which appeared to be less prejudiced against lower castes. Then the Congress threw off the yoke of Hindu Mahasabha and RSS in 1934.

Hindu Mahasabha, RSS : No Part in Freedom Struggle

The Congress had ostensibly remained engaged in the so-called fight against the British rulers throughout. In the beginning the Hindu Fundamentalists supported the Congress by being its members but later on they opted out of it and its so-called fight for freedom. Thus, the Congress came to be understood as an organisation of the liberal Hindus. The Hindu Mahasabha never took part in the struggle independently in the beginning and later on left the Congress alone to fend for itself. RSS is known to have been encouraged by the British rulers to deal with the Muslim militants, in order to serve their own vested interests, in case the latter became a problem for the former. It is also known to have been in receipt of grant in aid from the government, which can be construed to mean a sort of taking pledge of not working against the government or the British rulers.

Hindu Fndamentalists Distance From Gandhi

The Hindu fundamentalists distanced from the Mahatma as already stated after signing of the Poona Pact in 1932. Next occasion for their distancing from him came in connection with his favourable attitude towards Muslims and Pakistan. Next occasion arose, when the Mahatma himself suggested to the then Prime Minster to entrust the onerous task of Constitution-making to Dr. Ambedkar. Dr. Ambedkar resigned as Law Minister on his differences with the then Prime Minister Nehru over the question of Hindu Code Bill, which, of course, subsequently came to be enacted into Law in smaller parts. The Hindu fundamentalists traced the dilution of their Hindu law again to Mahatma Gandhi, through the agency of Dr. Ambedkar. Finally, one of the men of the Hindu Fundamentalists, Nathuram Godse, assassinated the Mahatma on 30 January 1948.

Hindu Fundamentalists Adopting Gandhi as Their Hero

After that the RSS remained a banned organisation for many years, stalling the progress of Hindu fundamentalism in India. But after having a foothold on the political ladder, the same Hindu fundamentalists adopted the same Mahatma Gandhi as their hero. At times, they also change their harsh attitude towards Dr. Ambedkar.

Mahatma Gandhi enjoys a definite veneration in international circles. He came to be known throughout the British Empire since 1915, when he was conferred the *Kaiser-I-Hind* (Emperor of India) Gold Medal by British rulers. Then he joined the Congress, which had been working for political reforms in India since 1885. Mahatma Gandhi became the lifetime dictator of the Congress with effect from 28.12.1921.

On Gandhi Being Chief Challenge to British Rulers

Thus, Gandhi became the chief challenge of the British rulers in India. The Hindus welcomed him generally in his new role. He started living and looking like a Hindu saint, within his own Ashram and, as such, he came to be known as a Mahatma. As Mahatma, he started preaching through his prayer-speeches and his papers the tenets of orthodox Hinduism. Thus, he began to enjoy reverence by Hindu fundamentalists. He invited the association of Hindu reform organisation Arya Samaj but soon severed connections with it in 1922. In this way, his reputation as an orthodox Hindu was automatically strengthened. During the same period he started repeatedly asserting that he was a *Varnashrami* Hindu. Further, as already stated, the Hindu Mahasabha leaders and later RSS leaders kept on enjoying dual membership with congress and their respective organisations. This fact also went to further confirm Gandhi as an orthodox Hindu. Thus, Gandhi and the Congress have been oscillating between orthodox Hinduism and liberal Hinduism like a pendulam.

Graduation of Gandhi from Orthodox to liberal Hindu

First jolt to Gandhi's orthodox character came to him, as we know, through Poona Pact with Dr. Ambedkar, which resulted in important concessions to Dalits. Although the Orthodox Hindus later ratified this pact, yet the concessions were not found by them to be in keeping with the spirit of the scriptures of Hinduism. On the other hand, the Mahatma established *Harijan Sewak Sangh* in 1933, which gave him publicity of being pro-Dalits. The orthodox Hindu Organisation, then started distancing from him. Hedgewar, the founder of the RSS resigned from the Congress, on the advice of Mahatma Gandhi tendered through Jamanalal Bajaj. This fact can be said to be indicative of the fact that the Mahatma had started enjoying his role as a liberal Hindu.

Nationalism, Popular BJP Slogan was Congress Slogan

There is an interesting sidelight to the so-called struggle for freedom of India. Today, the Hindutva forces are in the forefront in raising the flag of nationalism high up in the sky. Initially, the Congress had given the slogan for nationalism, which was successful in a way in bringing many Muslims under the banner of Indian nationalism. Today the same Congress has become suspect in the eyes of neo-nationalists, the Hindu Fundamentalists. On the other hand, the Muslims who had been regarding Hindu fundamentalism as their worst enemy, have already started lending their support to the latter by becoming the Vice-Presidents and the Spokesmen of the only Hindu Fundamentlists' political party, the BJP. Are the Muslims preparing to fall by being between two stools? Or, is India going to say good-bye to all trends of fundamentalism?

Hindu Mahasabha, RSS and Muslims

Initially, Hindu Mahasabha and RSS were never interested in having understanding with the Muslims. Thus, they consciously developed a reputation of being anti-Muslim. On the other hand, the political exigencies urged the Mahatma to have a constant dialogue with Muslims starting from 1921, the days of Khilafat movement. In

Round Table Conference, Gandhi agreed to give to the Muslims and other minorities the separate electorates. Dr. Ambedkar raised a demand for such electorates for Dalits also. Although the demand was resisted by Mahatma Gandhi by staking his life, yet the Dalits got away with reservations and a promise for removal of certain important disabilities concerning temple entry, drawing water from public wells and admission to schools and services. Gandhi's reputation as an orthodox Hindu naturally suffered on account of his pacific attitude towards Muslims.

Orthodox Hindu Anger against Gandhi and Congress

The Hindu fundamentalists can never forget this history and, therefore, their anger against the Mahatma Gandhi and his Congress. As already suggested, but for the Mahatma being made the Father of Nation, the Hindu fundamentalists would have buried the Mahatma very deep. But his memory is alive, because they cannot efface it. Since he is alive in public memory, the orthodox Hindu opinion continues to be divided over the question of veneration for him. But apparently it is more a matter of politics than anything else.

Relevance of Welfare of Masses

In any such choice, the welfare of the masses in general is a factor, which must become the ultimate deciding factor for true veneration for anyone. The most important aspect in the welfare of the masses is the social justice. Mahatma Gandhi as a liberal Hindu has also come to have a reputation for devoting his life to the question of amelioration of the Untouchables. Amelioration of the untouchables must tilt the balance in favour of the amelioration of other deprived sections of population also. But the Mahatma has come to develop that reputation with the support of the upper caste Hindus only. So far as the Dalits and other weaker sections are concerned, they regard only Dr. Ambedkar as their deliverer.

In this sense, Dr. Ambedkar poses definite danger to Mahatma Gandhi and Atal Bihari Vajpayee, L K Advani, Rajnath Singh, nay, all the Hindu fundamentalists, and their combined spokesman Arun Shourie and his present Avatar, Arun Jaitley in the matter of being declared as India's Man of Millennium for Social Justice. This danger presents a very serious question for all of them as to whether Dr. B. R. Ambedkar should be allowed to be declared India's Man of the Millennium for Social Justice.

Since the ball has been set rolling by by Arun Shourie, through a strategical endeavour to glorify Mahatma Gandhi, by dishonestly projecting him as a true God through a clever design to vilify Dr. Ambedkar by means of the book *Worshipping False Gods, and the facts that have been erased*, the book in hand unwittingly throws the ball back in the court of the fundamentalists. It goes in their court automatically since the perennial problem of survival of caste and exploitative caste organizations still persists.

Just as Shourie's book against Ambedkar has not been accepted as the last word on Gandhi, Ambedkar and the nature of true and false gods, the book in hand may also not accepted as the last word in favour of the proposition that Ambedkar is India's Man of Millennium for Social Justice, since acceptance of this proposition as a fact can mean the last nail in the coffin of organized exploitation, oppression, suppression of the weak and poor by the strong and the rich, and by the crafty of the simple folks or the lay masses.

However, where vested interests rule reason gets no hearing. Rather new reasons are imagined to defeat the absolute reason. In such a situation, the aggressor and the aggrieved cannot have a meaningful dialogue. The exploiters and the exploited and their advocates need to stand face to face. The weak and the exploited cannot take their arguments and their appeal to a disinterested arbiter, since it is not easy to find one. The weak has his reason but the strong has the power to ignore the reason.

Indian caste system has kept the beneficiaries and the victims of the system in separate compartments, separated by a thick but transparent wall. The parties can look at each other but cannot convince each other of the merits in reasoning of the opponent. Any Gandhi or any Ambedkar is bound to be caught in their game. Since the perpetrators cannot be forced to change their outlook, the victims have no option but to find some escape route. But escape is no solution and, therefore, all escape routes giving rise to new religions, new sects, new ideologies have been unable to cause any dent in the solid wall of exploitation, which goes on getting stronger and stronger, by applying the tact of *sama* (conciliation), *dama* (deceit), *danda* (force) and *bheda* (dissension), against particular bits and parts, which are found vulnerable to the dismay of the whole.

At times, natural catastrophes might force the parties to take over the roles of their opponent. But even then, the game must go on as before, and the same rules of game must go on operating. Master may become the slave and a slave may turn into master, but either one must feel forced to play the game as per the same rules of the game. Anyone, who decides not to play the game, may have the option of turning into a recluse, a *yogi* or a saint and witness the goings on as a disinterested entity. Such an entity may have a peace of mind but nothing of his own to keep his body and soul together.

8

Choosing Time of Attack on Ambedkar

Some of the mischievous individuals occupying important positions in Government and Hindu Fundamentalist organisations had devised a new method of celebrating the Golden Jubilee of their own independence. It appears from Shourie's book *Worshipping False Gods and the facts that have been erased* that they wanted to remind the Dalits that they would not have any future in free India, if they dared celebrate their independence and freedom from exploitation by expressing a sense of gratitude to their messiah, Dr. Ambedkar. The Dalits were also warned that they would be butchered on the pattern of the carnage that took place in Maharashtra after the desecration of the statue of Babasaheb Ambedkar. Do such mischievous people want to celebrate the freedom to demolish others' God and by scuttling any adverse reaction to such acts of vandalism?

Yes! The suggestion appears to be that in order to spare themselves of such tyrannies and indignities, the Dalits ought to meekly declare that they are no more interested in regarding Dr. Ambedkar as their messiah. The fundamentalists also want the Dalits to declare that they are ever ready to discard Dr. Ambedkar and erase his memory from their own minds, in order to purchase security for themselves from the die-hard Hindus.

Misleading Title of Shourie's Book

The title of the book in question wrongly suggests that some facts about Dr. Ambedkar have been erased. But the real objective of the book and of all those who are and have been behind its conception, appears to have the memory of Dr. Ambedkar erased from the minds of the public by attacking every thing the great man stood for.

It is clear that lot of prior preparations had gone in connection with the preparation of the case of vilification against Dr. Ambedkar. It is further evident that the timing for the release of the book in question had been deliberately determined to coincide with the Golden jubilee celebrations of India's independence. Mr. 'S' himself had made advance preparations for proper reception of the vilification campaign. His efforts had been supplemented by the BJP as a political party, which had also prepared the mood of its followers and Hindu fundamentalists through its *Yatras* and accompanying propaganda, which particularly tended to hit the Dalits in a special sense.

Web page created by *Vedam Books International* in connection with the Golden Jubilee of India's independence ran like this:

> *"The Golden Jubilee of India's Independence is a momentous occasion—an occasion to recall. Remember and recreate the spirit of freedom struggle, highlight the gains of fifty years of Independence and look forward with a vision for the future."*

Golden Jubilee Occasion: Account of Failures Absent

The scheme of the Constitution prescribed the best principles to run the government and the society. Proper system of checks and balances with regard to various Constitutional authorities of the country had also been prescribed. But much has been lost at the implementation level mainly because of lack of political will of the successive governments. All such governments had been more than willing to succumb to the vested interests on traditional lines. Most of the governments have been apologetic about the provisions of the constitution aiming at restoring social justice in stead of taking a genuine pride in them and whole-heartedly implementing them. There has been a sure tendency to drift rather than having a definite will to take a positive action in right directions in an absolute sense. This is why, after fifty years, India went through through a period of tremendous turbulence. The Vedam Site had rightly lamented as under at the state of affairs prevailing at that time:

> *"Despite the country making substantial and significant progress, the fact remains that vast masses are destitute. Neither*

democracy nor development seemed to have come anywhere closer to achieving the ideals of genuine equality or distributive justice."

Occasion for Evaluation of Achievements and Failures

The Golden Jubilee occasion should have been an honest attempt to assess and evaluate our achievements and failures during the last fifty years. The Government should have made a beginning in this behalf by itself presenting a balance sheet of achievements and failures. The government ought to have thereby invited the considered reaction from national leaders, freedom fighters, former VVIPs irrespective of their political affiliations, eminent jurists, diplomats, industrialists, political commentators, social activists as also from the spokesmen of the important political parties. In view of the complex nature of the Indian society in transition with all its travails and anxieties, the responses could be presumably diverse and even contradictory to the claims put forth by the government. But in the larger interests of the country and the society, a churning of all sorts of ideas should have been welcome to all concerned. But nothing like that happened.

No Party Found to be Sympathetic to Dalits

Incidentally, the actual working of democratic process in India shows that no government is particularly sympathetic to the Dalits. All the political parties are out to extract political benefits from the Dalits. Their importance consists for them in the large number of Dalits, in their poverty, in their ignorance, in their hunger and in their destitution. In 1997, there was Gujral Government in power, which was not of BJP. And, in 1992, it was Narasimha Rao Government which was again not of BJP; it was of the Congress. In 1991, it was of VP Singh, which again was not of the BJP; it was that of Non-Brahmin-Bania combine. But under all these governments the Dalits suffered with certain regularity.

All the parties have been having a definite attitude of *samabhava*, a feeling of equanimity and being equidistant, which may be regarded as a high quality in spiritual sense. They have **exhibited the policy of equal ignorance, equal exploitation, of equal browbeating, of equal lack of concern and, in particular situations, of equal enmity.** While conducting themselves they remain totally oblivious of the fact that the nature hits every one and when it hits, it does not produce the sound of hitting. All these political parties believe in practice in the message which is opposite to the teaching of the *Gita*, *karmanyeva adhikaras te ma* *phalesu kadaachana*, that is, your duty is to go on doing action without bothering for the fruit of labour. But they always aim at the fruits and never at performing honourable duties.

Misrepresenting Message of Gita

The message for all the politicians of all the political parties, constituted by the upper caste leadership, who declare themselves to be the ardent followers of the above-said message of the Gita has been modified as under:

> *"Your duty is to avoid action in all situations; you must allow the things to drift to the maximum possible extent. But you must always go on steadily exploiting all the situations, good or bad, only to your selfish ends. Never bother to be reminded of your duty to the poor, the needy, the destitute and so on. God has punished them by making them so. If you disturb God's scheme, He will be angry with you and punish you. Your duty is either to close your eyes towards them, or to help God in fulfilling His purpose, in a speedier manner. By acting that way, you are sure to earn a special merit."*

Seeking Solace through Policy of Unconcern

And, quite understandably, such parties and castes find solace through such policy of unconcern. Their Yoga tells them just to be witness to whatever may happen. They tell everyone that time is the best healer. So, they leave the matters to time for healing the diseases of all kinds. They tell you to bother for your own spiritual evolution as an individual. You came alone; you will leave this world alone. There is none who may be called as your own. So, there is no need to bother about any one. They derive inspiration in such matters from Saint Kabir: *Tuzh ko parai kya pari, apni niber tu,* that is, why to bother about others; you be concerned about fixing your own problems. This is the crux of all orthodox teachings, which suits those who believe in status quo.

No Participation of Minorities and Dalits In Golden Jubilee Celebrations

Should such a thing have happened in the year in which the nation was celebrating the Golden Jubilee of India's Independence? Incidentally, the Golden Jubilee had been advertised, *inter alia*, through a special Web Site created by or on behalf of Government of India. It had quoted highly inspiring thought of Rabindranath Tagore.

Celebration of Golden Jubilee is a national event in which the participation of all the citizens, irrespective of caste, creed, social or economic status, should have been encouraged. But in case of India, it appears that the occasion had been monopolised by the upper caste Hindus. There are reasons to believe that the minorities and weaker sections had been marginalised in advance.

Dalits Charged for Not Joining Fight for Freedom

So far as Dalits are concerned, they were publicised particularly through Shourie's book and vigorous publicity campaign as not having taken part in the fight for freedom, as being the followers and devotees of Dr. Ambedkar, who had also allegedly not taken part in the said fight. The messiah of the Dalits had also been declared to be anti Mahatma Gandhi, who has been credited with winning freedom for the country. He had also been alleged to have brought shame on the Hindus for their beliefs and culture with a view to helping the British to continue to rule over India.

Choosing Time for Attack

Under these circumstances, the timing of denigrating both Gandhi and Ambedkar had been decided upon by the fundamentalists out of power, but it seems, with the underhand approval of the then ruling party. The government and the nation were otherwise committed to the celebration of the Golden Jubilee programme more in the sense of a ritual. But the enthusiasm in this behalf was more in the fundamentalist quarters. Both the fundamentalists and the government of the day had thought it best to take the advantage of the Internet. As such, both of them had created their own Web Sites.

Planned Dampening of Dalits Enthusiasm

The result of all this was naturally to dampen the enthusiasm of the Dalits in celebrating the Golden Jubilee of Independence and to participate in such celebrations. Dalits also had started fearing the cat calls of the Hindus in general in public meetings, and their accusing fingers.

Dr. Ambedkar had been articulating his stand and his philosophy, throughout his life. As such, one does not have to take the help of imagination in order to understand his mind. He had duly explained every intention of his, which has been in print for decades. As to why he had not sided with the Congress or why he had been criticising Mahatma

Gandhi, in the matter of the latter's fight for freedom, or in that of the latter's lack of serious concern for the Untouchables, had been duly explained by Dr. Ambedkar himself. He had done it in the relevant contexts, more than half a century ago and even when the so-called 'Congress fight for freedom' was still on. The right time for reaching to Ambedkar and his thought was when he had launched the alleged attack. Any reaction after 50 years of independence could be aimed at hitting those, who have become the beneficiaries of his policy, and they are primarily the Dalits.

Failure to Give Other Side of Picture

Unfortunately, Mr. 'S' has contented himself with only levelling the charges and he has not considered his duty to present the other side of the picture which was clearly discernible from the same published works on which he claims to have prepared the charge-sheet against Dr. Ambedkar. Had he referred to other side of the picture, he would not have had the apparent justification for inflicting so heavy a volume on Dr. Ambedkar, on the devotees of the latter and on the unsuspected readers of the unnecessarily long book of its author, Arun Shourie.

Logically speaking, it should have been the Mahatma Gandhi and Dr. Ambedkar's contemporary Congressmen, who could have legitimately felt aggrieved and considered the necessity of expressing their resentment, at or around the very time when Dr. Ambedkar had allegedly criticised the Mahatma and the Congress. But those persons had not only taken no offence against Dr. Ambedkar in the matter, but they had themselves and voluntarily also invited him to undertake the most prestigious task of preparing the Constitution. And that invitation was accompanied by yet another invitation regarding Dr. Ambedkar's becoming the first Law Minister of Independent India, in addition to becoming the Chairman of the Drafting Committee of Constitution of India. Had Shourie mentioned these facts, he would not have been left with any justification for narrating the pejoratives against Ambedkar.

9

One Adversary Made Measuring Rod for Another

In Indian context, there may be different persons, who might be projected as being the greatest men of the millennium by different sets of people for different reasons. But two great men have surpassed all others in the sense that organised efforts have been made by different sets of people or groups to efface their names from the public memory. Such efforts have been presumably made with a view to make some pigmies to occupy the top place in history, if vacated by those who actually hold it. The top dignitaries who actually deserve such a position must include Mahatma Gandhi and Dr. B R Ambedkar since the former is known the Rashtrabapu or the Father of the Nation and the other as Babasaheb or Grandfather and the Father of Constitution of India. Attempts to efface the memories of both of them were made in the 50th year of Independence or in the Golden Jubilee year of India's Independence, namely, the year 1997.

Gandhi Used as Measuring Rod for Ambedkar

Shourie's book against Ambedkar appeared about the time, when the bug of man of millennium had already bitten the world. Did he decide to write his book anticipating the fear of someone suggesting his name for the top slot of Man of Millennium? He started the tirade against Ambedkar by making the Mahatma as the measuring rod for Dr. Ambedkar, as we already know. For various reasons the book against Dr. Ambedkar has been claimed to be the best seller by its author, Shourie and his associates. The book had also been reportedly purchased in bulk by certain political leaders of the upper castes appears to have already been prepared in favour of the Mahatma and against Dr. Ambedkar. If the said book has been the bestseller, the following questions seem to naturally arise:

Whether the book has been best seller, has it been so because it has been authored by Shourie? Or

Has it been so because Gandhi has been projected as True God? Or

Has it been so because Ambedkar and Gandhi have been contrasted against each other? Or

Has it been so because of the fact that a special propaganda was launched against Ambedkar to prove that the latter was a false god, which has thus far been described as *asura* or demon or *rakshasha?*

It is not easy to get to the truth of the matter. But a peep into the media hype and its analysis shows that Shourie has been largely condemned for levelling unverified charges against a celebrity (Dr. Ambedkar) and unnecessarily involving another one (Mahatma Gandhi) in idle controversy. It has also come to the fore that Gandhi who has been projected as a true god has also come to be exposed beyond proportion. It is also true that bad blood has been created between the followers of Ambedkar (who regard the latter as their deliverer) and the Hindu fundamentalists. This fact has obviously resulted in the generation of all round interest in Ambedkar as against Gandhi.

Besides, both Ambedkar and Gandhi have been vilified at about the same time, and by the persons of RSS background. Further, the number of persons who came forward to defend Ambedkar is extremely large as compared to those who cared to defend Gandhi. Rather, it appears to be nearer truth that there is hardly anyone, who has formally raised his pen in favour of Gandhi, but quite a few books have appeared in favour of Ambedkar and aiming at condemning Shourie.

All this must lead to the conclusion that the entire exercise of Shourie has misfired and boomeranged not only against himself but also against his favourite Gandhi. It has also been suspected that perhaps **Shourie's secret aim was to hit both Ambedkar nad Gandhi since the Hindu fundamentalists have been regarding Gandhi as liberal Hindu and Ambedkar as Anti-Hindu, who are equally disliked by Sangh Parivar, and therefore by Shourie, its ideologue.** Thus, Shourie had extended only a left handed and non-serious compliment to Gandhi, which failed to amuse anyone.

Still, it is a fact that the actual tie in the matter of occupying the top slot of Man of Millennium, for social justice must remain between Mahatma Gandhi and Dr. Ambedkar. The tie remained during their lifetime and it continues to be there after their deaths. But only one of them can succeed in the tussle. If one succeeds, the other must fail and vice versa. And, each of them has to be measured against the measuring rod of the other.

It is good that Shourie has set the ball rolling by trying to make Dr. Ambedkar appear pigmy as compared to Mahatma Gandhi. **Now, it is the turn of the Mahatma to be compared against the measuring rod of Dr. Ambedkar.** The views of Madhu Limaye, already referred to earlier, might appear to work, in a way, as those of a referee in this behalf. But now, the result must depend on the consideration of the case of each other in the background of absolute qualifications for a great man, since such qualifications alone can guard against the possibility of prejudice creeping in for or against either of them.

Gandhi and Ambedkar as Two Ends of Pole

It can be accepted as a fact that both Gandhi and Ambedkar had been projected for long as the two ends of the same pole. Accordingly, the job of the fundamentalists is becoming increasingly difficult in the matter of winning over the followers of both to their own side. Thus, in a way, **the fundamentalists gave up such followers altogether, and finally decided to render both Gandhi and Ambedkar, irrelevant, not through threadbare analysis of their respective ideologies and actions, but through their denigration on grounds unrelated to their respective ideologies or actions.** It appears to be under these circumstances that both Gandhi and Ambedkar came to be denigrated in the golden jubilee of independence.

Emergence of Omnibus Volume on Vilification

As regards Mahatma Gandhi, not many people might dispute his right to the position of his being one of the greatest man of the last millennium. Mahatma Gandhi has reasserted his claim to the said position since the time a relentless campaign for his vilification through the attempts of deification of his assassin, Nathuram Godse has been started.

Campaign against Dr. Ambedkar with the same object of effacing his memory from public minds was also started. Significantly, the campaign culminated in an omnibus volume authored by Shourie, already mentioned above.

More importantly, the weakest point about Dr. Ambedkar, that has been advanced by the author of the said book, is that the former had been the greatest Gandhi-hater. To state differently, Mahatma Gandhi has been assumed to be the perfect man to measure the size of Dr. Ambedkar. In other words, Mahatma Gandhi has been accepted as the measuring rod for assessing the personality of Dr. Ambedkar, who has been first decalred as Gandhi-hater or at least an adversary. Logically speaking both deserve to be measured against the measuring rod of each other, since they were working for particular ideologies, and were not engaged in personal warfare.

Reasons Behind Comparison

Why Dr. Ambedkar has been chosen to deserve the honour of being compared with the Mahatma has been explained by Shourie at the very start of his book by lamenting that no other person has been conferred with 'so great an honour' as Dr. Ambedkar. In other words, it has been assumed for the purpose of the book in question that only Mahatma Gandhi should have deserved so much honour, and not Dr. Ambedkar. The latter has been highlighted not only as Gandhi-hater but also as having opposed the freedom movement, which, according to Shourie, had been successfully led by Mahatma Gandhi.

Thus, the short question that can be said to have been put before the country is whether both Mahatma Gandhi and Dr. Ambedkar have a rightful place in the history of the country or not, and, if so, in what sense. If this question has been raised by interested parties in the fiftieth year of India's Independence, the same is likely to be reasserted with renewed vigour at the completion of the Century of Indian Independence, in the year 2047. There is every likelihood of the same question being agitated even earlier than 2047, when the Independence of India completes 75 years in 2022 AD.

Both Gandhi and Ambedkar Passed First Test of Survival

Both Mahatma Gandhi and Dr. Ambedkar have passed the first test of survival. Ambedkar has done so through the endeavours of the interested parties hinted above. These endeavours have, in a way, made him stand in comparison with Mahatma Gandhi, so far as the question of endeavours of certain people with a view to effacing their memories is concerned. This means that the tussle is now only between the two personalities and there is no third aspirant to the position of the Man of the Millennium.

In this light the natural question that emerges in this behalf is whether Mahatma Gandhi or Dr. B R Ambedkar is the rightful Man of Millennium.

Chances are that both of them might resurrect themselves, and survive the attempts at their second killings, though for different reasons since, according to many, both of them were obviously the two ends of the same pole, the human welfare. But it is also a fact that only he should be considered the Man of the Millennium, who has the real qualifications of a great man in an absolute sense, and in connection with ensuring social justice.

In Search of Objectivity

In this connection, the book of Madhu Limaye, *The Prime Movers: The Role of Individual in History* can be relevant in another sense. Limaye suggested, as per the estimate of this author, one of the most reliable criteria for the purpose in question. The suggestion, this author got from Limaye was that the honour of being declared to be the Man of the Millennium should go to a man, who has played the most decisive role in history.

If so, the next question can be as to the field in which such a role has been played. Justice and fair play have been the most wanted things in this world, since this world is believed to have been generally controlled and managed so far by the forces of injustice and exploitation.

Taking Help from Madhu Limay

Limaye's book had been published at a time, when the world had not yet been bitten by the Millennium bug. Naturally, Limaye had only the last two centuries in his mind. Only a few years ago, the search had been on for the greatest man of the 20th century. That kind of search appeared to be more exact and more manageable, in view of there being a better availability of reliable comparative data, within the scope of the frame-work to be determined by particular opinions. He had selected only 10 personalities from all over the world to deserve special treatment. He had also pinpointed the specific areas in which the concerned individuals had been operating throughout their life.

Out of those 10, only 5 happened to be the Indians. Out of the Indians, two personalities were Mahatma Gandhi and Dr. B R Ambedkar. Others were Gopal Krishna Gokhale, Vallabh Bhai Patel and Netaji Subhash Chandra Bose. Since no efforts have been made to efface the names of the said three Indians from the memory of the masses, they cannot be considered to be in the run for being declared as the Man of the Millennium. For that very reason, we need not discuss their personalities. Incidentally, the non-Indians included in the list of were Mohammed Ali Jinnah, Karl Marx, Bismarck, Justice Wendell Holmes and Harold Laski. Thus, out of the Indians, again only Mahatma Gandhi and Dr. Ambedkar can be said to have emerged to be the actual competitors for the purpose.

Relevance of Salvation of People and Intelligentsia

Anton Chekhov said that "the power and salvation of a people lie in its intelligentsia, in the intellectuals who think honestly, who feel, and can work."® Intellectuals are the people who have got special intelligence, which is described as "the faculty of manufacturing artificial objects, especially tools to make fools."- In this sense, Mr. 'S' can surely be considered as an intelligent person and the brand of people represented by him and his associates can be ironically called to be forming a band of intelligentsia.

It is obvious, that Mr. 'S' represents the obscurantistic die-hard Hindus, highly prejudiced against the masses, the Sudras, and the Dalits, the erstwhile Untouchables. They had adopted the creed of prejudice in order to become privileged persons. After they decided to become themselves privileged, it was only natural that they would make others deprived of all privileges and even of human rights.How far these observations apply to Mahatma Gandhi and Dr.Ambedkar will become evident from the following pages. However, this much can be straightaway said with a certain amount of certainty that considered in the light of the dictionary meaning of the word intelligentsia in an absolute sense, Dr. Ambedkar shall have a definite edge over Mahatma Gandhi.

Difficulty In Attempting Balanced Comparison

Mikhail Bakunin observed that "It is the peculiarity of privilege and of every privileged position to kill the intellect and heart of man. The privileged man, whether he be privileged politically or economically, is a man depraved in intellect and heart". If Mr. 'S' and his associates, and his supporters do consider themselves, as privileged, they should not be expected by any one to possess the quality of being dispassionate persons, possessing a definite amount of objectivity.

From such persons, no balanced comparison can be expected between the one who has been accepted as their own ideal and another who is regarded by them as an opponent of their own or of their accepted ideal. If Shourie being such a person has chosen Mahatma Gandhi as his ideal, can it be reasonably denied that the latter should automatically tend to lose some weight?

In view of this, the endeavour of Mr. 'S' was bound to be coloured from the stage of the very conception of the idea of undertaking the said endeavour. He started with a 'mission' of denouncing Dr. Ambedkar, and therefore, he had picked up the tools best suited for the purpose, or modified them in such a manner that they appear to suit the best, for the purpose.

In fact all comparisons should be meant for those endowed with a supreme sense of objectivity. If the audience is lacking in a sense of supreme objectivity, the real purpose of such comparisons must be lost.

Gandhi and Ambedkar Standing for Different Values

The mere fact that Mr. 'S' has decided to compare Dr. Ambedkar and Mahatma Gandhi, presupposes that there is, in public mind, already an impression that the two great men stood for different values. Mr. 'S' has thought it fit to highlight the area of disagreement between and about the two great men.

In view of the inherent nature of the comparisons, any expressions countered in the book under reference are not likely to be received as being satisfactory by the entire readership. The readership has to be divided for the simple reason that both the Mahatma and Dr. Ambedkar have come to be deified by different sections of population. Such sections of population are separated by their respective differences in religious, political, economic and political senses. Any deity comes to have a following of the people, who are generally intolerant to the criticism of their own deity. The intolerance does not permit them to bother about the merits of the criticism. The same thing can be true of the respective followers of Mahatma Gandhi and Dr. Ambedkar. But in a book, coming from one, who claims to be one of the most objective writers, the author, should have shown greater sense of responsibility and the consequent objectivity. Mr. 'S' has obviously miserably failed in this behalf.

Comparisons are odious

Any comparison unavoidably leads to some sort of competition with all its natural consequences. While the law [of competition] may be sometimes hard for the individual, it is best for the race, because it ensures the survival of the fittest in every department. We accept and welcome, therefore, as conditions to which we must accommodate ourselves, great inequality of environment, the concentration of business, industrial and commercial, in the hands of the few, and the law of competition between these, as being not only beneficial, but essential for the future progress of the race.

The book of Mr. 'S' has intended to give rise to some sort of competition, if not between the two great men, certainly between their respective devotees. Friedrich Engels had declared that "Competition is the most extreme expression of that war of all against all which dominates modern middle society."

The two great men had identified themselves with two different sets of sections of Indian population which had been traditionally forced to remain divided and set against each other by the force of circumstances and the machinations of the upper strata of society against the lower one. One set had been struggling for retaining their ill-gotten gains and superiority over the other, and the other section had been struggling for its existence against the injustice meted out to it through the strategies given the name of religion.

This sort of struggle for existence — which in extreme cases is a life and death struggle — is waged not only between different classes of society but also between individuals within these social groups. Every body competes in some way against everyone else and consequently each individual tries to push aside any one whose existence is a barrier to his own advancement. The Mahatma and the Doctor had made themselves identified with different sets of people and, therefore, they could be legitimately said to be in competition against each other. And, decidedly, they were in competition against each other over the question of keeping the Dalits on their side. We shall be discussing this aspect elsewhere in detail.

Need for Similarity of Field of Comparison

The field of comparison has been incidentally indirectly limited by Shourie to two main assumptions:

[1] That the national struggle was launched by Indian National Congress and it was led to success in its resolve to rid the country free of British rule under the leadership of Mahatma Gandhi; and

[2] That the main and final event in the history of freedom was the Quit India Resolution confirmed by the Congress in August, 1942 consequent upon which Mahatma Gandhi and his Congressmen had to lavish in Jail and suffer therein the atrocities of the British authorities and the British repression.

It is about these assumptions, that Shourie has attempted a comparison of Dr. Ambedkar with Mahatma Gandhi. It is said that comparisons are odious. The synonyms for the word odious given in the thesaurus are *despicable, abominable, detestable, excrecable, hateful, and invidious.* Whenever a comparison is attempted between any two persons or things, the naturally expected outcome thereof has to unavoidably describe with the suggestions thrown by the above-said words.

References

@ Arun Shourie; *Worshipping False Gods, Ambedkar and the facts which have been erased*; ASA Publications, New Delhi, 1997, pp. ix-XI

- Henri Bergson; *Creative Evolution*; Quoted in *Great Quotations.*

¬ Andrew Carnegie; The *Gospel of Wealth.* 1889; Quoted in *Great Quotations*

¯ Friedrich Engels; The *Condition of the Working Class in England.*

Part IV
Media Reaction for and Against Vilification

10. Politically Incorrect Hand Granade Tossed

11. Dalits Need Another Struggle for Freedom

12. Wildly Polemic and Incorrect Campaign of Vilification

13. Bringing Order in House of Disorder

10

Politically Incorrect Hand Granade Tossed

There should be some question of one's having a *locus standii* to rake up an issue. Arun Shourie (AS) does not have any *locus standii* to inflict such a volley of vilification as has been made by him the subject matter of his book in question. Even the mere lapse of more than a half a century after the event, should have been sufficient ground for stopping AS from such an act of vilification at least without analysing all the issues in a dispassionate manner. But here it appears that he has regarded his indiscretion as the best part of valour.

Indian Media is Caste Hindu Media

The media which is in India practically a Hindu media, had been giving wide publicity to the idea of vilification of Ambedkar much in advance of the publication of the book in question in 1997. General tone of such reports before and after was to give the maximum vent to the feelings against Dr. Ambedkar. Still, there were some honourable exceptions among the reviewers, of Shourie's book, who tried to give their balanced views. But the weight of their logic was so profound that the entire mist of calumny was cleared in no time at least among those readers who had a chance to look at the both sides of criticism. Among them one was Kancha Ilaiah, who in his story titled *Upholders of Utouchability* expressed his unconcealed yet a righteous agony on the manner in which AS had gone hysteric. He began by observing that

Arun Shourie's book *Worshipping False Gods,* through virulent publicity by the Brahminical media, is being put out as a 'magnum opus' for the simple reason that he presents 'facts' as he likes, to attack the Dalit God—Ambedkar — of contemporary India, whose spirits are creating a crisis in the very same state and civil society that AS and his ilk reaped all fruits without expending their labour whatsoever. Ilaiah says, "From the title page to the packed jacket back page (667+xli pages including introduction and index) the book is nothing but spitting venom against Ambedkar and untouchables (SCs) in the name of presenting facts." He holds AS responsible for instigating the happenings in Maharashtra and, of course, elsewhere.

Book Attacking Ambedkar, Unable to Demolish Him

Of course, what happened in Maharashtra on August 11, 1997, within a short time after the said book came into the market, Ilaiah felt, was an expression of that mindset. But both his book and the process of his "School of thought" initiated in Maharashtra **will only contribute to more and more statues of Ambedkar with officially paid guards to protect them, as is being done** in Maharashtra. Ilaiah feels that AS has failed in his mission against Dr. Ambedkar and the Dalits.

Arun Shourie's book attacks Ambedkar but is unable to demolish him either by means of dubious scholarship with which it is written or by the facts he repeatedly boasts to have mustered. Having written this book Shourie stands to lose everything except the fabulous money by selling the bulky volume full or repetitions, with a price (Rs. 450) to rob the public money from libraries. The book fails Shourie and his school on two important counts:

1. Methodologically, the book is based on paper foundation, not on a concrete foundation. Simply by employing a research scholar as Shourie did we can dig out archival material of praise from the same British rulers on Shourie's heroes — Gandhi, Patel, Subhash and so on — to prove that they too were British agents. British administrators noted different things at different times about all the leaders including Gandhi. **Different governors and viceroys had different views about almost all the national leaders.**
2. As E H Carl rightly put it, a fact is like a 'sac' and the interpretation changes the worth and value of that 'sac.' Constructing history should not be based on mere opinionated

> writings of an administrator and they cannot be shown as facts. If that is going to decide the patriotism of persons like Ambedkar, Gandhi, Nehru, Patel and so on, for that matter anybody can be proved anti-national and pro-British. **On all occasions when Gandhi withdrew Satyagraha British administrators issued statements and wrote letters appreciating and praising him**. That does not prove anything. A historical personality must be assessed on his/ her overall role and how that role empowered the poor, illiterate masses of a given country. This is where Ambedkar's godhead in so far as Dalit masses are concerned lies.

Readers might like to take note of the fact of repetition of the desecration of the statues of Ambedkar, in the same Maharashtra, and Marathwada region after 10 years, namely , on 10 April 2007 (The Tribune dated 11 April refers) and again leading to riots. Have Caste Hindus learnt any lession? Will anyone pause to think. what will happen on silver, golden and other jubilees of certain events that have been constantly bringing shame on Hindus? Or does the shame come on them when anyone happens to raise such questions?

Increasing Mass Support for Ambedkar And Decreasing for Gandhi?

Kancha Ilaiah makes a very pertinent point regarding the increasing mass support to Dr. Ambedkar as contrasted with the decrease of mass support to Gandhi:

> **Increasing mass support to Ambedkar and decreasing support to Gandhi lie in theoretical and political strategies that Ambedkar worked out for annihilation of caste.** His popularity among SC, ST and OBC is not because he wrote the Indian Constitution but more because he wrote Annihilation of Caste, Riddles of Hinduism, Revolution and Counter-revolution, Hindu Philosophy and so on. Ambedkar is to Dalit Bahujans more than what Marx was to European proletariat because apart from being a thinker and fighter, he was an organic intellectual of the untouchable people of this country. **Not even a fool from among the Dalit Bahujans expects Arun Shourie to appreciate Ambedkar**. If anybody does that it would be like expecting Edmund Burke to appreciate Marx.

Foregrounding of Attack

Shourie and Ambedkar were born in castes opposed to each other. A peep in the Shourie's background has taken Ilaiah to the mindset of Shourie, which would be found convincing by many disinterested scholars:

> The **foregrounding of Arun Shourie's attack** on Ambedkar is **embedded in an irrefutable fact that Shourie was born in a Brahmin caste whereas Ambedkar was born in its arch enemy Chandal caste.** Nobody, therefore, expects Arun Shourie to recognise the creative genius of Ambedkar just as his ancestors never did in the past. To him and his school of thought — Brahminism — **not just Ambedkar but all Dalit Bahujan Gods were only *Raakshasas***. Since the Dalit-Bahujan movement that Ambedkar initiated, injected some fear (not sense) into his mind, **he characterised him as a 'false God' and not as a *Raakshasa***. History, however, seems to be going against the wish of **Arun Shourie as his children and grandchildren will have no other way but to de-brahminise themselves and worship this 'false God.'**

Did Ambedkar Preach Non-Violence?

Kancha Ilaiah continues: "**According to Shourie, Ambedkar preached violent methods as against the non-violent methods of Gandhi**. But what about the worshipping by all his ancestors and his contemporary ***Hindutva* forces of violent killers — from Brahma to Krishna? Asks Ilaiah. He goes on,** "Their daily recitation of a text — the *Bhagavad Gita* —, which was a handbook of Gandhi — **preaches only violence**. Has it ever occurred to Shourie that it is **the only religious text that was constructed in a Yuddhabhoomi** (war theatre)? Can Shourie understand that his God Rama is not perceived in the same manner by **Dalit-Bahujans, the descendants of Shambhuka, Vali and Ravana?"** Kancha Ilaiah says in reply: "To understand that, he needs to give up his twin anti-human essences — Brahminhood and Aryanhood. Otherwise, as Shourie fears, civil war could break out. As after the American Civil War, perhaps casteists of Shourie's ilk can be cleansed and reformed."

Ambedkar Falsely Charged by a CIA Agent

Kancha Ilaiah tried to pay Shourie almost in his own coins, while making this observation:

> "If one builds an argument around a historical fact like Ambedkar working in the British government as a proof of his being a British agent, one can write a bigger book on Arun Shourie on how he was an American, more particularly, a CIA agent, who sat and operated from the worst imperialist institute — World Bank — for quite a long time before he joined the JP movement only to sabotage it from within."

Besides, will someone try to prepare a list of all those Indians, who had remained members of he Viceroy's Executive Council, and one of their progeny, who are playing important role in governing or misgoverning the present day India, before pointing an accusing finger on the likes of stalwarts like Ambedkar? Here, one example may suffice, which has been dealt with in detail in this author's *Indian Freedom Struggle: New Insight.* Gopal Krishan Gokhale, the mentor of Mahatma Gandhi, was such a member of the said Council, at the time Gandhi was operating in South Africa.

Gokhale was deputed by the British rulers to South Africa, in order to bring round Gandhi to the thinking of the rulers. Whereas Gandhi had been thrown out of one of the railway compartments, Gokhale was allotted the full saloon for one week, and was treated as the state guest by the same South African Government. Similarly, Rabindranath Tagore had sent his confident Andrews to Gandhi for similar purpose. It was as a result of such parlours that when Gandhi returned to India, in January, 1915, he was awarded by the then Viceroy, *Kaiser-I-Hind Gold Medal* also mentioned elsewhere in this book, on account of its publicity value. How is it that becoming a member of the said Council, is treated as a crime for Ambedkar but as an act of virtue for Gokhale and others including Motilal Nehru? Reverting to Ilaiah, it may be pointed out that he sarcastically remarked:

> "Shourie has every right to write anything on Ambedkar or on whomsoever for that matter, but the problem arises only when he wants to sell himself as a 'neutral fact-based' writer and scholar."

Shourie Cannot Invoke Gandhi and Lohia

Kancha Ilaiah asked, "Further, what right has Shourie, the worshipper of untouchability, as he calls himself, of the Brahminical social order, to invoke Gandhi and sometimes Lohia, who also conducted their own modes of struggle against caste?" He puts a very pertinent question about other Hindu leaders approaching sainthood not speaking a word against Caste:

Of all the top upper caste freedom fighters, why only Gandhi and Lohia made an attempt to fight caste (in different degrees)? Why did not Arun Shourie's own caste heroes — Ramakrishna Paramahamsa, Tilak, Rabindranath Tagore, Bankim Chandra and Radhakrishnan — speak a single word against untouchability and Casteism of their times?

A Peep into Mind of Gandhi

Kancha Ilaiah disclosed, "Gandhi and Lohia, fought against caste because as Baniyas they had their own experience of Brahminism." He asked, "Was not Gandhi attacked by the orthodox Brahmins when he threw away his sacred thread? Did not Arun Shourie read the very first sentence in Gandhi's autobiography "the Gandhis belong to the Baniya caste and seem to have been originally grocers"? What respect did Brahmins of that period had for grocers?

Brahmanas Ill-Treating of Gandhi and Lohia

Ilaiah had a dig at the Brahmanas by charging them of rejecting Gandhi and Lohia. "Gandhi, with his Harijanisation of untouchability, Lohia with his thesis that " lower castes are the earth and upper castes are seeds" in a way upset the order of the *Varnadharma*. For doing so both Gandhi and Lohia paid the price. One was killed by a Chitpavan Brahmin and the other was driven out of Congress, lest he should overtake Nehru — a Brahmin."

Gandhi's Rare Tribute to Ambedkar

More than any other two national leaders, Gandhi and Ambedkar shared a common meeting ground, pointed out Ilaiah. He maintains that therefore Gandhi wrote about Ambedkar participating in a debate on Ambedkar's book 'Annihilation of Cast:

> "He (Ambedkar) has carved out for himself a unique position in society. Whatever label he bears in future, Dr Ambedkar is not the man to allow himself to be forgotten."

Role of Gandhi Finished, of Ambedkar Continues

Ilaiah makes an un-analysed observation about Mahatma Gandhi that the latter had driven out the British and observes that "Gandhi was consistent about driving out the British." But he comes out with a balanced approach while judging both Gandhi and Ambedkar:

> "In any historical fight a step this side or that side by the maker of history does not matter so long as there is consistency about his/her main agenda. With British going out of India, Gandhi's role ended but Ambedkar's role continues to operate because caste has not yet been driven out."

Ilaiah wants Shourie and his ilk to realise that in the entire nationalist leadership Ambedkar was the only thinker and that his books were the researched ones. He discloses that "Neither Gandhi, not Nehru, nor Lohia did such a thoroughgoing reconstruction of history as Ambedkar did." Quoting Gail Omvedt he said:

> "the 'Dalit Democratic Revolution' that Ambedkar initiated began to unfold more vigorously after his death. Many upper caste leaders appreciate the role of Ambedkar because he averted a caste based civil war by introducing reservations."

Even Hindu Fundamentalism Dalitised

Ilaiah's attack against Shourie and Hindu fundamentalists remains fierce. He maintains:

> "In Hindu fundamentalism there is no place for even the Sudras and women, what to speak of the Dalits, the Untouchables and the minorities. But the rule of democracy in India has forced the fundamentalists also to have a Christian Union Defence Minister, A Muslim Vice President of the BJP, to have a Dalit as the Speaker of the Lok Sabha, and finally a Dalit as the President of the BJP, even after Shourie's publication of the Book against Dr. Ambedkar. Of course, they could not stall the election of a Dalit to the most August office of the President of India in the very month the book in question was released in 1997."

And, what would AS say about the year 2007, when a Muslim aNd the son of a fisherman, Kalam is the President of India, a Sikh, Manmohan Singh is the Prime Minister of India, again a Sikh is the Commander-in-Chief of Armed Forces, A Communist Hindu is the Speaker of Lok Sabha, and a Chrirstian, Mrs. Sonia Gandhi, is the President of UPA, which is ruling at the centre? Will AS lead a tirade against all of them, for not towing the line of Hindu fundamentlism or for not being the members of the fundamentalist Party? Even if he decides to do that, who cares?

Moreover, at that time the Hindu fundamentalist Party had been forced to induct some Governors of the States also from amongst the

Dalits, points out Ilaiah. But their biggest defeat had been, according to him, to enter into a compromise with the sworn enemy of the Hindu fundamentalists, the political party, known as the Bahujan Samaj Party, so that the Chief Ministership of UP, the heartland of Hindi region and Hindu religion, on terms which were most disadvantageous to the BJP. The worst thing to happen was that of the induction of Arun Shourie himself in the Union Ministry, who was at that time rumoured to be the mouthpiece of the then Prime Minister, Vajpayee, after the publication of the book in question. Only God of Shourie might know as to how he can feel reconciled with so many pro-Dalit things taking place in a party and the government of which Shourie himself was understood by many to be the hub." Shourie's assessment by Ilaiah may be pertinent to note:

> Obviously, Shourie wrote this book to re-educate his upper caste brethren (sisters are any way not listening as they are also revolting against Brahminical patriarchy) that they must resist the ' Dalit Democratic Revolution which has set a course of Dalitising every organisation. He expected the RSS, the BJP to resist this process but Ambedkar caused a crisis even in these organisations, forcing them to open up Dalit wings, Dalit Morchas and so on. The relationship between the BJP and the BSP leading to Mayawati's emergence as the Chief Minister of Uttar Pradesh frustrated Brahminical ideologues like Shourie. The book, thus, is an expression of the VHP standpoint on Ambedkar, *Varnadharma*, untouchability and reservation.

Shourie portrays cleverness but not scholarship when he drives a wedge between the traditions of Narayana Guru and Ambedkar, one as an upholder of the Hindu pantheon and the other as a demolisher of them. Ilaiah, then, puts quite a few questions to Mr. 'S':

> Shall Shourie attempt to write a book on Periyar and drive a wedge between Periyar and Ambedkar as the former led a movement to destroy all Hindu idols whereas the latter only criticised them in writing?
>
> Did Shourie read my book "Why I am not a Hindu," which was written in the tradition of Narayana Guru, Phule, and Periyar, having come from an OBC caste as they?
>
> Did Shourie read the classic "Hindu Imperialism "by Dharma Teertha who was a close disciple of Narayana Guru?

If AS has, he will realise that if Dalits are worshippers of "false Gods", the Brahminical forces have proved to be worshippers of killers and plunderers."

Psychology of the Book *Worshipping False Gods*

Next is the review by Sunil Khilnani which provides a bird's eye view of the psychology behind the production of the book *Worshipping False Gods*, and suggests sufficiently directly that Shourie is posed to advance one of the two main parties, which have emerged after the decline of the Congress Party since 1980, and simultaneously to finish the other party, BSP, which has in turn risen on the strength of the ideological foundations provided by the philosophy and the practices of Dr. Ambedkar.

Reaction Reveals Nation's Historical Memory

Khilnani points out, "When people burn a book, it is essential to take notice of it. During a summer in which India marked its 50th year of freedom from British rule, *Worshipping False Gods,* written by Arun Shourie one of India's most eminent journalists, was set alight in various parts of the country. Understanding why it has provoked such a violent reaction reveals much about the current mood of Indian politics and about the nation's historical memory in a year when such memory has been assiduously massaged and manipulated by current pieties."

Shourie's Purpose: Bitter Polemic

Then Khilnani, while tracing the purpose of the book in question writes, "Shourie's book has one very simple purpose. It is an extended—indeed, overextended—bitter polemic against those who, driven by current political ambitions, wish to rewrite the history of Indian nationalism and the early years of the foundation of the Indian republic. More specifically, Shourie takes to task those who downgrade the prominent role of Indian leaders such as Mahatma Gandhi and Jawaharlal Nehru, while elevating lesser figures like B.R. Ambedkar."

However, Khilnani reminds Indians that Ambedkar was always regarded with respect across the spectrum of Indian politics, but in recent years he has been transformed from a notable historical figure into something approaching a saint, venerated by growing lower-caste movements and the parties of the Dalits and Bahujans (as members of the Scheduled Castes now call themselves).

BJP and BSP Legitimise Their Own Aspirations

It has been noted that some lower-caste parties have emerged in the wake of the Congress Party's historic decline since the late 1980s.

The party which had emerged after the decline of the Congress is of the Hindu nationalists, then represented in parliament by the Bharatiya Janata Party (BJP). It has been stressed that inevitably, each of the parties, comprised of the Upper castes and of the lower castes has "embarked on rewriting Indian history in order to legitimise its own current aspirations." A particular note had been taken out of the developments in Uttar Pradesh, in the following words:

> "Nowhere have these developments been more strikingly apparent than in India's most populous region, the 140 million-strong state of Uttar Pradesh. Here, the lower-caste parties, led by the Bahujan Samaj Party (BSP), and the Hindu nationalists are locked in a struggle for power that produced a bizarre shotgun marriage (the two parties recently fell out over a deeply uncomfortable arrangement where each took a turn governing the state for a six-month period). The BSP's leader, the feisty Mayawati, takes her inspiration from Ambedkar and during her six months in office engaged in a frenzy of naming parks, buildings, and development projects after her hero, while also commissioning thousands of his statues (thus producing a severe shortage of skilled statue makers) and ordering the publication of new school and university textbooks that "properly" reflect Ambedkar's contribution to India's history."

Shourie Tossed Politically Incorrect Hand Grenade

Khilnani finally came to the conlusion which is couched in this language: "Into this atmosphere of uncritical veneration, Shourie has tossed a politically incorrect hand grenade. He sets out to demolish two myths that in recent years have calcified into truths: that Ambedkar was at the forefront of the national struggle for independence from the British and that he played a decisive role in drafting the constitution. Shourie amasses a catalogue of Ambedkar's doings during the 1930s and 1940s that establishes that he often sided with the British against the Congress Party in return for British support for the claims of India's untouchables."

Reminder to Explore Complexities

Khilnani's final comments are: "*Worshipping False Gods* is said to have served the important purpose of reminding Indians of the need *"to explore fully the complexities and ambiguities of their recent past, rather than merely to succumb to a caricatural history in which heroes and villains enact mythic struggles.*" If Indians continue to burn books like Shourie's, they will remain prisoners of the very past whose legacies they wish to escape."

11

Dalits Need Another Struggle for Freedom

Amberish K Diwanji is another scholar, who wrote a review of the book in question, which is available on the Net@. Its title is *Ambedkar's opponents were not the British but the Hindus,* who were unwilling to change or compromise. First of all he takes up the point of Ambedkar not taking part in Freedom Movement, and tells his readers that Shourie misses a point. He asks: But who did? Diwanji continues:

> He (AS) misses the point completely about Ambedkar not taking part in the Independence movement because Ambedkar was primarily concerned with the plight of some people who were then treated as 'untouchables', 'unapproachables', and the worst, 'unseeables'. India has got her freedom, **millions of Dalits** and Adivasis have not. **For them, the British raj has been replaced by Brahmin raj.** So much for 50 years of non-independence.

India Needed Complete Renaissance

Diwanji emphasised that "In the turmoil that preceded India's independence, different people had different agendas, and rightly so, because **India did not just need political freedom but a complete renaissance and reformation, and economic upliftment**." Ambedkar's goal was very clear, he tells us. "He **[Ambedkar] wanted to help his people**, the Dalits or depressed classes. And he had to help them **because no one else was willing to do so**, least of all the **Brahmins and Banias who thronged the Rashtriya Swayamsevak Sangh and rightwing parties, or the Congress."**

Diwanji points out the failure of Shourie to realise certain important aspects of freedom movement, apparently due to the latter's natural hatred of the Dalits because of his RSS leanings:

> In his prejudice, **Shourie fails to realise that Ambedkar probably feared a political freedom, which once again gave the Brahmins the right to practice untouchability**. The upper castes did precious little to reform Hinduism or improve the plight of the untouchables (who then were treated as such). [Emphasis has been supplied]

"Mahatma Gandhi spoke of Ram Rajya with panchayats (village councils), **never realising that these same villages kept the untouchables out of the village**, did not let them draw water from the wells, never let them enter the temples, did not let them take part in the decision-making process, and **denied them decent employment and education,"** maintains Dewanji. Moreover, the recent cases of atrocities in Haryana, involving massacres, loot and arson of Dalit houses also confirm an old pattern. The worst atrocites take place in a district, which has a Dalit District Magistrate or District police chief or both. But the latest case of atrocoties is believed to have taken place at a time when even the Home Secretary and the Director Genral of Police were both Dalits. Such officers help the government to come out clean by making the reports for media consumption that when the state is headed by such high level Officers of Dalits, it should be beyond imagination that such like incidents can take place.

British First to Do Some Favour to Dalits

He raises a questioning finger even on **Nehru**, and disclosed that the latter revealing his brahmanical prejudice **always ignored the Dalits**. He ridicules Nehru for emphasising secular character of Varanasi by giving an example that a Muslim played the shehnai at the Kashi Vishwanath temple and points out that Nehru never realised that the same temple barred Dalits from entering it. Dewanji gives examples of the Hindu atrocities against Dalits:

> **During the Peshwa rule of the Maratha confederacy, Mahars were not allowed to enter villages and were treated in a most inhumane fashion**. That is a known historical fact, but not necessarily remembered. However, the **British were more kind to the untouchable Indians than the Hindus**. They created a Mahar regiment, employing and educating them.

By citing the above example, he ridiculed Shourie by sarcastically saying that the latter "may soon write a book on the treachery of the Dalits for siding with the British!" He raises a pertinent question: **"Is it any wonder that the Mahars preferred to fight with the British against the Brahmin Peshwas** in the Anglo-Maratha wars, because if the latter won, the Mahars would once again have become untouchables?" He emphasises: "The British rule was their emancipation, not the Peshwa's. The **British army gave Ambedkar's father access to education, and he would later become a schoolteacher** in the Mahar regiment. In turn, Ambedkar could study right up to his Ph. D and more."

Dewanji's penetration is deeper. He points out: "Certainly, the cruelty of the Hindus was not forgotten in a hurry. Ambedkar, and many others, must have been **worried that if India got independence without a reformation, the plight of the Dalits would be as bad as before.** Dewanji reminds Shourie: "Let us also remember that **social reforms**, which started at the beginning of the 19th century, were **slowly pushed aside as the political agenda moved to centre stage**. The **Social reforms Committee was not allowed to participate in the Indian National Congress meetings** from the beginning of this century. Which is why even today, caste oppression continues and in 1986, a woman committed sati. India's reform process remains mostly incomplete..."

Gandhi's Insignificant Contribution for Dalits

Again, somewhat sarcastically, Dewanji goes on, "Mahatma **Gandhi did contribute his mite** towards helping the Dalits. He **gave them the name Harijan** (which today has been rejected but was certainly an improvement then), **cleaned the toilets of Dalits** (shocking the upper castes), and **fought with his supporters** and benefactors to ensure **that Dalits could stay in his ashram** in Ahmedabad. **Gandhi** had, after all, **suffered the pain of untouchability:** he had been thrown out of a train in South Africa simply because of what he was, just as Dalits are denied numerous facilities simply for being.

Has Dewanji also been partial to Mahatma Gandhi while making the above remarks? Perhaps yes. If the latter had become a **Mahatma**, the orthodox rules permit a Mahatma freedom to mix up with persons of all castes. Such a Sadhu is called *Sarbhangi* in Hindi belt. The orthodox Hindus have been approaching *Sarbhangis* with respect for securing material gains through miraculous powers of such a Sadhu. If such a Sadhu has an ashram, he has the freedom to have his own rules therein. But he **has no right to challenge the orthodoxy as a reformer**. But Mahatma Gandhi did not become even a *Sarbhangi,* since he had made arrangements for his own food in his ashram, and thus, he did not have to beg for food like an ordinary saint. In this sense, he was a queer character. Was he patently modelled like that by the Brahmanas in consultation with their sympathetic masters and collaborators, the British rulers, in order to serve their mutual vested interests?

Gandhi Never Challenged Orthodox Hindus

Mahatma **Gandhi**, accordingly, **never challenged the orthodox** Hindus, **not even his own sister, who observed untouchability.** He **never suggested any alternative rules** of behaviour to the householders, in supersession of the rules of the Smritis and the Puranas. Thus, **his own experience** of being treated as untouchable **in South Africa had no effect** on Mahatma Gandhi. He never revolted against the South African Whites and never revolted against the orthodox Hindus. So much so, he never revolted against Lord Krishna, who called Sudras and the Vaisyas as *Papayonayah,* literally, the outcome of womb of sin. On the other hand, he had always been assuring the orthodox people that he was equally orthodox. He did so by repeatedly emphasising that he was a *Varnasrami* Hindu.

Dewanji asks, "Also, **how could you fight racism in India while condoning Casteism within the Hindus?** Unfortunately, many Indians did not share the same principle or logic. They were keen to overthrow the 100-year-old British raj, but also sought to preserve their 2,000-year-old caste prejudices." It is unfair to the Mahatma to charge him with fighting racism in India. He did not lead any such fight and he never made any claim of leading such a fight. **The Indians, who were keen to overthrow the British, were the revolutionaries but not the Congress or its lifetime dictator Mahatma Gandhi at least at anytime before 1942**.

Gandhi's Aim: Independence for Upper Strata

It has been pointed out that "Gandhi's main aim was political, which culminated in Independence". But Dewanji again becomes partial to the Mahatma. His partiality is evident from the following statement of his:

> **One can see today that while he defeated the British totally, his work regarding the Dalits remained incomplete.** The sheer pressure of time and the political tasks ensured that Gandhi could never devote sufficient time and energy for the cause of the Dalits.

Gandhi Defeating The British is Debatable

That Gandhi defeated the British is totally debatable. The subject matter has been dealt with in detail in this author's book already referred to earlier, which is titled *Indian Freedom Struggle: New Insight*. **To say that Gandhi's work regarding the Dalits remained incomplete is to mislead the readers**. The survey of the whole life of Mahatma Gandhi does not disclose that he had any specific programme for the emancipation of the Dalits, apart from mildly suggesting to the Hindus to stop observing untouchability. That was also done by him more in the interests of the Caste Hindus, than in that of the Untouchables, so that the former could pose to be human to the outside world. His task consisted in making mild suggestion to the orthodox Hindus, to that extent Mahatma Gandhi's mission was complete.

Again we find it difficult to agree with Dewanji that the political pressures ensured that 'Gandhi could never devote sufficient time and energy to the cause of Dalits.' In fact, it cannot be said that in absolute sense, there was any clash between the so-called political work and the cause of Dalits. If this argument were admitted to be sufficient, it would mean that all the present day political parties can seek shelter behind the respective political pressures for continuing to ignore the cause of Dalits.

Explanation for Gandhi's Failure

Dewanji makes amends for his mental aberration by hastening to provide explanation for Gandhi's failure to engage himself to the cause of the Dalits:

> But more important, to do so would risk offending his main supporters: caste Hindus. **Hence, Gandhi would make contradictory statements like he believed in the varnashram, but opposed untouchability!**
>
> Maybe there was little else he could do. **A leader, after all, is a representative of his people. He leads them, even a little in directions they dislike**, but can never be too different from their aspirations, or too radical for their consumption.

Gandhi Wanted Just to Count Dalits Among Hindus

Mahatma Gandhi's role as a Hindu Mahatma and his faith in *varnasrama* had left no sense of responsibility in him towards the Dalits excepting for the purpose of continuing them to be counted among the Hindus for the purpose of Census. In that case, the Hindus would not become a minority as compared to the Muslims. At least to that extent, Mahatma Gandhi could be said to be against social and political justice, unlike Dr. Ambedkar.

Dewanji does **another favour to Mahatma Gandhi**, when he declares the latter to be the leader of the masses:

> *Gandhi was a leader of India's masses, and Indians then were (and to a large extent even now are) extremely caste conscious. The people would follow him to fight the British, not their own caste prejudices. They were unwilling to reform Hindu society beyond certain symbolic gestures; even Gandhi could not force them. To do so would mean no longer being their leader, someone else would have led India to freedom.*

The above **observation is self-contradictory**. The people always signify the majority. The Sudras and the Dalits constitute the Hindu majority. Both these groups are denied human rights under the Hindu scriptures. If Mahatma Gandhi could afford to ignore the masses in favour of the handful of the Upper Castes, he cannot deserve to be called a mass leader. He should be logically called the Upper Castes' Leader. In fact it is in realisation of this fact by the Sangh Parivar that he is being claimed by a section of the Parivar, which is expressing these days its renewed faith in his Swadeshi Programme, the race for multinationalism and globalisation notwithstanding.

Questions Never Raised Before

One point made by Dewanji makes him outstanding as compared to all the orthodox Hindus put together. He has raised the questions never raised by anyone so far. These question are at the same time elevating for Dr. Ambedkar and they go to castigate the entire Hindu leadership, past and present:

> A question to ask is what would Ambedkar have gained by being part of the freedom struggle?
>
> Would it have helped the cause of the Dalits?
>
> Would the upper castes in the Congress have had time for this Mahar, no matter how erudite?

Would they have listened to him, followed him? And,

Was it only a coincidence that no Dalit could reach the top echelons of the Congress party before 1947?

Replies to all these questions can be logically in the negative. If so, the fault must lie with the Congress or the Caste Hindus rather than with Dr. Ambedkar. While collaborating with the British, Caste Hindus wanted to enlarge their own areas of freedom. Dr. Ambedkar wanted first to come to the level of the Caste Hindus before being able to think on their lines and along with them. The Caste Hindus were opposing him at that time in the matter of emancipation of Dalits and today also they are trying to reverse the process of further emancipation of theirs and, of course, that of the masses.

Example of Caste Hindu Collaboration with British

The same caste Hindus had been only collaborating with the British rulers at least up to 1942, for a very long period of 57 years. Thus, the Caste Hindus were not even treating the British as enemies. How could they expect those who were their enemies to treat the British as the enemies of those others? If they had done so, they could be dismissed with the help of an Urdu phrase, which is commonly used in criminal proceedings, *Muddai sust, and Gawaah chust.* This signifies a situation in which a prosecution witness proves to be smarter than the complainant himself does. In the instant case, when the Caste Hindus were not fighting the British, they need not find fault with Dr. Ambedkar or the Dalits as a class.

There is another point worth pondering at this stage. The Congress had been spurning all attempts by any one of their own people, including those of Subhash Chandra Bose, at making the British uncomfortable, before 1942. Whatever had happened in 1942 cannot be explained with the help of normal rules of behaviour of the Congress. Therefore, its conduct of asking the British to 'Quit India', looks somewhat strange and, therefore, calls for a closer look. So far, the Caste Hindus have been forcing their own opinions on others, including their opponents and the adversaries. But is it not logical to ascertain the views of others also at least for a change?

No History of Caste Hindus Fighting Foreigners

The Caste Hindus do not have a history of fighting the foreigners. But they do have very long history of collaboration with the invaders and foreign rulers. The Hinduism is basically a religion of the Brahmanas, by the Brahmans and for the Brahmanas. The Hinduism is a disguised form of Vedic religion and its leadership rests only with the Brahmanas. The Brahmans have been treating lower Varnas as their enemies, rather than the foreign invaders or rulers. They have preferred the foreign rulers as compared to the rulers from the lower Varnas, if the latter choose to rule otherwise than the rules made by such Brahmanas and incorporated in the scriptures, attributed to God Himself.

Quit India Resolution: Truth Behind

The caste Hindus under the leadership of the Brahmanas had been happy being ruled by the British in exchange for the specific benefits for particular Varnas, which were normally in keeping with the rules of Manu-Smriti. In 1942, the British rulers perhaps for reasons of seeking excellence, offered membership of the Viceroy's Executive Council to one of the Untouchables, that is, to Dr. Ambedkar. This had been done for the first time in the history of such Councils starting from the day India came to have a Viceroy, in place of Governor-General. Ambedkar was one of the 14 Indians members, who included C.P. Ramaswamy Aiyar, J.P. Srivastava, H.P. Modi, M.S. Arey, N.R. Sarkar and Joginder Singh.

This action of the British rulers regarding appointment of an untouchable to such a high office was not in keeping with the rules of *Varna-vyavastha* of Manu-Smriti. Dr. Ambedkar had taken over only on 20 July, 1942. This appointment was treated as the worst challenge to the Caste Hindu supremacy after signing of the Poona Pact in 1932. According to the perception of the Dalits, Quit India Resolution was passed immediately after the appointment of Dr. Ambedkar. Naturally, it could be said to be an act of retaliation to the British act of appointing Dr. Ambedkar as above. If so, how could they expect Dr. Ambedkar to express a sense of solidarity with the Congress, which was considered by him as one made up and fed by the Caste Hindus?

These orders were passed on 2 July, 1942. The Congress Working Committee passed Quit India Resolution on 14th July, which was ratified on 8 August. Quit India movement was started on 9 August. Has Dewanji tried to put this historical version under the carpet by making a statement like the one reproduced below?

> There was little for Ambedkar to contribute to the political freedom struggle from within the Congress; no party outside it

really bothered to have Political independence except the Muslim League, whose reasons were rather different.

Even the case of reserved constituencies came after a bitter battle, made possible only after Gandhi went on a fast to oppose separate electorates for the Dalits. After Ambedkar was forced to relent, caste Hindus temporarily showed some consideration towards India's worst-off. Gandhi too would try and "do his best" to alleviate their miseries after his fast, but with limited success. And then politics came back.

Ambedkar's opponents were not the British: it was the Hindus who were unwilling to change or compromise. In fact, since the British were the first to help the Dalits, their longer presence was better, thus thought Diwanji.

Ambedkar's Place in History for Freedom for All

Diwanji points out that Ambedkar has his place in history. When Columbia University put up his bust on its campus, they did not link him to the struggle to India's freedom, but to the far more important struggle for freedom for all Indian people. Justice, Liberty, Equality, and Fraternity may mean little to many, but they were what Ambedkar sought to put into practice and to give to every Indian, regardless of his caste or creed. Today, millions in India revere him for the same reason. They do so because he led the cause of emancipation of India's most oppressed, and also gave our country a Constitution, which even the lousiest politicians have not been able to destroy. He struggled to give more humane and just laws to Hinduism, but was unable to do so completely because of rightwing opposition. Most important, he gave the former untouchables a voice, and an awareness of their rights. The result: from being denied the chance to attend school, today we have a learned Dalit as India's first citizen, Dewanji Stated. Even the successor of K.R. Narayanan, Shri Abdul Kalam Azad the present President of India, is coming from a similar background of fisherman, who has been the top nuclear scientist of India.

Fundamentalist Gurus: Contribution to Freedom?

Incidentally, along with Ambedkar, others too had their own missions, most of whom were at cross-purposes. For instance, Diwanji asks, What did Shourie's ideological gurus, the rightwing parties, do? And, he replies, they couldn't prevent Partition; they did little for freedom and even less for the Dalits. What was their contribution to Independence besides some of its members assassinating Gandhi? Or opposing liberal laws in the name of protecting Hinduism?

Shourie's Ridiculous Logic

"Today, Shourie believes that if you were not for Independence, you were against India. By his ridiculous logic, all the Indians who worked for the British in some way or the other, were traitors fit to be shot dead: the policemen, the soldiers, civil servants, the whole lot who kept the British administration running," The learned reviewer observed. In this long list, all the Congress moderates could be included.

Whole Groups Not Supporting Freedom Struggle

But the reviewer seems to have omitted some very important organisations, which, applying the logic of Mr. 'S', could deserve treatment similar to the one suggested by the reviewer. The BJP's past avataras, like the RSS, the Hindu Mahasabha, the Arya Samaj, and Brahmo Samaj also never took part in freedom struggle started by the Congress. Similarly, the Communist Party of India, which has assumed the best responsibility to save the country from the Hindu fundamentalism, had also never fought for freedom. The learned reviewer disclosed:

"There were many great Indians who did not participate directly in the freedom struggle but helped India to end — economists (C D Deshmukh), technocrats (Visvesvarya), etc. In fact, think of the freedom struggle and one subconsciously thinks of Gandhi, Patel, Nehru, and the Congress party. But we know that others too were involved."

But perhaps Diwanji forgot to mention that there were still more notable individuals, who include the 'true Gods' of Mr. 'S', kept away from the freedom movement. They included Swami Vivekananda, who had time to attend the parliament of world religions in 1893, 8 years after the formation of the Indian National Congress, in 1885. They included Aurobindo Ghosh, reputed to be the best exponent of the Hindu sastras. They included Ravindranath Tagore, who had brought unprecedented honour to the country by being the first recipient of the Nobel Prize, on his Gitanjali, and who gave National Anthem to India.

Why was Ambedkar alone Hit?

Also to damn someone for his shortcoming alone is to miss the complete picture. Every Indian leader had major flaws, which is why our Independence came with a price. Congress greed and Jinnah's ego and vanity created Pakistan, Gandhi's tactics had their limitations,

Nehru's socialist ideas of yore hurt India's economy, his secularist ideas made a mess of Kashmir; Patel was considerably less secular, but is called India's Bismark! Diwanji gives all these examples.

Each of our leaders is revered for his contribution, and should be criticised for his shortcomings. The same for Ambedkar. But you cannot dismiss any of them completely; to do so is to be arrogant and biased, rightly maintains Dewanji.

Shourie No Disinterested Scholar

While judging Shourie's work, "one must be clear whether his work was done by a disinterested scholar seeking the truth, or by someone seeking to propagate his ideology. Shourie has written against the Muslims, Communists, and the secularists, all seen or perceived to be the opponents of the Hindu rightwing. Now, Rightwing (mainly the upper caste) Hindus cannot accept Ambedkar because Dalit emancipation for them means weakening of the Brahmins' and upper castes' power and privileges." Dewanji laments: "That it also strengthens India's social and political base is obviously not their concern."

References

1. Courtesy; IRB Home; On The NeT; Indian Book Review; 62 A, Ormes Road, Kilpauk, Chennai [India].
2. Courtesy, *Deccan Herald* and *Modern Rationalist* On The NeT.
3. *IndiaStar Review of Books*; —bookreview; On the NeT.
4. Subject: The Wages of Calumny: Arun Shourie; From: Dinesh Agrawal <DXA4@PSUVM.PSU.EDU> ; Date: Mon, 21 Mar 1994.
5. P Sunil Khilnani teaches Politics at Birkbeck College, University of London; *components/heading.htm* On the NeT.
6. S Swapan k. Biswas; Gods, False Gods and the Untouchables; Published by Smt. Maya Devi, Munshi Ganj, Sita Pur [UP], on behalf of Dalitbahujan Intellectual Forum of India; 1998.
7. Rediff On the Net.

12

Wildly Polemic and Incorrect Campaign of Vilification

Opinion of N. Ramesh, Ph.D., Associate Professor, Communication, Truman State University, Kirksville was equally scathing. Ramesh found the book of Shourie as rather aimless and wildly polemic. It has already been described as being politically incorrect" for being pro-BJP, pro-Hindutva, and pro-Hindu nationalism? There has been a studied silence on the book in question amongst the Caste Hindu scholars. Some of the papers have, of course, produced some articles but they have been generally lacking in analysis.

Reaction Shows India Belonging Only To Caste Hindus

Ramesh write, "The reaction available in the press goes to show as if the Indian world belongs to only the Caste Hindus and that the OBCs, the Dalits and Minorities have no business to feel concerned about topics of national interest. Even the minorities have ignored the book in question as if it has nothing to do their lives. These facts go to make the mockery of democracy in India."

Discomfort of Liberal Hindus Mainly Political

According to him, there are some people amongst the Caste Hindus, who feel uncomfortable with the Hindu fundamentalists, but their discomfort is mainly political and they seldom touch the questions concerning the human rights and real social justice. When they do write about such rights and justice, they write about children, women and labour welfare in general terms, without referring to the maladies caused to the masses because of pernicious Varna system. Such writers perhaps in order to be noticed by the Sangh Parivar, seem to have shown marked preference for papers issuing from abroad. But the pro-BJP elements do feel uncomfortable thereon and they spend their energy in order to "understand the mindset and ideology" of opinion makers that some foreign papers favour. One of such papers *is India Abroad,* appearing from USA.

Fabrication on Way to Funeral

For those interested in the ICHR issue, Ramesh directs them to Arun Shourie's Column titled "Fabrications on the way to the Funeral" that has been praised as hitting the left historians in connection with the controversy centring around Indian Council for Historical Research. None has suggested that the books like the one against Dr. Ambedkar are also a fabrication of the Hindu Fundamentalists, which is likely to take them on the way to their own funeral, in the manner, they had been experiencing for a full millennia because of their policy of Divide and Rule translated by them in the theory of Varnasrama.

Billions Lost on Research in support of Varna System

One Rao appears to be a great admirer of AS, whom Ramesh quotes: "Twenty seven years have gone by. Not a few lakhs, instead two crores of Rupees have been spent. The project is lost in the wilderness in one of the major scandals of Indian academia. Not just that. These were leftists. At various stages, the leftists had done their best to thwart the Freedom Movement. Salivating at the thought that by doing so they would attract Muslim youth to their fold, the Communist Party had supported the demand for the Partition of India. And so, the dedicated historians who had been conveniently handed the project, did everything to suppress documents, and derail volumes which could not but have brought the facts about the left on record. That is history. That is objective history...."

In reply to that he maintains,that while there may be lot of truth in the above observation, similar charges can be levelled in regard to the research in the Universities also in relation to the social sciences. The universities have been churning out numerous Ph.D scholars, for dittoing the Varna system as sanctioned in the Hindu scriptures. Had the Universities been objective enough, the whole Hindu society would not have felt shaken by less than half A dozen books by Dr. Ambedkar. He asks, "Could Shourie estimate the national loss caused by the social scientists and the language teachers ever since the establishment of the first Universities of Calcutta, Bombay and Madras in India in the 1850's?" And he himeslf replies, "No the matter does not interest a Hindu fundamentalist like Shourie."

While refering to Shourie's obsession of Partition, Ramesh observes, "He blames everyone for supporting the idea of Pakistan but the Caste Hindus and their leaders. The fact is that it was the Hindu majority areas of the concerned States, which had recommended the formation of Pakistan rather than the Muslim majority areas. A country is not partitioned by the opinions of some individuals or by those of some political parties. In the matter of voting, the decision lay with the majority of the Hindus in the concerned States and the Partition took place as a result of the Hindu votes favouring the Partition. He has developed a habit of charging others in a sense of refrain with a view to denying others the opportunity of expressing on the subject."

Need for Shourie's Self-Survey

Would Shourie and 'people of his ilk permit applying such criticism to his own book against Dr. Ambedkar? Does he consider himself having "the right and a monopoly in usurping and claiming the moral, intellectual, and political high ground" in the matter of condemnation of Dr. Ambedkar, even when he [Dr. Ambedkar] had been praised by his contemporaries and opponents, who included the very persons in whose comparison Dr. Ambedkar has been condemned?

How many Hindu scholars of today can answer the myths and illusions attacked by Dr. Ambedkar in *Riddles in Hinduism?* Who has ever cared to reply to his *What Gandhi and Congress have done to Untouchables*? which is a masterpiece on Gandhi's failure in the matter of emancipation of Dalits and in that of granting human rights as ensuring social justice?

Understanding Mindset of Opinion-makers

As already pointed out, the book of Shourie itself is rather *aimless and wildly polemic*. It has already been described as being *politically incorrect*" as being *pro-BJP, pro-Hindutva, and pro-Hindu nationalism*? There has been a **studied silence on the book in question amongst the Caste Hindus scholars**. But by now, the criticism has died along with the political career of Shourie. None has heard about him after the fall of Atal Behari Vajpayee's government, excepting in his own papers. With regard to vilification of Ambedkar, some of the papers produced some articles but they were generally lacking in analysis. Even the minorities had ignored the matter in question as if it has nothing to do their lives. Do such facts do not make the mockery of democracy in India?

There are some people amongst the Caste Hindus, who feel uncomfortable with the Hindu fundamentalists themselves. **But their discomfort is mainly political as they are never known to touch the questions concerning the human rights and real social justice.** Whenever they talk about such rights and justice, they do so about children, women and labour welfare in general terms, simply because they affect their own women and children also. But they hardly refer to the maladies caused to the masses because of pernicious Varna system.

If something appears in of the type "*BJP is more comfortable with mythology than history,"* the fundamentalists find such reports so much objectionable that they hasten to suggest careful dissection of such articles. But none has thought of dissecting the book against Babasaheb Dr. Ambedkar. Is it so because he is not a caste Hindu?

Even among the Dalits there are hardly any scholars, who can exhibit the courage to say "that **unless these articles are dissected carefully and shown what they really convey we will continue to be inflicted by these ideologues."** Apparent reason therefor is that most of them are co-opted like their political leaders. In fact, it is wrong to call the co-opted persons as leaders, since they themselves are led and often to an altar. Either their eyes are shut to reality or they have no courage to open their mouth, since, in the words of Dr. Ambedkar, they have become used to open theri mouth only when they have to yawn.

Many areas of darkness have escaped the attention of ideologues like Shourie, which were pointed out by Ramesh Rao as under:

1. None from among the caste Hindus has ever suggested the dissection of the Pauranic stories and the TV serials based on Hindu Mythology, which have been steadily poisoning the minds of the Upper castes against the lower sections of the society, and which have been preaching the philosophy of discrimination

even between man and woman on the authority of scriptural sanctions.

2. None has suggested the dissection of the fake history of freedom movement, which gives the entire credit for the freedom of the country to Mahatma Gandhi and his Congress, by ignoring the role of the revolutionaries.
3. None has suggested the examination of the role of all the Indian members of the Viceroy's Executive Council since the time of start of the practice of appointing them probably since 1909.
4. None has suggested the dissection of the activities of the RSS, the Hindu Mahasabha, the Arya Samaj, the Ramakrishna mission, the Brahmo Samaj, and the Communist Party of India in connection with their lack of interest in freedom of the country throughout.
5. None has suggested the examination of the role of the princely states in connection with the freedom movement, even though most of them are today sharing the political power with others in various capacities.
6. None has bothered to go into the history of those, who belong to the families, which had been conferred the titles like Rai Sahib, Rai Bahadur, Choudhary, Malik and so on, whose progeny is still ruling the country as the new masters.
7. None has suggested the dissection of the role of the Brahmins and the Banias, who had been competing with each other in the matter of the best of the openings in the administration in exchange for loyalty to the British Empire.
8. None has suggested the dissection of the events leading to the calling of agitations by Mahatma Gandhi, whenever success was in sight.
9. None has suggested the dissection of the role of Nehrus, as to how theirs had become the richest and the most influential family, and how it had emerged as the best freedom fighter in spite of enjoying the best trust of the British rulers.
10. None has suggested the dissection of the background of Mahatma Gandhi, who belonged tot he family of the prime ministers of quite a few states, which position could not be acquired without the best support of and loyalty to the British rulers.

11. None has suggested the dissection of the role of the Mahatma during the period between his publishing of the Indian Home Rule in 1908, and when he returned to India in 1915, he was obviously unknown to the Indians and he became famous through the stroke of pen granting him the *Qaiser-I-Hind Gold Medal*, for performing the most outstanding services to the British Empire.
12. None has suggested that the books like the one against Dr. Ambedkar are also fabrications of the Hindu Fundamentalists which are likely to take them, to borrow the phrase coined by Shourie himself, *on the way to their own funeral*, in the manner, they had been experiencing for a full millennia because of their policy of *Divide and Rule* translated by them in the theory of Varnasrama.

Obviously, Rao had used the phrase quoted above in connection with the controversy started by Shourie regarding the ICHR historians. He had referred the critics of Shourie to the latter's Column titled *Fabrications on the way to the Funeral'.*

Rao goes to the extent of asking: "Why is Shourie being exempted from the duty of 'rigorous analysis or substantiation' so far as his book against Ambedkar is concerned?

Review of A Rejoinder to Shourie's Book

This author finds that there has been a more serious and better endeavour as a rejoinder in the form of a book, by SK Biswas, which was reviewed by Pankaj Kumar Mandal for The Statesman. In the said review, which appeared in The Statesman dated 21 July 1998, Mandal has made the following concluding observations:

> *All said and done, SK Biswas has made an attempt to talk down Shourie, though hurriedly and inadequately. Diamond should be cut with diamond and the arguments should be met with stronger arguments but here Biswas proved to be weak and emotional. Then, the huge mass of materials collected by Biswas needed to be screened carefully, verified and analysed meticulously for refuting the allegations forcefully and logically… It is almost axiomatic that where the objections are stronger, the replies should be couched in more elegant language. Contrary to this, Biswas has used highly uncharitable comments about Hindu Gods and Goddesses and some national leaders like Gandhiji which could have easily been avoided.*

According to this author, in spite of these and other flaws, some of which are the same from which book of Mr. 'S' itself suffers, Biswas provides some new insight into the questionable conduct of the Upper Caste people, during the so-called freedom struggle, which can surely be helpful in better appreciation of the role of those who are termed as **False Gods**, as compared to those who have been placed by Mr. 'S' in the category of **True Gods.**

Further, Biswas has committed a mistake of referring to the so-called true Gods of the conception of Mr. 'S' as real Gods. The use of the said phrase tends to give a mistaken impression that Biswas means to suggest that the true Gods as above, as opposed to the false Gods, are the real gods in absolute sense. The plain reading of the relevant passages makes it clear that Biswas has used the phrase, in fact, in a sarcastic manner. But then, he should have made the sarcasm obvious at least by keeping the word real within the single inverted commas, since he does not mean to suggest that the said 'real' Gods are his ideals. The work of Biswas has been summed up in the following words of Mandal:

> *Of course, S K Biswas has located the reason for Shourie's outburst in the contempt, which is in-built in the Brahminical Social order. According to this order, "the Shudras (Touchables and untouchables) are the divine-slaves, one of the natural means of production. Themselves being property, created by the divinity to serve the gods of the governing classes, they were denied any property rights. How can the divine-slaves or their leaders who were antagonists of slavery be considered as gods? Hindu Devatas, the gods and the Bhu-Devatas, the Brahmins refused to recognise the Untouchables even as human beings. They are not, even today, in this scientific advancement, ready to give these autochthons, their human-personality. They have denied the equal status of human beings to them, in the name of God by imposing Shudrahood and Untouchability. And the Brahminical Social order acquired religious sanctity behind this act.*

But one thing is obvious that Biswas fully understood where the shoe pinches. He was angry and anguished but apparently failed to offer equally forceful and fitting reply, chapter by chapter, page by page, duly supported by documents, which have not been erased at all.

Important Points About Shouire's Misadventure

Before ending this discussion, let us have a quick look at the points of criticism listed by the commentators whose opinions have been discussed in the last few chapters in detail.

Ambedkar was always regarded with respect across the spectrum of Indian politics, but in recent years he has been transformed from a notable historical figure into something approaching a saint, venerated by growing lower-caste movements and the parties of the Dalits and Bahujans (as members of the Scheduled Castes now call themselves).

Kancha Ilaiah's condemnation of Shourie was forceful and direct. He maintained that **Indian Media is Caste Hindu Media, that mass support has been Increasing for Ambedkar, decreasing for Gandhi, that Foregrounding of Attack were embedded in the fact that Shourie and Ambedkar were born in castes opposed to each other, namely, Brahmana and Mahar, that Ambedkar never preached non-violence in the sense done by** Brahma and Krishna, that Ambedkar was falsely charged by a man who had himself been a CIA Agent, that a peep into mind of Gandhi cannot hold Ambedkar wrong, that Shourie could not invoke Gandhi and Lohia since Brahmanas had been ill-treating both of them, and that **Shourie Tossed Politically Incorrect Hand Grenade against Ambedkar.**

Important points form opinion of N. Ramesh, who was at that time Associate Professor, Communication, Truman State University, Kirksville, included the ones like that **reaction shows India was belonging only to caste Hindus, that discomfort of liberal Hindus was mainly political, that fabrication attempted by Shourie was on way to funeral, that billions were being lost by the country on research in support of Varna System.**

With reference to Shourie's charge against Ambedkar, Ramesh pointed out that at various stages, **the leftists had done their best to thwart the Freedom Movement**., that in order to attract Muslim youth to their fold, the **Communist Party had supported the demand for the Partition of India**. It was also said that even RSS, who has raised trhe banner of nationalsm today to the highest level, had not supported the freedom movement.

References

1. Courtesy; IRB Home; On The NeT; Indian Book Review; 62 A, Ormes Road, Kilpauk, Chennai [India].
2. Courtesy, Deccan Herald and Modern Rationalist on the NeT.
3. IndiaStar Review of Books; -bookreview; on the NeT- Subject: The Wages of Calumny: Arun Shourie; From: Dinesh Agrawal ; Date: Mon, 21 Mar 1994.

4. Sunil Khilnani teaches Politics at Birkbeck College, University of London; components/heading.htm on the NeT.
5. Swapan K. Biswas; Gods, False Gods and the Untouchables; Published by Smt. Maya Devi, Munshi Ganj, Sitapur [UP], on behalf of Dalitbahujan Intellectual Forum of India; 1998.
6. *Ibid.*
7. Rediff on the Net.

13

Bringing Order in House of Disorder

Ramachandra Guha published in 2001 a book titled as *An Anthropologist Among The Marxists and Other Essay*. Some extracts from that book deserve to be extensively quoted for the book in hand. He is a historian, biographer and cricket writer. Once a visiting professor at Stanford University, Oslo University and the University of California at Berkeley, he is now a full-time writer based in Bangalore. For want of time and in view of certain personal difficulties of this author at the age of about 75, who had to take sanyas from his kith and kin about 18 years ago, he finds it difficult to take permission for borrowing from the book of Ramachandra Guha. Still, he cannot avoid the urge for quoting from the said very illuminating book in order to bring its valuable contents to the notice of larger readership. This author hopes to be excused for his anxiety to serve better public interest.

Unsatisfactory Comparison between Two Icons

'Inside every thinking Indian there is a Gandhian and a Marxist struggling for supremacy,' says the above said noted historian and biographer Ramachandra Guha. With reference to Shourie's book of vilification mentioned earlier, he straightaway came to the conclusion that the latter had endeavoured an unsatisfactory comparison between Gandhi and Ambedkar and that Shourie had done injustice to both the icons. Starting with Gandhi he said:

> *Mahatma Gandhi was not so much the Father of the Nation as the mother of all debates regarding its future. All his life he fought in a friendly spirit with compatriots whose views on this or that topic diverged sharply from his. He disagreed with Communists and the bhadralok on the efficacy and morality of violence as a political strategy. He fought with radical Muslims on the one side and with radical Hindus on the other, both of whom sought to build a state on theological principles.*

According to Ramachandra Guha, Gandhi raised many questions before the Indians and the world at large, which had never been raised before:

> *He (Gandhi) argued with Nehru and other scientists on whether economic development in a free India should centre on the village or the factory. And with that other giant, Rabindranath Tagore, he disputed the merits of such varied affiliations as the English language, nationalism, and the spinning wheel.*

Gandhi was Suspicious of State

Guha made a significant observation that any discussion on Gandhi or Ambedkar would remain incomplete without weighing their views against those of each other. He described Gandhi as a *crypto-anarchist* who favoured non-violent protest while being suspicious of the state, but Ambedkar was a steadfast constitutionalist, who worked within the state and sought solutions to social problems with the aid of the state. He gave an example like this:

> *In some ways the most intense, interesting and long-running of these debates was between Gandhi and Ambedkar. Gandhi wished to save Hinduism by abolishing untouchability, whereas Ambedkar saw a solution for his people outside the fold of the dominant religion of the Indian people. Gandhi was a rural romantic, who wished to make the self-governing village the bedrock of free India; Ambedkar was an admirer of city life and modern technology who dismissed the Indian village as a den of iniquity.*

As to the difference between them, Guha said that perhaps the most telling difference was in the choice of political instrument. For Gandhi, the Congress represented all of India, the Dalits too ... Ambedkar however made a clear distinction between freedom and power. The Congress wanted the British to transfer power to them. But according to Ambedkar, to obtain freedom, the Dalits had to organise themselves as a separate bloc, to form a separate party, so as to more effectively articulate their interests in the crucible of electoral politics. Guha noted that in his lifetime, and for long afterwards, Ambedkar came to represent "a dangerously subversive threat to the authoritative, and sometimes authoritarian, equation: Gandhi = Congress = Nation".

Ongoing Arguments between Two Parts of Hindu

Guha believes that there has been an argument between one part of the Hindu who is keen to retain and reform caste and the other part who is keen to do away with caste altogether. The former is represented by the caste Hindu, and the latter by a weaker section Hindu. During freedom movement this position became evident through the personalities of Gandhi and Ambedkar. Gandhi in a way came to be rejected by both the parts of Hindu, but Ambedkar was adopted as a Messiah by the second part of Hindu. Even among the weaker sections, there are two parts of theirs. One is that which wants to remain a Hindu and still be an Ambedkarite. The other one is out to do away with Hinduism and follow his mentor to Buddhism. Here it is to be underlined that Ambedkar's following consists of both parts of weaker sections.

The tragedy from Gandhi's point of view was that his colleagues in the national movement either did not understand his concern with untouchability or even actively deplored it. According to Guha, priests and motley Shankaracharyas thought Gandhi was going too fast in his challenge to caste. They even seemed to ask as to why he did not first take their permission?

On the other hand, he maintained, "Communists wondered why he wanted everyone to clean their own latrines when he could be speaking of class struggle. And Congressmen in general thought Harijan work came in the way of an all-out effort for national freedom. Stanley Reid, a former editor of the Times of India quoted a patriot who complained in the late thirties that "Gandhi is wrapped up in the Harijan movement. He does not care a jot whether we live or die; whether we are bound or free."

Gandhi was through and through *Varnashrami* Hindu

But the fact is that all of them had perceived Gandhi in their own subjective way. A closer view of Gandhi makes him through and through a *Varnashrami* Hindu, as good or as bad as the Arya Samajis. This has been clearly established in another chapter. Ambedkar had no doubt about these antecendants and beliefs of Gandhi. Still, **both of them**

tried in their own way to improve the acceptability of Hinduism to the weaker sections, one by sticking to caste and the other by annihilating the same caste. According to Gandhi, Hinduism has survived because of caste, but as per Ambedkar, the country has been ruined because of the same caste. To Ambedkar survival of private and public morality was more important than that of a questionable dogma.

Politician Gandhi Bows before Fundamentalists

Politician in Gandhi made him bow before the fundamentalists, so that, at one stage, in a bid to win over the serious protagonists of caste, he did try to assuage the feelings of the Hindu conservatives by saying good bye to the reform movement of Arya Samaj leader, Swami Shradhhananda, as aback as 1922. By his said action, he had said good-bye to all the reform in Hinduism so much so that even the discussion of social questions on Congress platform was made a taboo.

Gandhi made it clear through his action that there could not be any co-operation between those who even dared talk of reform in Hinduism on one hand, and the Hindu fundamentalists, on the other. It is said that a man between two stools must fall, and therefore, he remained a suspect not only for both the reformers and the Hindu fundamentalists, but also for Muslims and the Depressed Classes. In this connection, Guha observed as under:

> The opposition that he faced from his fellow Hindus meant that Gandhi had perforce to move slowly, and in stages. He started by accepting that untouchability was bad, but added a cautionary caveat - that inter-dining and inter-marriage were also bad. He moved on to accepting inter-mingling and inter-dining (hence the movement for temple entry), and to arguing that all men and all *Varnas* were equal. The last and most far-reaching step, taken only in 1946, was to challenge caste directly by accepting and sanctioning inter-marriage itself.

Then, Guha diverts his attention to Shourie, who had maligned Ambedkar to the maximum possible extent. Referring to Shourie's book *Worshipping False Gods,* Guha maintains that Arun Shourie takes all of 600 pages to make two points: (i) that Ambedkar was a political opponent of both Gandhi and the Congress, and generally preferred the British to stay; and (ii) that Ambedkar cannot be called the "Father of the Constitution" as that implies sole authorship, whereas several other people, such as K.M. Munshi and B.N. Rau, also contributed significantly to the wording of the document.

Shourie is Pamphleteer Parading as Historian

Guha observed that one might likewise conclude that it has been mistakenly advertised as being the work of one hand. He made an interesting disclosure that the entire chapters are based entirely on one or other volume of the Transfer of Power, the collection of official papers put out some years ago by Her Majesty's Stationery Office. The editor of that series, Nicholas Mansergh, might with reason claim co-authorship of Shourie's book. In a just world, he would be granted a share of the royalties too. Guha attacks Shourie with reference to the latter's own past deeds:

> *Practised in the arts of over-kill and over-quote, Shourie is a pamphleteer parading as a historian. He speaks on Gandhi only as "Gandhiji" and of the national movement only as the "National Movement", indicating that he has judged the case beforehand. For, to use the suffix and the capitals is to simultaneously elevate and intimidate, to set up the man and his movement as the ideal, above and beyond criticism.*

Guha, also questions the Congress' claim to represent all of India which was always under challenge, by saying:

> "The Communists said it was the party of landlords and capitalists. The Muslim League said it was a party of the Hindus. Ambedkar then appended a devastating caveat, saying that the party did not even represent all Hindus, but only the upper castes."

He believes, and perhaps correctly, that Ambedkar preferred the British to the Congress is entirely defensible.He points out that here is a relevant remark of the 18th-Century English writer Samuel Johnson. When the American colonists asked for independence from Britain, Johnson said: "How is it that we hear the greatest yelps for liberty among the drivers of Negroes?" Ambedkar argued that untouchability was to the Indian freedom movement what slavery had been to the American struggle. He had obviously addressed to himself and then to Hindus and the British rulers that the untouchables were also humans and, as such, were entitled to freedom just like other human beings.

Persons like Arun Shourie give a misleading impression that there were no leaders before Ambedkar who thought on lines similar to those of his. Before Ambedkar, there was another outstanding leader of the lower castes, Jotiba Phule, who also distrusted the Congress, which was dominated in his times by Poona Brahmins. Guha points out:

> *Jotiba Phule too preferred the British, in whose armies and factories low castes could find opportunities denied to them in the past. Further he says that the opening up of the economy and the growth of the colonial cities also helped many untouchables escape the tyranny of the village. The British might have been unwitting agents of change; nonetheless, under their rule, life for the lower castes was less unpleasant by far than it had been under the Peshwas.*

One of the reasons therefor could be that the British themselves had their own grievance against the Caste Hindu leadership. Such leadership treated even the British as untouchables and would not allow devout Hindus to mix up with the former and even banned them to accept the jobs of domestic help in the houses of Europeans, who were treated as *Mlecchas* or degraded foreigners. For this reason, the British felt forced to encourage the Untouchables to work as domestic help and to perform other odd jobs.

Guha suspects that Shourie is unaware of work by worthy historians on low-caste movements in other parts of India, and discloses the facts in this behalf which are obviously not within the knowledge of the likes of Shourie, otherwise, the latter would not have expressed annoyance against Ambedkar to the extent exhibited by him in his book of vilification referred to above. Guha discloses:

> "Mark Juergensmeyer has documented the struggles of untouchables in Punjab, which under its remarkable leader Mangu Ram, rejected the Congress and the Arya Samaj to form a new sect, Adi-Dharm, which was opposed to both. Sekhar Bandyopadhyay has written of the Namasudras in Bengal, who like Ambedkar and his Mahars, were not convinced that a future Congress government would be sympathetic to their interests. And countless scholars have documented the rise of the Dravidian movement in South India, that took as its point of departure Brahmin domination of the Congress in Madras: the movement's founder, E. V. Ramaswami "Periyar", also fought bitterly with Gandhi.

Guhas maintains, "The leaders of these movements, and the millions who followed them, worked outside the Congress and often in opposition to it. Enough reason perhaps for Shourie to dismiss them all as anti- national. Indeed, **Shourie's attitude is comparable to that of White Americans who question the patriotism of those Blacks who dare speak out against racism** (Emphasis has been supplied). For asking Blacks to stand up for their rights, men of such stature as W.E.B. Du Bois and Paul Robeson were called all kind of names, of which "anti-American" was much the politest. Later, the great Martin Luther King was persecuted by the most powerful of American agencies, the Federal Bureau of Investigation, whose director, J. Edgar Hoover, equated patriotism with acquiescence to White domination."

The British had even promised the Untouchables the redemption from the age-old social and religious slavery by inviting them to become Christians on terms of equality. It was the result of such a policy that Ambedkar's father around the time of Ambedkar's birth was working as Subedar Major in the army. The office of Subedar-Major was probably the highest office offered by then to any Indian, by the British rulers. It was that high working status allowed by the British to the Untouchables, which naturally made Ambedkar suspicious about the fate of Depressed Classes in independent India, in view of the provisions of Hindu scriptures, particularly, Manu-Smriti, which was used as Constitution in Hindu monarchies.

Under these circumstances, the idea of seeking certain safeguards for such classes by Ambedkar was regarded by Guha, as natural. The importance of this idea cannot be appreciated by the likes of Shourie or those suffering from the myopic vision caused by the inhuman teachings and practices of Hindu *Varna-vyavastha.*

Guha is apparently unhappy to note that time and again Shourie equates Ambedkar with Jinnah as an "accomplice of Imperial politics". He points out that Shourie dismisses all that Ambedkar wrote about Hinduism "caricature" and "calumnies". Guha's righteous anger deserves to be appreciated:

> *Not once does he (Shourie) acknowledge that there was much truth to the criticisms. There is not one admission here of the horrendous and continuing sufferings of Dalit at the hands of caste Hindus that might explain and justify Ambedkar's rhetoric and political choices. For Shourie, the fact that Ambedkar disagreed long and often with Gandhi is proof enough that he was anti-national. He even insinuates that Ambedkar "pushed Gandhi to the edge of death" by not interfering with the Mahatma's decision to fast in captivity. Of the same fast other historians have*

> *written, in my view more plausibly, that by threatening to die Gandhi blackmailed Ambedkar into signing a pact with him.*

That Shourie's venom against Ambedkar is misplaced can be appreciated from the following assertion of Guha:

> Somewhere in the middle of *Worshipping False Gods*, the author complains that Ambedkar's "statues, dressed in garish blue, holding a copy of the Constitution - have been put up in city after city." However, this aesthetic distaste seems rather pointless. For the background to the statues and the reverence they command lies in the continuing social practices of the religion to which Shourie and I belong. If caste lives, so will the memory of the man who fought to annihilate it. The remarkable thing is that 50 years after independence, the only politician, dead or alive, who has a truly pan-Indian appeal is B.R. Ambedkar. **Where Gandhi is forgotten in his native Gujarat and Nehru vilified in his native Kashmir, Ambedkar is worshipped in hamlets all across the land. For Dalits everywhere he is the symbol of their struggle, the scholar, theoretician and activist whose own life represented a stirring triumph over the barriers of caste.** (Emphasis has been supplied.)

Guha traces the history of Shourie and his attacks on Dalits and their hero. He points out that Shourie's books attacking Communists, Christians and Muslims, follow in quick succession. He finds that the only category of Indians he has not attacked - and going by his present political persuasion will not attack - are high-caste Hindus. Further, he discloses that "this bilious polemicist and baiter of the minorities was once an anti-religious leftist who excoriated Hinduism." To see Shourie's career in its totality Guha recalls these words of Issac Deutscher, on the communist turned anti-communist:

> *He brings to his job the lack of scruple, the narrow-mindedness, the disregard of truth, and the intense hatred with which Stalinism has imbued him. He remains sectarian. He is an inverted Stalinist. He continues to see the world in black and white, but now the colours are differently distributed ... The ex-communist ... is haunted by a vague sense that he has betrayed either his former ideals or the ideals of bourgeois society ... He then tries to suppress the guilt and uncertainty, or to camouflage it by a show of extraordinary certitude and frantic aggressiveness.*

He insists that the world should recognise his uneasy conscience as the clearest conscience of all. He may no longer be concerned with any cause except one - self- justification.

This sort of chastisement should have been enough for Mr 'S' to realise the blunder of comming out with a book of wholesale vilification against ambedkar, the Man of Millannium for Social Justice, by ignoring the facts of history and saying good-bye to all sense of objectivity. Moreover, after throwing an incorrect hand granade - social, political and religious - Mr. 'S' has acted in the most cowardly manner by refusing to come out in his own defence, in response to series of rejoinders to his book of vilification.

Part V
Ambedkar-Haters in Dock

14. Wages of Ambedkar Bashing

15. Unseemly Tool of Hindu Fundamentalitsts

16. Arun Shourie and Nathuram Godse : A Comparison

14

Wages of Ambedkar Bashing

Before publishing his book *Worshipping False Gods, Ambedkar, and the facts that have been erased*, in 1997, Arun Shourie (AS) was known only as a journalist of good standing. But the said book made him known in political circles as someone who could dig the graves of dead men and thereby could make them resurrect into life as also someone who always likes to create and remain in controversies. The avowed purpose of AS and his associates, whoever they may be, was obviously to stall the election of a Dalit to the august office of the President of India, as will be shown later. Having failed in that, the Hindu fundamentalists became more serious.

Shourie's Wages of Ambedkar-Bashing

Significantly, the I K Gujral Government at the Centre fell as a consequence of the tirade against Dr. Ambedkar and the BJP, known to be the only Hindu communalist party of India, came to power in 1998 elections. This event went to make AS emerge as a prominent Hindu chauvinist, which fact brought him some other obvious material gains that include the following:

1. The first ostensible importance came to AS through large number of Web pages on the Internet. A cursory look at those pages shows that the number stood at 320 in November 1999. This had also a positive effect for Dr. Ambedkar, who had come to have more than 1568 web pages, which were almost five times more than those of AS did.

Thus, it can be said that AS had become instrumental in rousing the interest of many educated people in Dr. Ambedkar and his philosophy, not only in India but also throughout the world. Thus, the enemies of Dr. Ambedkar wanted him to make irrelevant in India but he has become all the more relevant and in more than one sense. This academic interest is bound to result in better resurrection of Dr. Ambedkar in political sense also, sooner or later.

2. The second good that came to accrue to AS was by way of his being made a member of the Rajya Sabha, the upper house of the Indian Parliament, on the BJP ticket.
3. The third good came his way in 1999 Lok Sabha elections, in which AS became the official spokesman of BJP, in which capacity he could be often seen on Door Darshan, the Indian Television.
4. The fourth good came to him in the third week of November 1999, when was made a Union Minister of State, by the BJP Government.
5. Earlier, another reward came to the share of AS. A book on Astrology titled *Pre-Eminent Horoscopes* was published by someone. The said book reproduced the horoscopes of more than 120 "eminent personalities" of the world. The horoscope of Mr. 'S' found a prominent place therein. In the small write-up, the book *Worshipping False Gods* was specially mentioned.

Astrology is the mainstay of the orthodox Hindus, who are particularly represented by the Sangh Parivar. According to them, it is also the highest science. Presenting of the horoscope of any living or dead person for public information, means the highest recognition to the individual concerned. In this sense, AS has been made by the Hindu astrologers a celebrity among the 120 "pre-eminent luminaries" of the world in this limited sense.

Interestingly, while AS had tried to vilify Dr. Ambedkar, to the maximum possible extent, he came to be rewarded through the same Dr. Ambedkar, to the maximum possible extent. Probably, Dr. Ambedkar 'in heaven' had taken note of the good turn done by AS to him by way of causing his second resurrection, since the first resurrection of his was caused by V P Singh as Prime Minister only a few years before. He was instrumental in organising the centenary celebrations of Dr. Ambedkar and in conferring the Bharat Ratna, the highest civilian award of India, on the latter, posthumously.

The obvious reason therefor seems to be that only the book on Dr. Ambedkar became really controversial which specially aroused interest of the political and religious leaders of Hindu Orthodoxy, which can be described by omnibus term Sangh Parivar, of which the BJP is the political wing. All other parties, with the exception of Bahujan Samaj Party [BSP] equally welcomed it. The obvious reason therefor can be traced behind the fact that the leadership of all such political parties comes from the upper caste Hindus, irrespective of the fact whether they like to be called as the secularists or the leftists of various hues. A contributory factor behind this truth can be that none of the said parties has been able to use the Dalits as its vote bank, since the emergence of Bahujan Samaj Party. The leadership of BSP rested from the beginning on the duo constituted by BSP Superemo Kanshi Ram and the Vice-President Ms Mayawati. After the demise of Kanshi Ram, Ms. Mayawati is the Supreme Commander. Ms.Mayawati has performed a miracle of becoming the Chief Minister of Uttar Pradesh for the fourth time, by securing the absolute majority for BSP. Now, her gaze is fixed on the office of Prime Minister of India. At present, she has established herself as the best ruler, who has exhibited the courage of getting an M.P. of her own party arrested, who involved himself in a serious criminal case, on 30 May, 2007.

It appears that at that time, all the said political parties other than BSP, decided to stall the rise of BSP in importance, which has started gathering the support of Other Backward Classes, and the Minorities. All such parties had realised that the BSP and its followers had started using Dr. Ambedkar and his philosophy, which is now referred to as Ambedkarism, as the ultimate source of inspiration. The significant factor behind that had been that Dr. Ambedkar had been the first person after the Buddha who had challenged the so-called Hinduism, (which has started taking shelter behind Vedic religion, discarded by the Hindus themselves centuries ago), through thread-bare analysis of their scriptures.

Both the Ambedkarism and the Buddhism are indigenous in character, content and origin. If not checked, there is every possibility of all the Dalits going Buddhists, sooner or later. Once that happens, many of the OBCs are also likely to follow suit. Consequently, the Sikhism can also claim its own share from the so-called Hindus. If that becomes true, the Hinduism can be left with only the Brahmanas and the Banias, who may not be more than 7 percent of the Indian population. In that position, they will be numerically less than every other major class. Brahmans and the Banias have got their own private financial resources, which surpass those of all others taken together. Then they are utilising almost the entire governmental resources to the research on the question of their own survival under various pretexts. The more they research the subject, the more vulnerable they find themselves. The more vulnerable they feel the more effectively they try to hit the target groups.

This author has come to form an impression, which may not be confirmed by the inerested parties, that the Indian publishers do not feel free to publish the books which are crititical of the views of the establishemnt or even to promote the sales of such books, which tend to criticise or honestly analyse the views of the establishment, in the present case, Hindu religious establishment, which seems to be in firm control of the Universities and other educational establishements and even the government. Those who tend to disagree with this view of this author, should feel free to have a public debate on the issue, if so advised. Anyhow, the idea is best illustrated by an Urdu couplet:

Muhabbat ke liye kuchh khaas dil maqhsoos hote hain
Yeh woh naghmaa hai jo har saaz pe gaayaa nahin jaataa.

That is,

Only certain chosen hearts stand earmarked for love songs, since, this is a song, which cannot be sung on every musical instrument.

Since the challenge thrown by Dr. Ambedkar could not be met by all the fundamentalists, they put the like of a *Sikhandi*, of Mahabharata fame, in the form of Arun Shourie to shoot at modern Bhishma, or Ambedkar, from behind the shoulder of another. In the Mahabharata, Shikhandi killed Bhishma in the ordinary sense of the word, but till today, nobody regards Shikhandi as a hero and nobody slights Bhishma as a villain. Bhishma is still immortal but Shikhandi is also remembered along with him, although the latter was already worse than dead even while living. Most likely, the same is going to be true in case of Shourie in relation to Dr. Ambedkar. History has never remembered with approval anyone who has stabbed another in the back.

But the fact of conferment of *Freedom to Publish Award* on Shourie, has added another dimension to the controversy. Henceforth, Shourie cannot complain of being singled out for the purpose of his face having been blackened. He has been now joined by the whole body of so-called Indian Publishers, who have formed themselves into Federation of Indian Publishers. The news-item regarding the said Award had in fact amused many. When this author came to know about it, he entertained the fear that in this Indian world of Hindu fundamentalists, it is not possible to have a word of dissent published, through the Indian publishers, since they have formally aligned with Shourie and stood against the spirit of the likes of Ambedkar. The Federation along with the chief guest on the concerned occasion, I K Gujral, had described the works of Ambedkar as a current and the book by Shourie as a work of dissent. What a fall!

In this sense, all of them volunteered to join the whole body of helpless people like the Dalits. Ambedkar's soul must be rejoicing wherever it might be now, if at all, at this revolution in his India, that is Bharat, where the prepetrators of all kinds of injustice have volunteered to be treated as victims of Ambedkarism, and accepted the fact of being swept away by the force of its current. The book in hand might provide them yet another occasion to assemble again and celebrate the anniversary of their organised helplessness against another current, which might be caused by the book in hand. But let this author stop day-dreaming, since what the Federation, Shourie and I K Gujral did was nothing short of a drama. And, it was in that mood of enacting a drama that Gujral had spoken in praise of dissent by his concealed enemy, Shourie.

In fact, Shourie and his clout are patently wrong in treating what he wrote against Ambedkar as dissent. It is very much in keeping with the mood and fashion of Hindu fundamentalists. And, this mood is both traditional and modern. Actually, Shourie has endeavoured to kill by deceit, the dissent attempted by Ambedkar. After all, it is the fate of the gods, to resort only to deceit for the purpose of killing an Asura, whose modern form is False God.

15

Unseemly Tool of Hindu Fundamentalists

As a Hindu fundamentalist, Shourie has done something obvious, something which is expected of him as a writer. That way there is nothing to qualify him for any honour. He has done a given job, but he has made it appear to have been independently done by him. Those who do a given job are known as clerks in government offices. And, their status is just above that of a peon or a class 4 officer. Such a person can at best deserve a pat but never an honour. Shourie must be content to receive such a pat from the one, whose voice he has tried to become.

Moreover, the honour comes to one who has suffered for a cause, for standing firm on principle against heavy odds. Can it be argued that someone was forcing AS not to write a word against Dr. Ambedkar? Has he suffered a term of imprisonment as a consequence of such writing? Has his property been attached as a result? Has he lost his job for engaging in an act of chivalry or heroism? Obviously not. He has only performed a job of hitting Dalits, which is no offence according to rules of Manu-Smriti, the *Vedas*, *Puranas*, the two epics of the *Ramayana* and the *Mahabharata*, the *Gita*, the astrological treatises and the like.

The Dalits have continued to be hit for ages. They along with OBCs or Sudras have been made to be punished and humiliated according to Tulsidas, the author of *Rama-Charita Maanas* or Hindi *Ramayana*. According to Hindu tradition, they have no business to pray to God also by sitting in tapasya, otherwise, it is the duty of Lord Rama to kill them on the analogy of Shambooka. It is their duty to remain at the service of the upper three Varnas, without expecting any rewards or demanding any wages. They are so vulnerable and devoid of any means to defend themselves.

Shourie has only tried to crush a blade of grass, which was already lying on the ground. Still, the grass is very much there. But during the crushing, some grains of sand went up in the air, which caused an eyesore to him. Does this event not call for a celebration? Rationally speaking, those who conferred the so-called honour, namely, the whole body of the Federation of the Indian Publishers, deserve pity for indulging in such a mindless action, of honouring a man like Shourie. It should have been equally wrong for Shourie to accept such a tainted award, and for I K Gujral to be the Chief Guest at the concerned function. But who will tell whom about the simple rules of good behaviour to those, who, in the words of Lord Christ, know not what they are doing. An Urdu couplet makes apt comments on such a situation:

Ek hi ulloo kaafee hai barbaad gulistaan karne ko,
Har shaakh pe ulloo baithaa hai, anjaam-I-chaman phir kyaa hogaa?

That is, only a single owl is enough for devastating the entire garden. Here every branch has an owl perched on itself. What will be the fate of this garden?

Kabir had said *andhaa andhai theleyaa daunvain koop padant*, that is, if a blind man tries to push another blind man, both of them are bound to go down the ditch. In the instant case, both Shourie and the so-called Federation of Publishers of India, have placed themselves in such a tricky situation.

Analytically speaking, if a group of exploiters 'honour' their own chief, can the said action bring an honour to both the parties, in an absolute sense? Can the same ink remove the spot caused by itself? Besides, it is misnomer to call the said federation as that of Indians. India belongs to the majority. The federation can be said to represent the top layer of the top, namely, the minority of the Caste Hindus. Whether the said top can be compared to the cream over the milk or the algae of a stagnant pool, has yet to be distinguished by the disinterested experts. Do we have such a body of experts in a society, which believes in the unity and brotherhood of each of the stratified groups in an exclusive sense? No! We do not have.

Hitting Adversary Group: No News

Here, Shouries and Ambedkar represent two different and exclusive groups, whose interests are self-contradictory. Shourie is sitting at the top layer of frogs of a folk tale; Ambedkar is placed below all the rest crushed under the weight of all the rest. Shourie can afford to indulge in an idle talk to discuss weather, when there is nothing else worthwhile to do. Ambedkar has neither any time for such useless pursuit, nor has he any inclination to indulge therein.

Judged in the above background, the whole activity of honouring a member by his brethren is meaningless or at least a clannish activity. If one does not have the correct perception of the standards of ethics and public and private morality, all labour put by them in any direction has to be simply fruitless in an absolute sense. But such people are not likely to appreciate the truth behind such words, in the light of the Kautilya's declaration *Arthi dosho na pasyati*, that is, a selfish man does not see any harm [in his pursuit]. As such, the fact of Shourie's having been honoured the way it has been done is no less than an organised dishonour. The whole act is suggestive of all round mental bankruptcy.

All said and done, if it was the easiest act of Hindu Fundamentalists, it could be fine for them. But what was I K Gujral doing there, who had been ousted from power precisely by the machinations of such fundamentalists, who had begun with the preparations for production of the book against Ambedkar and the desecration of his statues? Did Gujral go there to witness the *Jashn-I-Barbaadi*, or the to celebrate his political holocaust? If the Hindu Fundamentalists had organised such a celebration, it could be said to be all right, in the background of their limited objective. But to see Gujral participating therein must have disappointed many members of the AJGR communities, namely, Ahirs, Jats, Gurjars, Rajputs and if he went as Vibheeshana from Lanka of AJGRs, it could, of course, mean something else. But only time will tell the real story.

Gujral: Tool of Brahmin-Bania Combine

It is evident that Gujral has acted as willing tool of the Brahmin-Bania combine after giving up his allegiance to the AJGR Combine, for reasons best known to him. By doing so, he has tended to sabotage the solidarity of the AJGR Combine and strengthen the Brahmin-Bania Combine. The fact of his joining the function in question as a chief guest, has conveyed the sure message that he had already been won over or brow-beaten by the Brahmin-Bania Combine even when he was the Prime Minister. However, he had perhaps failed to realise that that he was being stabbed in the back

Gujral to Share Credit or Blame with Shourie Brahmin

Had I K Gujral this much sense of history, he would have perhaps declined the offer to be the chief guest on the occasion of Shourie being 'honoured' as already discussed above. But, there is a point, which might have provided justification to Gujral to be the chief guest as above. Shourie had shot his book in question against Dr. Ambedkar, at a time, Gujral was the Prime Minister of India. By being present on the occasion, he had probably wished to leave an important piece for the consumption of the nation that he was very much one with Shourie in the act of vilification of Dr. Ambedkar.

If so, whatever may the result of the reaction to Shourie's action and that of the book in hand, Gujral must become entitled to share the credit or the blame with Shourie in equal measure. Hopefully, the book in hand will reach Gujral also. If it does, he should be under a duty to respond to it for public consumption. If he fails to volunteer to act that way, some of the discerning readers might require him to give his considered opinion after having the other side of the picture being provided to him through the book in hand.

Who is Helpless Before Whose Current?

Incidentally, the words of Gujral expressed by him on the occasion referred to above, provided another insight, which went to support the thinking of Shourie expressing his helplessness before the Dalit youth blackening his face, as per the incident recorded by him in his own book against Dr. Ambedkar. Gujral stoically said that fundamentalism was not confined to one religion but it exists in all religions. "Fundamentalism questions the right to dissent and treats those who differ as blasphemous". Since the occasion was obviously to honour Shourie for dishonouring Dr. Ambedkar, any criticism of Shourie or his works that might have taken place was sought to be described as being blasphemous by Gujral. He had also felt that society had lost the capacity to face the truth. "The myths that we have constructed have become dearer to us", he had said. He went on "Far from not facing the facts, we now uphold the inverse of the truth. All this is not because of liberalism. It is because of an enfeebled state and an enfeebled society." Perhaps, he forgot to use the words "the enfeebled *dvijaṣ or* Upper three *Varnas*" or did he mean to say "enfeebled Manu-Smriti and enfeebled monarchy" of Manu's connotation?

Whose Voice is Voice of Dissent?

In the said function referred to in the preceding chapter, I K Gujral, who was the Prime Minister at the time of starting of the vilification campaigns and at that of desecration of the statues of Dr. Ambedkar, had made a statement that smacked of academic dishonesty. He had said that "right to dissent" was an integral part of democracy and was also the touchstone of the freedom of speech and expression, and that dissent was a wide concept and apart from politics, it also encompasses "saying things which are not acceptable at the moment".

Deliberate Distortion of Democracy

It does not need to be explained that the democracy referred to in his statement was not the democracy in which Dalits or the OBCs or the Minorities were to enjoy equal rights. But it was the democracy exclusively meant to be of the Caste Hindus, for the Caste Hindus and by the Caste Hindus. Gujral, being a Sudra [as per the Sankaracharyas' declaration that today 'there are no Kshatriyas]' but 'labouring under the impression that he is definitely a Kshatriya', has to perforce perform the role of being a reliable and robot-like tool in the hands of the Brahmanas.

In that sense, the status of Kshatriya is comparable with that of an office, to which one is appointed for a specified term for performing a specified job and the said job can be held as long as Brahmans are not displeased. As per the *Manu-Smriti,* the Brahmanas have been declaring many foreigners like Khasa, Hunas, Abhiras and so on as Kshatriyas, in order to have the existing Kshatriyas defeated for the sin of challenging the Brahmanas.

Varnasrama Dharma versus Nationalism

In the face of the supreme object of the *Smriti*, it is inconceivable for a Brahmana to talk of nationalism. For him, the *Varnadharma* is supreme. If a foreigner agrees to leave *varnasrama dharma* undisturbed, he is free to rule India. Most of the foreign invaders have ruled over India, under such an arrangement and with tacit co-operation of the Hindu leadership. Otherwise, it would not have been possible for Dara Shikoh, a brother of Emperor Aurangzeb, to find and collect most of the 200 *Upanishads*, in *Deva-vani*, Sanskrit or the exclusive language of Brahmanas. Similarly, it would not have been possible for the Europeans to translate long and tedious Hindu scriptures and write commentaries on them, into European languages.

As such, the first given duty of Gujral, regarding himself as Kshatriya, was to ditto whatever a Brahmana Shourie says. And for a Brahmana, every matter is a religious matter, and only Brahmanas can give the final verdict on it. According to Manu Smriti, in the absence of the prescribed number of "qualified" Brahmanas, even one qualified Brahmana is enough to give the final verdict. In the instant case, the verdict against Dr. Ambedkar had been given by a *jnaani* [all knowing] Brahmana, in the shape of Arun Shourie. After that verdict, there cannot be *reason why, there is but to do or die*. And, interestingly, no petition had been made to such a Brahmana by anyone. He had assumed the inherent jurisdiction comparable with that vesting in a High Court, to take *suo moto* notice of any event.

Was Gujral Happy to Step Down for Fundamentalists?

According to *Manu-Smriti,* the greatest merit of a Sudra is to die while defending or while being in service of a Brahmana. As per that rule, Gujral does not have to repent over his own political death, because, after all it pleased the Brahmana masters, the subsequent rulers of India. Gujral, in fact, died a political death, for the sake of Brahmanas, and in favour of Brahmana Bajpai. With the grace of Brahma [that is, the whole body of Brahmanas, acting through modern Brahma, in the shape of the then Prime Minister], Gujral can be made to achieve *moksha* [redemption] by being sent to *Vaikuntha*, a place in heaven reserved by Lord Vishnu for Brahmana-haters, who can rest there in "peace" but only after death. Alternatively, he can be rewarded here itself, so that he can pass the remaining days of his life with some satisfaction.

Traditional Condition for Rise in India

Did Gujral hope to again rise in India through playing as bard of Brahmin-Bania combine? **In the history of Hinduism, only they have risen, who have abdicated Hinduism. It was true in case of the Buddha, Lord Mahavira, all the unorthodox Hindu saints [who were born in Sudra families], Guru Nanak, and finally Dr. Ambedkar. Any one giving up Hinduism becomes immortal after death and he becomes entitled to kingdom in heaven.** This means that he is remembered with respect after his death. Through such remembrance, he becomes immortal. Such examples are provided by Charan Singh, VP Singh, Chandra Shekhar, Devilal, Devegauda, and I K Gujral, to name a few.

The heterodox religions had arisen as a direct consequence of the rebellion of Kshatriyas against the Brahmanas. The Kshatriyas had revolted because of the fact that organised game of exploitation carried out by the Brahmanas with the help of the *Vedic* sacrifices had been thoroughly exposed. The Kshatriyas had taken along with them the Sudras, with whom the former had been comparatively in direct touch as compared to the Brahmanas. Naturally, the Sudras were encouraged by the Kshatriyas to come socially near themselves obviously reducing the rigours of segregation.

Later on, Vaisya opposition of Vedic religion and their preference to a modified version of Buddhism in the form of Jainism, also became more inviting to the Sudras. Then the Brahmanas concealed themselves among the priests of the two heterodox religions and started to work for revival of the modified version of their *Vedic* religion. Consequently, they also had to be at least outwardly much more liberal with a view to misleading the followers of those religions over to their own side.

Tradition Favours Rise of Sudras

Obviously, the **Sudras had become comparatively speaking much sought after class**. Firstly, they were welcomed into the Buddhist order. Secondly, Jainism also gave them the opportunity to become *Munis*, a counterpart of *Vedic Rishis* and Buddhist *Bhikshus*. The Buddhist alternative to *Vedic Rishi, namely Bhikshu,* was more appropriate and even more telling. Since, they were directly referred to as B*hikshus* or beggars. Analytical study of the priestly functions of *Vedic* religion in relation to the means of livelihood, leaves one in no doubt that, at one stage, begging had become the mainstay and the monopoly of the Brahmanical priests, which had been snatched from them by Buddhist Bhikshus.

Revival of the *Vedic* Religion was to Embrace Sudras : A Hint for Fundamentalists

Revival of the *Vedic* religion had also to perforce embrace the Sudras and to take kindly to the uplift of women, the two categories, thus far, denied the right to *Vedic* knowledge. This had to be done by way of imitating the ways of Buddhism and Jainism and alternatively with a view to torpedo the said two religions. The method employed by the revivalists was much subtler in view of their being guided by the well-tried method of their ideological enemies.

The revivalists had studied the pattern of the religious life of the non-Aryans and enumerated their deities, both male and female. They found that primarily the non-Aryans were following the mother cult and they worshipped the supreme power in the form of *Kali,* the Dark Woman. The non-Aryans also believed in lesser goddesses and male gods like *Rudra* [male counterpart of fierce-looking *Kali],* Bhairon, *Ganapati* or *Ganesa* and so on

The revivalists sent their missionaries to the non-Aryan pockets and settlements and offered to undertake the worship of their gods and goddesses. On being accepted as priests by the non-Aryans, the Aryans had started indulging in sexual exploitation of non-Aryan black women, thereby to create a new progeny. This progeny was easier for the Brahmanas to train in the homely environment, with an ultimate motive of achieving their real hidden expansionistic objectives. Similarly, they encouraged their own women to have promiscious relations with non-Aryan males of dark complexion, which is confirmed by the introduction of worship of *Siva-Linga*.

Ratio of any foreigners in any country at any given point of time, settling in a new country has to be insignificant. The same was true of the Aryans in ancient times coming to India. Since they had become victorious in political war, they had dual purpose of maintaining their racial purity and of being acceptable to the non-Aryan majority. The surest method was through adopting the non-Aryan culture but by stratigically keeping their own upper hand. This process involved a series of new and unprecedented steps.

16

Arun Shourie and Nathuram Godse : A Comparison

We already know that a Marathi play titled *Mi Nathuram Godse Boltoy* (I am Nathuram Godse speaking) was banned by the state in Maharashtra. Nathuram Godse was Bapu Gandhi's assassin. The play claims that it gives the assassin's side of the story. After killing the memory of the Mahatma, the idea behind the play is to make Godse the new hero of India, in place of Mahatma Gandhi.

The spirit behind the play is Gopal Godse, the brother of Nathuram Godse, who was a co-accused with the latter, and who has come out of the jail a few years ago after serving a-life term, in connection with the cold-blooded murder of Gandhi. One Dalvi has prepared the script of the play.

AS has authored the book of vilification against Babasaheb Ambedkar. He has tried to hit the Messiah of the down-trodden, the weak, the exploited, the have-nots of India, and the one who had restored the human rights to the masses of India who stood condemned in Hinduism as *Sudras* and *Ati-Sudras*. The idea of AS is to render Dr. Ambedkar irrelevant in India particularly for the Dalits, who have challenged both the Hindu religion and Hindu fundamentalist politics. If Ambedkar's memory were erased as per the plans, the man who should live in his place would be the killer of that memory, namely AS.

Similar Scene

Those behind making Nathuram Godse stand in comparison with the Father of Nation were generally the activists of Sangh Parivar, but more particularly, the Shiv Sena and the BJP. The scene of operation was Maharashtra. All concerned had tried to hit the Mahatma who is a very important Icon of India. Their idea was to demolish Gandhism, which rightly or wrongly came to be known as the respecter and the promoter of the goodwill and understanding between the Hindus and Muslim. In case of Ambedkar also the scene was Maharashtra.

Similar People in Background and Similar Targets

Those behind the endeavours of effacing Gandhi's memory were the men having RSS background. And, the activists of Sangh Parivar, both Godse and Shourie are the Brahmins. The target in the shape of Gandhi is a Bania, who is described in the Gita as *Papayoni*, one born from the womb of sin. The one in the shape of Ambedkar is a born Untouchable. Gandhi agreed to act as Hindu Mahatma, the defender of Hindu faith but who failed to perform as expected by the Brahmin Godse.

An Untouchable was not expected to study and comment on the Hindu *sastras*. But Ambedkar studied all the *sastras* and then subjected them to threadbare analysis and proved them to be unworthy of claiming to be serving the human interest and honouring the human dignity of the masses. As an Untouchable, it was the duty of Ambedkar to die for the sake of Hinduism, but on the contrary he stood against the same religion and ultimately walked out of its fold along with 5 lacs of his followers.

Similar Fears

Gandhi was feared to pose danger to Hinduism because of policy of appeasement of the Muslims. Ambedkar was considered to threaten the very existence of Hinduism by challenging all its fundamentals and by starting the policy of conversion from Hinduism into another religion, Buddhism, which could not be dismissed like Christianity and Islam as the religion not born in India.

Similar Level of Scholarship of the Critics

The commentators on Godse want us to believe that he was not a crazy fanatic but a man of learning and an uncompromising patriot.

Similarly, Shourie also describes himself to be the best investigative journalist and as the most decorated media man. Since he has the books to his credit against all the major religions and Ambedkar, one of the best brains ever produced by India. Shourie also wishes to be considered as a good scholar [*Vidwana*] in his own right. The admirers of Godse want us to believe that since he was a Brahmin scholar, his defence must be received with due care and proper respect, preferably before the court of only Veda-knowing Brahmanas. Similarly, AS and his admirers want us to take the criticism of Ambedkar on its face value and gulp it as a whole, without entertaining any doubt about its veracity. His criticism is to be accepted as *swatah-pramana*, like the contents of the Veda, since it has issued from the mouth of a Brahmana.

Similar Motives

The defenders of Godse, wish us to consider the greatness of the assassin of Gandhi, for the reason that he did not try to escape from the scene of murder unlike the assassins of Lincoln and Kennedy, and for the reason that he did not fire at Gandhi from behind. As such, Godse is being presented as a hero to be worshipped like a hero or *avatar*.

Similarly, AS also has started with the airs of hitting Ambedkar, who had so far appeared invincible. Then, AS like Godse has fired upon Ambedkar from the front and in full view of his worshippers and the concealed admirers like VP Singh and others in all the political parties. In other words, both Godse and Shourie have proved through their respective actions that they are bold & brave, and that each one of them had justifiable grounds to hit his target in defence of his country and his faith, the Hinduism. Particularly, Shourie believes that he has "killed" Ambedkar through latter's own words, speeches and writings or, in other words, through the gun in the armoury of Ambedkar himself. The claim of Godse is also similar. Both Godse and Shourie are not at all repentant on what they have done. And, both of them had started receiving hero's welcome in the same home, namely, Hindu fundamentalism.

On the other hand, there is another similarity also. Congress party consciously used the issue of Gandhi's murder to eliminate Hindu fundamentalists from politics. In last four decades, Maharashtra did not have any Brahmin occupying the office of power, namely, that of Chief Minister since Brahmins are vilified as Gandhi's assassins. The same Congressmen raised a lot of hue and cry over the publication of the book against Ambedkar.

Similar Background and Same Caste of Critics

Godse was the RSS (Rashtriya Swayamsevak Sangh) activist. But his action was reportedly strongly condemned by RSS leaders. But AS was not so condemned by Sangh Parivar or the BJP or the Shiv Sena etc. Perhaps RSS had done so in case of Godse in order to save itself from its own involvement by the then Congress government. There was no such fear in case of AS and he could be left to go scot-free even on the commitment of something, which can be compared with one of the most heinous crimes.

According to Milind Thate, Godse was initially used as a whip to hit RSS, and is still used to crucify RSS as murderer of Gandhi. Who knows a stage might come when AS is also used to whip the same RSS or Sangh Parivar, when politics of the country takes a reverse turn. Shouldn't AS prepare a suitable alibi in his future defence?

Similar Dangers

In any case, Thate had warned us of the dangers of suppression: "I warn the Hindu fundamentalists of the dangers of suppressing Ambedkar. Ambedkar is not a man. He is an institution, which represents the sense and common sense, in the non-sense, that has been going on since times immemorial in the name of religion and spirituality, which, of course, has been posing the greatest danger to sense of unity, to human values, to private and public morality. He is the last chapter in the book whose important chapters have been existing in the sense of Ajivikism, Jainism, Buddhism, Sikhism, the medieval saints, and any thing that has been hitting at the forces of exploitation of man by man, of woman by man, of the poor by the rich, of the weak by the strong and so on."

Thate has positive thinking about Ambedkarism. He unlike Shourie has great hope from this ism. He is of the firm view that it cannot be suppressed and that the danger of suppression is more for those who want to suppress it. Here are his own words:

> Ambedkarism consists in a voice of righteous protest and therefore is supported by the saner feelings of a man truly spiritual, and is set against false sense of religiosity and useless dogma. Ambedkarism can never be suppressed but those aiming at its

suppression are themselves bound to be suppressed to the extent, which cannot b e foreseen by them with their the help of their myopic vision.

Shourie seems to have given rise to another Ism, *the Ism of killing Ambedkarism*. For this crime of his, innocent followers might have to suffer in future the consequences of their own unclear beliefs, since they would be known as the followers of a philosophy given birth to by an instigative journalist rather than by an 'investigative' journalist. The future generations of Indians are, therefore, more likely to be Ambedkarites than Shouriests or rabid fundamentalists.

Similar Repercussions

Thate pointed out that Congress has staged a violent attack on the "Mi Nathuram..." play. He cautions: "that does not mean that the Congress love Gandhi, they simply found the timing and a topic that would embarrass the BJP govt. in the state and the union. BJP's knee-jerk reaction is another trick of politics. They also have no love for Gandhi." The same can be said of the Congress condemnation of Shourie's vilification of Ambedkar. The Congress men being the true followers of Gandhism, could not be expected to have any love for Ambedkar, but they had to stage a drama since they happenned to be in the opposition of the BJP, the party of Shourie.

Similar Mistakes

Every Society has its icons of honour. India is country of many sections having self-contradictory vested interests and philosophies. Each section may have its own icon. Gandhi is icon of the upper caste Hindus. Ambedkar is the icon of the weaker sections, particularly, the Dalits. Both the sections have been co-existing since time immemorial. They are bound to co-exist forever on account of being needed by each other. Therefore, the followers of one cannot wish away the existence of the other.

If Gandhi as an icon is hurt, the Gandhian society is hurt. If Ambedkar as an icon is hurt, all the Ambedkarites are hurt. Ancient Hindus have been hurting the ancient icons of the Dalits by referring to them as *Asuras* and *Raakshasas*. The process is continuing till today. They had added another icon in the category of those to be so hurt. He was Lord Buddha. Modern Hindus have added Dr. Ambedkar to the the said list. Buddha had been chosen for attack because he had been instrumental in wiping out the Vedic religion from the face of earth. The same danger now lurks for Hinduism at the hands of Dr. Ambedkar.

Similar Impact

Milind Thate in one of his articles dated 24 July 1998, made an interesting observation, which he applied to Godse, but which applies with equal vigour to Arun Shourie also:

> This reminds me of Albert Einstein's childhood memoirs: One day his teacher in the school told the children that "Jesus Christ was crucified" and then looking at Albert, she said "by Jews". Then the whole class looked at little Albert with such disgust as Christ's murderer. Brahmins have suffered similar disgust in every field of social life, simply because one of them murdered Gandhi. This has had a bounce-back effect on Brahmins. A lay Brahmin hates Gandhi and preaches Godse.

This fact points out to another disturbing factor in Hinduism. Brahmanas may accept the icons from other communities as measure of rule of adversity. They had done so in case of Kshatriya Rama and Sudra Krishna. In independent India, they adopted a Bania Gandhi for the time being as one of their working icon. But soon they reverted to a Brahmin, just as they had never forgotten their own Ravana and Parasurama. They haven't forsaken their Brahma and are keeping him alive for all the Hindus under a rule according to which all the pilgrimages will be fruitless unless at the end one does obeisance to Lord Brahma at Pushkara, Rajasthan.

But they cannot get reconciled to Ambedkar, unless he also becomes or is made the author of epics like Mahabharata and Ramayana on the analogy of Vyasa and Valmiki, aimed at perpetuation of slavery of the Sudras and excommunication of the Dalits. They would have accepted Ambedkar also but his writings and speeches in this electronic age are presenting the greatest hurdle in this behalf. Hence, there has to be a parallel impact of Brahminism and anti-Brahminism.

Similar Protection

Any icon, which may be in any form: 'a book, a statue, or a living person' is protected against all attacks. As such, Ambedkar having become an icon in more than one sense must be protected by its own intrinsic worth. He cannot be killed by hundreds of Shouries. There was a stage when Atal Behari Vajpayee, had strategically declared as the chief guest of Dalit Sahitya Academy function a few years ago that "Ambedkar was modern Manu, and he himself was *Manu-vadi.*"

The same Vajpayee as Prime Minister, in changed circumstances said on 14 April 2000, that he was not a believer in *Manu-Smriti*, but a believer in the Constitution of India, which was a *Bhim-Smriti*. Judged in the light of this statement, Shourie is not being defended by his own Prime Minister. While speaking for Ambedkar, the Prime Minister was denouncing what Shourie had done to Ambedkar. In this connection, the words of Milind Thate deserve to be quoted:

> The society, that cherishes the icon revolts when there is attack. Take the instance of Ambedkar, Ambedkar is an icon for a section of the society. Even if a statue of him is molested, that society revolts.

Difference

But there are certain differences between the reactions to the actions of Godse and Shourie:

1. Nathuram Godse belonged to the Brahmin community of Maharashtra. Brahmins were believed to have been killed, looted, raped, and their properties were believed to have been burnt, after it was known that Gandhi's assassin was a Brahmin. But nothing like that has happened in case of Shourie, excepting that his face was blackened by some Ambedkarites as per Shourie's own admission made by him in his own book of vilification.
2. Godse had to die for the crime of killing a member of *dvijas*, Gandhi. But Shourie was made suddenly to climb the political staircase for his feat of killing an Ati-Sudra, so that he had become a spokesman and a celebrity of the Sangh Parivar. Both these consequences were in keeping with the spirit of Manu-smriti. Manu-smriti exhorts Brahmanas and Kshatriyas to stay united and to keep Vaisyas and Sudras divided. For this also, cooperation of Gandhi and Ambedkar or of Gandhism and Ambedkarism had to become a suspect inviting fatal consequences for both, at least through death of their respective icons and ideologies.

These differences are explainable in the fact that at the time of murder of Gandhi, the Congress was in power but at the time of Shourie's trying to efface the memory of Ambedkar, the Sangh Parivar was in power. There is Hindi saying *Sanyiya bhaye kotwaal ab dar kahe ka?* That is, now my master has become the head of the police station, so whom I have to fear?

In this sense, the feat of Shourie must appear less spectacular and more cowardly and more futile. It is true that on the day the book was published BJP was not in power at the Centre, but it was so in Maharashtra all right. But the day BJP came to power. Shourie received his 'well-deserved' award for killing the memory of an Untouchable, or in his own words, a false God.

Difference in Acceptance of Gandhism and Ambedkarism

The problem is that Gandhi's own men disown him. They are the people for whom he worked and for whom he died. On the other hand, the people for whom Ambedkar primarily worked are worshipping him. He is being accepted by more and more sections of people, who are learning from the example of his followers, and who are increasingly realising the reality of their own existence threatened by the forces of exploitation.

Ambedkarism is silently influencing and serving the newer and newer sections every day and, thus, it is eating into the vitals of the exploitative system and the exploitative society.

In the process, the fundamentalism is in danger of extinction. Gandhism is also threatened with such extinction so far as it tends to be used to favour the forces of exploitation. But Gandhism standing for feelings of tolerance and mutual understanding must remain alive forever. More and more people of the world are also accepting Gandhi for that reason. But it is not the Gandhism of the description of Hindu fundamentalism; it is Gandhism of non-violence and of passive resistance against tyranny, which is nearer Ambedkarism.

In Event of Logic Living or Dying

According to Thate "when logic dies, a leader degenerates into an icon." These words can be made justifiably applicable to Hindu fundamentalism in one sense and to Gandhi in another sense. The logic of Hindu fundamentalists and that of Gandhi as a defender of such a brand of Hinduism has already died. It seems to be alive because of the violent groups of RSS. Any idea, which needs the support of organised force, must be considered as already dead.

The present day logic is in favour of those who give a hope for freedom from exploitation of all sorts. Therefore, the balance of convenience lies overwhelmingly in favour of Ambedkarism as against Gandhism based on Varnasrami Gandhi. Even in India, Gandhi was not revered on account of his being a Varnasrami Hindu, but because he was able to pose as the uplifter of the lowliest of the lowly and as the treader of middle path of the description paved by Buddhism. Ambedkarism is alive because of its natural attraction. Gandhism is alive because of its posing to deserve some attraction. Gandhi is a mere icon and as such he must die in due course. Thate maintains:

> His [Gandhi's] advice to dissolve Congress was never followed by Congressmen. His teachings of "building the nation from below" were turned upside down by Nehru. His idea of Graam-Swaraj (self-reliant village) lost its sway to globalisation. His teaching of peaceful resistance (Satyagraha) became futile in independent India. Peaceful movement often died without success. All movements became prone to violence and their voice reached the Government only through the barrel. Gandhi is nowhere in practice; he is a dead icon.

Neither Congress nor anyone else has followed Gandhi. And hence, they have no stature, no authority to stand by Gandhi, says Thate. If so, Gandhism has no legs to stand on. On the other hand, the words of Thate about Ambedkar are worth quoting: -

> India has witnessed and accepted - though unwillingly - criticism against many of its icons. Even gods like Rama and Krishna were not spared. "Riddles of Hinduism" by Ambedkar criticised the gods, and rocked the society. "Worshipping false gods" by Arun Shourie targeted and maligned Ambedkar. Rama and Ambedkar have not lost their cherished place because of these works.

On Strength and Weakness

Is Gandhi so weak an idol that he will be broken by a stage-play? Asks Thate. He himself replies, "I do not think so. Gandhi had and has his own glory, which cannot be molested by small people. Someone has a desire to spit at Sun, let him spit. In democracy, it is his right!"

One generally comes across a real dispassionate defence of one's icons. But Thate has to be considered among the exceptions. Here is an illustration:

> Let Gandhi face what Ambedkar faced. If he was great, he was. Trust in him, nothing will happen to him the row over the play shows that they do not have trust in him. When Shourie's book on -Ambedkar was published, a similar hullabaloo was launched by some people. A ban on the book was demanded,

but Ambedkarites intellectuals gathered and proclaimed that let the book be in the open. We will face it. The self-proclaimed Gandhiites neither have these guts nor do they think Gandhi as capable of facing attacks.

In conclusion it can be said with a sense of certainty that the fate of Nathuram Godse and Shourie is going to be similar. They are likely to be remembered by fanatics as long as fanaticism survives. But ultimately the reason has to triumph. If so, the moment of such triumph shall be the moment of certain death of whatever Godse and Shourie and the pillars of of their misconceived strength stand for.

Part VI
Ambedkar's Search for Alternatives

17. Ambedkar on Hindu Attitude to Problem of Caste

18 Ambedkar on Annihilation of Caste

19. Ambedkar on Shakti and Kaliyuga

20. Ambedkar's Search for Alternatives

17

Ambedkar on Hindu Attitude to Problem of Caste

There are many sets of people within Hinduism. According to Ambedkar, there is one set, which finds neither peculiar nor odious in the Caste System of the Hindus. Such Hindus cite the case of Muslims, Sikhs and Christians and find comfort in the fact that they too have castes amongst them. He advises us at the outset to bear in mind that nowhere human society is one single whole. It is always plural. He wishes the society to be an ideal society. In this connection, he says that the questions to be asked in determining what is an ideal society are:

How numerous and varied are the interests which are consciously shared by the groups?

How full and free is the interplay with other forms of associations?

Are the forces that separate groups and classes more numerous than the forces that unite?

What social significance is attached to this group life?

Is its exclusiveness a matter of custom and convenience or is it a matter of religion?

It is in the light of these questions that Ambedkar asks us to decide whether caste among Non-Hindus is the same as caste among Hindus.

Survival of Hinduism, No Matter of Consolation

Ambedkar mocks the idea that most Hindus seek comfort in the view that the Hindus have survived and take this as a proof of their fitness to survive. They argue through their celebrities like S. Radhakrishnan, that its historic records date back to over four thousand years and even then it had reached a stage of civilisation, which had continued its unbroken course until the present day and that it has stood the stress and strain of more than four or five millenniums of spiritual thought and experience. But here also Ambedkar raised quite a few questions :

> Whether what is referred to as Hindu civilisation, represents co-mingling of non-Hindu cultures and civilisations like those of Ajivikism, Jainism, Buddhism, Sikhism, Christianity, Islam and various primitive religions, which have been influencing and modifying the course and content of Indian culture and civilisation for centuries and millennia, in their own way?
>
> Even if it is argued that whatever is indigenous in culture can be said to stand for Hinduism, even then it may be asked as to what is indigenous at a particular stage of history, after being influenced by foreign elements?

Still, it is being urged that though peoples of different races and cultures have been pouring into India from the dawn of History, Hinduism has been able to maintain its supremacy by influencing all others. But influence is two way process. If you influence, you are also influenced to an agreed extent, Ambedkar points out.

On Question of Level of Survival

Ambedkar concedes that the Hindu culture possesses some vitality, which seems to be denied to some other more forceful currents. He agrees that it is no more necessary to dissect Hinduism than to open a tree to see whether the sap still runs. But he expressed the fear that such statement may become the basis of a vicious argument that the fact of survival is proof of fitness to survive. It seems to me, he says, that the question is not whether a community lives or dies; the question is on what plane does it live. He argues that there are different modes of survival, but all are not equally honourable. For an individual as well as for a society, there is a gulf between merely living and living worthily. He clarifies:

> "To fight in a battle and to live in glory is one mode. To beat a retreat, to surrender and to live the life of a captive is also a mode of survival. It is useless for a Hindu to take comfort in the

fact that he and his people have survived. What he must consider is what is the quality of their survival. If he does that, I am sure he will cease to take pride in the mere fact of survival."

According to him, a Hindu's life has been a life of continuous defeat and what appears to him to be life everlasting is not living everlastingly but is really a life which is perishing everlastingly. It is a mode of survival of which every right-minded Hindu, who is not afraid to own up the truth, will feel ashamed. Therefore, he tells the Hindus that they cannot progress without changing their social order. He warns:

> There is no doubt, in my opinion, that unless you change your social order you can achieve little by way of progress. You cannot mobilize the community either for defence or for offence. You cannot build anything on the foundations of caste. You cannot build up a nation, you cannot build up a morality. Anything that you will build on the foundations of caste will crack and will never be a whole.

Ways to Reform Hinduism

Ambedkar, knowing full well that there are serious limitations to changing and, as such, he gives careful thought to question of Hindu reform. He is conscious of the fact that Hindus claim to have had numerous reformers but most of them have tried to ask the Hindu leadership to revert to their "pristine glory" of having the pure Varna system, which has and continues to be the bane of Indian society. But Ambedkar is the one person who has had the guts of asking the Hindus to annihilate caste system, which is the legitimate son of Varna system. After coming to this conclusion he maintains:

> The only question that remains to be considered is - How to bring about the reform of the Hindu social order? How to abolish caste? This is a question of supreme importance. There is a view that in the reform of caste, the first step to take is to abolish sub-castes.

Ambedkar told the Jat-Pat-Todak Mandal, which had become instrumental for the production of his treatise *Annihilation of Caste* that "the real remedy for breaking Caste is inter-marriage. Nothing else will serve as the solvent of Caste. Your Jat-Pat-Todak Mandal has adopted this line of attack. It is a direct and frontal attack, and I congratulate you upon a correct diagnosis and more upon your having shown the courage to tell the Hindus what is really wrong with them."

But the history of independent India has shown that to Hinduism caste is more sacred than the country and, therefore, we are regularly seeing so many murders of their sons and daughters, for daring to marry outside their caste even in the year 2007. What is more shocking is that the state has never been able to register any case of murder committed in full view of public and the state. This can only mean that India, in this sense, is still happy living at the most primitive stage, when loyalty to clan used to be the only test of loyalty. Such are the glaring examples of social tyranny, about which Ambedkar had said:

> Political tyranny is nothing compared to social tyranny and a reformer, who defies society, is a much more courageous man than a politician, who defies Government. You are right in holding that Caste will cease to be an operative force only when inter-dining and inter-marriage have become matters of common course.

He had, in the circumstances, decided to leave the matter, in the first instance, to Hindu leadership itself by telling them:

> You have located the source of the disease. But is your prescription the right prescription for the disease? Ask yourselves this question: Why is it that a large majority of Hindus do not inter-dine and do not inter-marry? Why is it that your cause is not popular?

Hollowness of Reform of Arya Samaj

Ambedkar had volunteered to tell the Hindu leadership, "But there is a set of reformers who hold out a different ideal. They go by the name of the Arya Samajists and their ideal of social organisation is what is called *Chaturvarnya* or the division of society into four classes instead of the four thousand castes that we have in India. To make it more attractive and to disarm opposition the protagonists of *Chaturvarnya* take great care to point out that their *Chaturvarnya* is based not on birth but on *guna* (worth). At the outset, I must confess that notwithstanding the worth-basis of this *Chaturvarnya*, it is an ideal to which I cannot reconcile myself. In the first place, if under the *Chaturvarnya* of the Arya Samajists an individual is to take his place in the Hindu Society according to his worth, I do not understand why the Arya Samajists insist upon labelling men as Brahmin, Kshatriya, Vaishya and Shudra."

Objections to the Continuance of Caste Labels

Referring to the habit of Hindus to pick up only the individuals for honouring for certain outstanding performances, Ambedkar articulated himself as follows:

> A learned man would be honoured without his being labelled a Brahmin. A soldier would be respected without his being designated a Kshatriya. If European society honours its soldiers and its servants without giving them permanent labels, why should Hindu Society find it difficult to do so is a question, which Arya Samajists have not cared to consider? There is another objection to the continuance of these labels. All reform consists in a change in the notions, sentiment and mental attitudes of the people towards men and things. It is common experience that certain names become associated with certain notions and sentiments, which determine a person's attitude towards men and things.

Varna Names Associated with Fixed Notions

Ambedkar told the Hindus that Brahmin, Kshatriya, Vaishya and Shudra, are names which are associated with a definite and fixed notion in the mind of every Hindu. That notion is that of a hierarchy based on birth. So long as these names continue, Hindus will continue to think of the Brahmin, Kshatriya, Vaishya and Shudra as hierarchical divisions of high and low, based on birth, and act accordingly. The Hindu must be made to unlearn all this. But how can this happen if the old labels remain and continue to recall to his mind old notions? If new notions are to be inculcated in the minds of people it is necessary to give them new names. **To continue the old name is to make the reform futile.** To allow this Chaturvarnya, based on worth to be designated by such stinking labels of Brahmin, Kshatriya, Vaishya, Shudra, indicative of social divisions based on birth, is a snare.

TV Serials Using Caste Names Spread Poison of Disunity

In stead of paying any heed to this advice of Ambedkar India of 2007 continues to exhibit a new trend of strengthening the venom of caste system through its electronic media. All the TV serials are using the caste titles like Chopras, Khannas, Malhotras, Guptas, Aggarwals, Sharmaji, Thakurji and so on, which are hammered hundreds of times every day to remind the concerned persons belonging to such castes of the privileges of theirs as against the weaknesses and disabilities of the lower castes and of persons belonging to other religions.

The authors of such serials are indirectly telling the persons belonging to the so-called higher castes that they are the people who possess superior status to others and that they are the only ones possessing the greatest merit. But there is nobody to remind the cream of the Hindus appearing as the announcers of TV that *dopahar* is the Hindi word to describe noon time at 12 O'clock in the day and any time after 12 till evening time is described as afternoon, for which the Hindustani word is *baad-dopahar*. But all the announcers are heard daily wrongly telling the TV viewers that such and such programme would be telecast at *teen baje dopahar* (at 3.00 noon) or *chaar baje dopahar* (4.00 noon).

Besides, in all the big scams involving thousands of crores of public money, the news papers indicate that almost invariably the culprits belong to the upper castes, occupying the strategic positios in any organisation. All of them have gone up with the help of their so-called merit. Does anyone condemn the caste of these people for their misdeeds? No! Condemnation of this type is reserved for the persons belonging to the weaker sections. During the elections, the higher caste politicians are normally but always informally accused of purchasing the votes of poor voters. Such voters are blamed but never those who exploit the poverty of the hapless. Ambedkar had expressed his agony about *Chaturvarnya* in the following words:

> To me this Chaturvarnya with its old labels is utterly repellent and my whole being rebels against it. But I do not wish to rest my objection to Chaturvarnya on mere grounds of sentiment. There are more solid grounds on which I rely for my opposition to it. A close examination of this ideal has convinced me that as a system of social organization, *Chaturvarnya* is impracticable, harmful and has turned out to be a miserable failure. From a practical point of view, the system of Chaturvarnya raises several difficulties which its protagonists do not seem to have taken into account.

Ambedkar asks, "How are you going to compel people who have acquired a higher status based on birth without reference to their worth to vacate that status? How are you going to compel people to recognize the status due to a man in accordance with his worth who is occupying a lower status based on his birth? For this you must first break up the Caste System, in order to be able to establish the Varna system. How are you going to reduce the four thousand castes, based on birth, to the four Varnas, based on worth?"

Impossible to Classify People into only Four Clases

Ambedkatr maintains, "*Chaturvamya* presupposes that you can classify people into four definite classes. Is this possible? In this respect, the ideal of Chaturvarnya has, as you will see, a close affinity to the Platonic ideal. To Plato, men fell by nature into three classes. In some individuals, he believed mere appetites dominated. He assigned them to the labouring and trading classes. Others revealed to him that over and above appetites, they have a courageous disposition. He classed them as defenders in war and guardians of internal peace. Others showed a capacity to grasp the universal reason underlying things. He made them the law-givers of the people. The criticism to which Plato's Republic is subject, is also the criticism which must apply to the system of *Chaturvarnya*, in so far as it proceeds upon the possibility of an accurate classification of men into four distinct classes. The chief criticism against Plato is that his idea of lumping of individuals into a few sharply marked-off classes is a very superficial view of man and his powers. Plato had no perception of the uniqueness of every individual of his incommensurability with others, of each individual forming class of his own. He had no recognition of the infinite diversity of active tendencies and combination of tendencies of which an individual is capable."

Ambedkar concludes that the utilisation of the qualities of individuals is incompatible with their stratification by classes, since the qualities of individuals are so variable. Chaturvamya must fail for the very reason for which Plato's *Republic* must fail, namely, that it is not possible to pigeon men into holes, according as they belong to one class or the other. That it is impossible to accurately classify people into four definite classes is proved by the fact that the original four classes have now become four thousand castes.

System That Requires Penal Action for Maintenance is No System

Ambedkar raises another pertinent question, "How are you going to maintain the system of *Chaturvarnya*, supposing it was established? One important requirement for the successful working of *Chaturvarnya* is the maintenance of the penal system which could maintain it by its sanction. The system of *Chaturvarnya* must perpetually face the problem of the transgressor. Unless there is a penalty attached to the act of transgression, men will not keep to their respective classes. The whole system will break down, being contrary to human nature. *Chaturvarnya* cannot subsist by its own inherent goodness. It must be enforced by law. That, without penal sanction the ideal of *Chaturvarnya* cannot be realized, is proved by the story in the Ramayana of Rama killing Shambuka..... Ram Raj was a Raj based on *Chaturvarnya*. As a king, Rama was bound to maintain *Chaturvamya*. It was his duty therefore to kill Shambuka, the Shudra, who had transgressed his class and wanted to be a Brahmin. This is the reason why Rama killed Shambuka. But this also shows that penal sanction is necessary for the maintenance of *Chaturvarnya*. Not only penal sanction is necessary, but penalty of death is necessary. That is why Rama did not inflict on Shambuka a lesser punishment. That is why *Manu-Smriti* prescribes such heavy sentences as cutting off the tongue or pouring of molten lead in the ears of the Shudra, who recites or hears the *Veda*. The supporters of *Chaturvarnya* must give an assurance that they could successfully classify men and they could induce modem society in the third millennium to reforge the penal sanctions of *Manu-Smriti*.

Varna System Cannot be Applied to Women

The protagonists of *Chaturvarnya* do not seem to have considered what is to happen to women in their system. Ambedkar asks, "Are they also to be divided into four classes, Brahmin, Kshatriya, Vaishya and Shudra? Or are they to be allowed to take the status of their husbands. If the status of the woman is to be the consequence of marriage what becomes of the underlying principle of *Chaturvarnya*, namely, that the status of a person should be based upon the worth of that person? If they are to be classified according to their worth is their classification to be nominal or real? If it is to be nominal then it is useless and then the protagonists of *Chaturvarnya* must admit that their system does not apply to women. If it is real, are the protagonists of *Chaturvarnya* prepared to follow the logical consequences of applying it to women? ... Given these difficulties, I think no one except a congenital idiot could hope and believe in a successful regeneration of the *Chaturvarnya*, concludes Ambedkar.

18

Ambedkar on Annihilation of Caste

Reformers working for the removal of untouchability, including Mahatma Gandhi, do not seem to realise that the acts of the people are merely the results of their beliefs inculcated upon their minds by the Shastras and that people will not change their conduct until they cease to believe in the sanctity of the Shastras on which their conduct is founded, Ambedkar told *Jat-pat Todak Madal,* in his address referred to in the previous chapter. He maintained that there is "no wonder that such efforts have not produced any results. You also seem to be erring in the same way as the reformers working in the cause of removing untouchability. To agitate for and to organise inter-caste dinners and inter-caste marriages is like forced feeding brought about by artificial means." He exhorted the reformers:

> *Make every man and woman free from the thraldom of the Shastras, cleanse their minds of the pernicious notions founded on the Shastras, and he or she will inter-dine and inter-marry, without your telling him or her to do so. How Shastras are understood is important, not quibbles.*

Difficulties in Destroying Caste

Ambedkar saw no use in asking people o give up caste, unless the bias taught by religious notions was changed. He said :

> *To ask people to give up Caste is to ask them to go contrary to their fundamental religious notions...The Hindus hold to the sacredness of the social order. Caste has a divine basis. You must, therefore, destroy the sacredness and divinity with which Caste*

> *has become invested. In the last analysis, this* ***means you must destroy the authority of the Shastras and the Vedas.***

Ambedkar emhasised that knowing the proper ways and means is more important than knowing the ideal. If you do not know the real ways and means, all your shots are sure to be misfires. "If my analysis is correct then your task is Herculean. You alone can say whether you are capable of achieving it," he declared.

Attitude of Hostility

Ambedkar said everything in unequivocal terms with all his sincerity. He told the Jat Pat Todak Mandal, that he saw the task to be well nigh impossible. And, for the reasons, he came out as under:

> *Out of the many reasons, which have led me to take this view, I will mention some, which I regard much important. One of these reasons is the attitude of hostility, which the Brahmins have shown towards this question. The Brahmins form the vanguard of the movement for political reform and in some cases also of economic reform. But they are not to be found even as camp followers in the army raised to break down the barricades of Caste. Is there any hope of the Brahmins ever taking up a lead in the future in this matter? I say no.*

Imagining that it was not easy for his audience to admit the significance his words, he said that they might argue

> *That there is no reason why Brahmins should continue to shun social reform;*
>
> *That the Brahmins know that the bane of Hindu Society is Caste and as an enlightened class could not be expected to be indifferent to its consequences; and*
>
> *That there are secular Brahmins and priestly Brahmins and, if the latter do not take up the cudgels on behalf of those who want to break Caste, the former will.*

Ambedkar said that all this, of course, sounds very plausible. But in all this it is forgotten that the **break up of the Caste System is bound to affect adversely the Brahmin Caste**. Therefore, Ambedkar asked:

> *Having regard to this, is it reasonable to expect that the Brahmins will ever consent to lead a movement the ultimate result of which is to destroy the power and prestige of the Brahmin Caste?*

Is it reasonable to expect the secular Brahmins to take part in a movement directed against the priestly Brahmins?

And, he replied himself as follows:

In my judgement, it is useless to make a distinction between the secular Brahmins and priestly Brahmins. Both are kith and kin. They are two arms of the same body and one is bound to fight for the existence of the other.

To Save Hinduism, You have to Kill Brahminism

While talking of profession of a Hindu priest, Ambedkar observed that it was the only profession which was not subject to any code. He was emphatic in making the following conclusion:

Mentally a priest may be an idiot, physically a priest may be suffering from a foul disease, such as syphilis or gonorrhoea, morally he may be a wreck. But he is fit to officiate at solemn ceremonies, to enter the sanctum sanctorum of a Hindu temple and worship the Hindu God. All this becomes possible among the Hindus because for a priest it is enough to be born in a priestly caste. The whole thing is abominable and is due to the fact that the priestly class among Hindus is subject neither to law nor to morality. It recognises no duties. It knows only of rights and privileges. It is a pest which divinity seems to have let loose on the masses for their mental and moral degradation.

Whenever Ambedkar raised a question, he always came out with the well-considered answer to that. About the problems of Hinfu priests, the Brahmans, he suggested:

The priestly class must be brought under control by some such legislation as I have outlined above. It will prevent it from doing mischief and from misguiding people. It will democratise it by throwing it open to every one. It will certainly help to kill the Brahminism and will also help to kill Caste, which is nothing but Brahminism incarnate.

Brahminism As poison,

Ambedkar distingushed between Brahmins and Brahminism. He thought that the former could improve but that the latter was incorrigible:

Brahminism is the poison, which has spoiled Hinduism. You will succeed in saving Hinduism if you will kill Brahminism. There should be no opposition to this reform from any quarter. It should be welcomed even by the Arya Samajists, because this is merely an application of their own doctrine of guna-karma.

Annihilation of Caste, is the master-pece of Ambedkar in which he has talked at length about the topics which covered the entire gamut of Hindu society in all possible sense. The topics covered included the ones to which an average Hindu has probably never bothered to think upon. They include Hindu Responsibility to Caste, Hindu Tolerance Indicates Weakness, Higher Caste Hindus Preventing Lower Ones From Improving Levels. It might be eye-opener for the Hindus but Ambedkar does point out that there is No Sangathan among Hindus.

He went on to point out that All Hindus Are Slaves Of Caste And Slaves Are Not Equal, that Intellectual Class was Confined To Brahmin Caste, that there is No Scope For Liberty, Equality And Fraternity In Hinduism, that there is Hollowness in Reform Of Arya Samaj,that Chaturvarnyam is the Most Vicious System, that Chaturvarnyam is the Most Degraded System, Chaturvarnyam And Social Revolution Are Incompatible, that in Hinduism Rationalism is Regarded As Wicked As Atheism.

While admitting that Hindus are not prepared to accept any reforms in Hinduism, he still suggested Ways to Reform Hinduism, and that the foemost way is to Annihilate Caste He dwelt at lenght to talk about Caste Consciousness of Hindus, Caste and Common Activity, Brahmin's Primary Concern, Castes as Warring Groups, Brahmanas' Insults to Shivaji, Millions Excluded as Savages in Midst of Civilization, Cardinal Items in Reform, Sanctity of Shastras and Need to Destroy their Sanctity, To Save Hinduism, You have to Kill Brahminism.

Final Words of Advice To Hindus

Ambedkar advised the Hindus through his *Annihilation of Caste*, to necessarily give a new doctrinal basis to their religion-a basis that will be in consonance with Liberty, Equality and Fraternity, in short, with Democracy. In this connection, he raised some questions which he considered very vital and invited them seriously to consider the same.

In the first place, the Hindus must first make an attempt to find out what kind of morality, beliefs, habits and outlook have worked best and have enabled those who possessed them to flourish, to go strong, to people the earth and to have dominion over it. In this connection he cited Prof. Carver:

> "Morality and religion, as the organised expression of moral approval and disapproval, must be regarded as factors in the struggle for existence as truly as are weapons for offence and defence, teeth and claws, horns and hoofs, furs and feathers. The social group, community, tribe or nation, which develops an unworkable scheme of morality or within which those social acts which weaken it and unfit it for survival, habitually create the sentiment of approval, while those which would strengthen and enable it to be expanded habitually create the sentiment of disapproval, will eventually be eliminated. It is its habits of approval or disapproval (these are the results of religion and morality) that handicap it, as really as the possession of two wings on one side with none on the other will handicap the colony of flies. It would be as futile in the one case as in the other to argue, that one system is just as good as another."

Ambedkar insisted, "Morality and religion, therefore, are not mere matters of likes and dislikes. You may dislike exceedingly a scheme of morality, which, if universally practised within a nation, would make that nation the strongest nation on the face of the earth. Yet in spite of your dislike such a nation will become strong. .... The Hindus must, therefore, examine their religion and their morality in terms of their survival value."

Secondly, the Hindus must consider whether they should conserve the whole of their social heritage or select what is helpful and transmit to future generations only that much and no more. He derived support from Prof. John Dewey, his teacher, and said:

> "Every society gets encumbered with what is trivial, with dead wood from the past, and with what is positively perverse... As a society becomes more enlightened, it realises that it is responsible not to conserve and transmit the whole of its existing achievements, but only such as make for a better future society."

Ambedkar suggested that even Burke, had had been compelled to admit: "A state without the means of some change is without the means of its conservation. Without such means it might even risk the loss of that part of the constitution which it wished the most religiously to preserve." Then Ambedkar maintained that what Burke said of a State applies equally to a society.

Thirdly, Ambedkar advised the Hindus to cease to worship the past as supplying its ideals. About the baneful effect of worship of past, he again took support from Prof. Dewey who maintained:

"An individual can live only in the present. The present is not just something which comes after the past; much less something produced by it. It is what life is in leaving the past behind it. The study of past products will not help us to understand the present. A knowledge of the past and its heritage is of great significance when it enters into the present, but not otherwise. And the mistake of making the records and remains of the past the main material of education is that **it tends to make the past a rival of the present and the present a more or less futile imitation of the past."**

Ambedkar continued that the principle, which makes little of the present act of living and growing, naturally looks upon the present as empty and upon the future as remote. Such a principle is inimical to progress and is an hindrance to a strong and a steady current of life.

Fourthly, he told the Hindus to recognise that there is nothing fixed, nothing eternal, nothing sanatana; that everything is changing, that change is the law of life for individuals as well as for society. He went on "In a changing society, there must be a constant revolution of old values and the Hindus must realise that if there must be standards to measure the acts of men there must also be a readiness to revise those standards."

In his humility Ambedkar said that all he claimed wass to have told them candidly his views for their consideration in their own interest and that he had little to recommend them but some study and a deep concern in their destiny. He made it clear that these were the views of a man, who has been no tool of power, no flatterer of greatness. He stressed:

> *They (the views) come from one, almost the whole of **whose public exertion has been one continuous struggle for liberty for the poor and for the oppressed and whose only reward has been a continuous shower of calumny and abuse from national journals and national leaders, for no other reason except that I refuse to join with them in performing the miracle -I will not say trick- of liberating the oppressed with the gold of the tyrant and raising the poor with the cash of the rich**.*

*But he cautioned, "All this may not be enough to commend my views. I think they are not likely to alter yours. But whether they do or do not, the responsibility is entirely yours. You must make your efforts to **uproot Caste, if not in my way, then in your way**. I am sorry, I will not be with you. I have decided to change. This is not the place for* *giving reasons. But even when I am gone out of your fold, I will watch your moment with active sympathy and you will have my assistance for what it may be worth."*

Ambedkar continued:

> *Yours is a national cause. Caste is no doubt primarily the breath of the Hindus. But the* ***Hindus have fouled the air all over and everybody is infected, Sikh, Muslim and Christian****. You, therefore, deserve the support of all those who are suffering from this infection, Sikh, Muslim and Christian.*

While refering to sawaraj, he observed:

Yours is more difficult than the other national cause, namely Swaraj. ***In the fight for Swaraj you fight with the whole nation on your side. In this, you have to fight against the whole nation and that too, your own. But it is more important than Swaraj.*** *There is no use having Swaraj, if you cannot defend it.*

But here also Ambedkar did not forget to remind the Hindus, in his parting words of his address, what was more imPortant to them than even the swaraj:

More important than the question of defending Swaraj is the question of defending the Hindus under the Swaraj. In my opinion only ***when the Hindu Society becomes a casteless society that it can hope to have strength enough to defend itself. Without such internal strength, Swaraj for Hindus may turn out to be only a step towards slavery.***

Impossible to Reform Hinduism

What is regarded by the Hindus as their strength was interpreted by Ambedkar as theri weakenss. Instead of being led by the group, he emhasised the value of individiual opinions. He said **caste was powerful weapon for persecuting the reforms and for killing all reform:**

> The assertion by the individual of his own opinions and beliefs, his own independence and interest as over against group standards, group authority and group interests is the beginning of all reform ... Now a caste has an unquestioned right to excommunicate any man who is guilty of breaking the rules of the caste and when it is realised that excommunication involves a complete process of social intercourse it will be agreed that as a form of punishment **there is really little to choose between excommunication and death.** No wonder individual Hindus have

not had the courage to assert their independence by breaking the barriers of caste ... But as it is, **even law gives each caste an autonomy to regulate its membership and punish dissenters with excommunication.** Caste in the hands of the orthodox has been a powerful weapon for persecuting the reforms and for killing all reform.

True Religion: Not Religion of Rules

Ambedkar condemns a Religion of Rules, but still he considers religion as necessity for a religion since he agrees with Burke when he says, "True religion is the foundation of society, the basis on which all true Civil Government rests, and both their sanction." While urging that these ancient rules of life be annulled, he is anxious that its place shall be taken by a Religion of Principles, which alone can lay claim to being a true Religion. In view of this being his opinion about religion, outlines cardinal items in the reform of Hinduism as under:

(1) There should be one and only one standard book of Hindu Religion, acceptable to all Hindus and recognised by all Hindus. This of course means that all other books of Hindu religion such as *Vedas, Shastras* and *Puranas*, which are treated as sacred and authoritative, must by law cease to be so and the preaching of any doctrine, religious or social contained in these books should be penalised.

(2) It should be better if priesthood among Hindus was abolished. But as this seems to be impossible, the priesthood must at least cease to be hereditary. Every person who professes to be a Hindu must be eligible for being a priest. It should be provided by law that no Hindu shall be entitled to be a priest unless he has passed an examination prescribed by the State and holds a *sanad* from the State permitting him to practise.

(3) No ceremony performed by a priest who does not hold a *sanad* shall be deemed to be valid in law and it should be made penal for a person who has no *sanad* to officiate as a priest.

(4) A priest should be the servant of the State and should be subject to the disciplinary action by the State in the matter of his morals, beliefs and worship, in addition to his being subject along with other citizens to the ordinary law of the land.

(5) The number of priests should be limited by law according to the requirements of the State.

Destroy Sanctity of Sastras

According to Dr. Ambedkar, the real remedy is to destroy the belief in the sanctity of the Shastras. He asks, "How do you expect to succeed, if you allow the Shastras to continue to mould the beliefs and opinions of the people? Not to question the authority of the Shastras, to permit the people to believe in their sanctity and their sanctions and to blame them and to criticise them for their acts as being irrational and inhuman is a incongruous way of carrying on social reform."

19

Ambedkar on Shakti and Kaliyuga

In this chapter, we are going to examine the views of Ambedkar about the Hindu goddesses, who are known as *ardhanginis* or wives of the gods who form Hindu trinity. In the process, he raises many questions which are important for the unity and strength of the country.

Ambedkar felt repeatedly intrigued while going through the mythological stories and the philosophic treatises of Hindu philosophy. Instead of glossing over the intrigung portions as is the habit of the blind followers of religion, he tried to raise questions and find appropriate answers so that he could educate himself and those to whom he felt a definite responsibility. We have already noted his sense of exasperatin with regard to the Hindu social orgnisation in previous chapters, but in this chapter we propose to have a peep into his mind about why and how the pernicious Hindu social organisation came to take the present shape.

Ambedkar noted that Brahma, Vishnu and Siva are the members of Hindu trinity, that they have wives in the shape of *Saraswati*, *Laxmi* and *Parvati*, respectively, that these wives are the *shaktis* (power) of their male consorts. But he also notes that the shakti of different gods opertate in different manners. He also notes that Siva has many wives but even they do not act in a uniform manner. He felt puzzled to note that Saraswati and Lakshmi have killed no Asura and have in fact no deed of valour. Question is why?

Brahma and Vishnu had Shakti, which in conformity with the theory must have dwelt in their wives. Why then did Saraswati and *Lakshmi* not take part in the battle with the Asuras? This part is only reserved for the wives of Shiva. Even here Paarvati's role is quite different from that of Durgaa. Like *Durgaa*, *Parvati* is also the *Shakti* of *Shiva*. Why was *Shiva's Shakti* dwelling in Parvati so dull, so dormant, and so inactive as to be non-existent?

According to him, the second point is that though this doctrine may be a good justification for starting the worship of Goddesses independently of Gods, it is difficult to accept either the logical or historical basis of the doctrine. Looking at it purely from the point of view of logic if every god has Shakti then even the Vedic gods must have had it. Why then was this doctrine not applied to the wives of the Vedic gods? Looking at it from the point of view of history, **there is no justification for saying that the *Pauranic* gods had *Shakti* in them.**

Further he asks himself as to why the Brahmins do not seem to have realised that by making *Durgaa* the heroine who alone was capable of destroying the Asuras, they were making their own gods a set of miserable cowards. It seems that the **Devas [gods] could not defend themselves against the Asuras** and had to beg their wives to come to their rescue. According to him, one illustration from the *Maarkandeya Purana* is enough to prove how imbecile the Pauranic Gods were shown by the Brahmins against the Asuras. Says the Maarkandeya Purana:

> *"Mahisha, king of the giants, at one time overcame the gods in war, and reduced them to such a state of want that they wandered through the earth as beggars. Indra first conducted them to Brahma, and then to Shiva; but as these gods could render no assistance, they turned to Vishnu, who was so grieved at the sight of their wretchedness, that streams of glory issued from his face, whence came a female figure named Mahamaya; [another name of Durga]. Streams of glory issued from the faces of the other gods also, which in like manner entered Mahamaya, in consequence of which she became a body of glory, like a mountain of fire. The gods then handed their weapons to this dreadful being, who with a frightful scream ascended into the air, slew the giant, and gave redress to the gods."*

> *How can such cowardly gods have any prowess? Dr. Ambedkar had asked. He continued that "If they had none, how could they give it to their wives. To say that Goddesses must be worshipped because they have Sakti is not merely a*

riddle but an absurdity. It requires explanation why this doctrine of Sakti was invented. Was it to put it a new commodity on the market that the BRAHMINS started the worship of the Goddesses and degraded the gods?"

The most important riddle pointed out by Dr. Ambedkar concerns the Hindu imagination of *Kaliyuga*. According to him **the significance of this assumption is that all wrong doers, criminals, and immoralists have been made immune from suffering any consequences for their actions since they can always take shelter behind 'assumptions' that whatever they have done, has been under the influence of *Kaliyuga* for which they cannot and need not be punished by anyone**. In this connection, it will be important to peruse the words of Dr. Ambedkar himself.

Riddles about Kali-Yuga?

Ambedkar argued, "If there is any notion widespread among the Hindus and understood by every man and woman adult or old, mature or immature, it is that of the *Kali-Yuga* and that they are living in the *Kali-Yuga*. The theory of *Kali-Yuga* has a psychological effect upon the mind of the people. It means that it is an unpropitious age. It is an immoral age. It is, therefore, an age in which human effort will not bear any fruit." He, therefore, considered it necessary to enquire as to how such a notion arose. He argued as under:

> There are really four points, which require elucidation. They are [1] What is *Kali-Yuga*? [2] When did *Kali* begin? [3] When is *Kali* to end? And [4] why such a notion was spread among the people?
>
> His answer to 'What is *Kali-Yuga*?' was as follows:
>
> *Kali is one of the cycles made up of four Yugas: Krita, Treta, Dwapar, and Kali. The terms Krita, Treta, Dwapara and Kali are known to have been used in three different connections. The earliest use of the term Kali as well as of other terms is connected with the game of dice.*

Then he found that "From the Rig-Veda it appears that the dice that was used in the game was made of the brown fruit of the Vibhitaka tree being about the size of a nutmeg, nearly round with four sides instead of five. Each side was marked with the different numerals 4, 3, 2, and 1. The side marked with 4 was called Krita, with 3 Treta, with 2 Dwapar, and with 1 Kali. Shamshastry gives an account of how a game of dice formed part of sacrifice and how it was played".

Kali as one of Five Dices

Ambedkar consulted the commentaries of the foreigners and found that Prof. Eggling's references to the Vedic literature leave no doubt about the prevalence of the game of dice almost from the earliest time. It is also clear from his references that the game was played with five dices; four of which were called *Krita* while the fifth was called *Kali*. He also points out that there were various modes in which the game was played and says that according to the earliest mode of playing the game, if all the dice fell uniformly with the marked sides either upwards or downwards then the player won the game. The game of dice formed part of the *Rajasuya* and also of the sacrificial ceremony connected with the establishment of the sacred fire.

Kali as Unit of Time

These terms Krita, Treta, Dwapar and Kali —were also used in Mathematics. This is clear from... passage from Abhayadevasuri's Commentary on *Bhagvati Sutra* a voluminous work of Jain religion. Whatever the meaning in which the words *Kali* and *Yuga* used at one time, the term *Kali* has long since been used to designate a unit in the Hindu system of reckoning time. According to the Hindus there was a cycle of time, which consists of four *Yugas* of which *Kali Yuga* forms one. The other *Yugas* are called *Krita*. *Treta*, *Dwapar*.

When Did Present Kali Yuga Begin?

Ambedkar maintained that there are two different answers to the question. According to the *Atereya Brahmana* it began with Nabhanedishta son of *Vaivasvata Manu*. According to the *Puranas* it began on the death of Krishna after the battle of Mahabharata. The first has been reduced to time term by Dr. Shamshatry who says that *Kali Yuga* began in 3101 BC. The second has been worked out by Mr. Gopal Aiyer with meticulous care. His view is that the Mahabharata war commenced on the 14th 0f October 1194 BC. He places the death of Krishna 16 years after the close of the War basing his conclusion on the ground that Parikshit was 16 years when installed on the throne and reading it with the connected facts, namely, that Pandavas went on Mahaprasthana immediately after installing Parikshit on the throne and this they did on the very day Krishna died. This gives 1177 BC as the date of the commencement of the Kali Yuga.

We have [thus] two different dates for the commencement of the *Kali Yuga* 3101 B.C. and 1177 B.C. This is the first riddle about the *Kali*

Yuga. Two explanations are forthcoming for these two widely separated dates for the commencement of one and the same *Yuga*. One explanation is 3101 B.C., which is the date of the commencement of the *Kalpa* and not *Kali* and it was the mistake on the part of the copyist who misread Kalpa for Kali and brought this confusion, The other explanation is that given by Dr. Shamshastry. According to him there were two *Kali Yuga* Eras which must be distinguished. One beginning in 3101 B.C. Another beginning in 1260 0r 1240 B.C. the first lasted about 1840 years and was lost.

Different Theories About Beginning of Kali Yuga

Indian Astronomer Gargacharya in his Siddhanta when speaking of Sailisuka Maurya the fourth in succession from Asoka makes the following important observation:

> *Then the viciously valiant Greeks, after reducing Saketa, Panchala country to Mathura, will reach Kusumadhvaja [Patna]: Pushpapru being taken all provinces will undoubtedly be in disorder. The unconquerable Yavanas will not remain in the middle of the country. There will be cruel and dreadful war among themselves. Then after the destruction of the Greeks at the end of the Yuga, seven powerful Kings reign in Oudha."*

First of all, it must be noted that in some of Hindu scriptures, the past events - actual or imagined - were described in future tense. Ambedkar's comments on the above extract are pertinent. He says that the important words are "After the destruction of the Greeks at the end of the Yuga.' These words give rise to two questions [1] which Yuga Garga has in mind? and [2] when did the defeat and destruction of the Greeks in India take place? Now the answers to these questions are not in doubt. By Yuga he means Kali Yuga and the destruction and defeat of the Greeks took place about 165 BC. It is not mere matter of inference from facts. There are direct statements in chapters 188 and 190 of the Vanaparva of the Mahabharata that the Barbarian Sakas, Yavanas, Bahlikas and many others will devastate Bharatvarsha 'at the end of the Kali Yuga'. Ambedkar concluded about the age of Kali as under:

> *The result which follows when the two statements put together is that the Kali Yuga ended in 165 BC. There is also another argument which supports this conclusion. According to the Mahabharata, Kali Yuga was to comprise a period of 1000 years. If we accept the statement that the Kali Yuga began in*

1171 BC and deduct one thousand years since then we cannot escape the conclusion that Kali Yuga should have ended by about 171 B.C., which is not very far from the historical fact referred to by Garga as happening at the close of the Kali Yuga. There can be therefore no doubt that in the opinion of the Chief Astronomer, Kali Yuga came to an end about 165 BC. What is however the position? The position is that according to the Vaidika Brahmins, Kali Yuga has not ended. It still continues. This is clear from the terms of Sankalpa, which is a declaration which every Hindu makes even today at the time of any religious ceremony.

The question we have to consider is, Ambedkar says, why and how the Vedic Brahmins manage to keep the Kali Yuga going on when the astronomer had said it was closed. The first thing to do is to ascertain what is the original period of the Kali Yuga.

Use of Kali Yuga as Adharma or non-Righteousness

The *Kali Yuga* means an age of *adharma*, an age which is demoralised and an age in which the laws made by the King ought to be obeyed. One question at once arises. Why was the *Kali Yuga* more demoralised than the preceding *Yugas*? what was the moral condition of the Aryans in the *Yuga* or *Yugas* preceding the present *Kali Yuga*? Anyone who compares the habits and social practices of the later Aryans with those of the ancient Aryans, will find a tremendous improvement almost amounting to revolution in their manners and morals.

Peep Into Religion of Aryans

According to Ambedkar, the religion of the Vedic Aryans was full of barbaric and obscene observances. Human sacrifice formed a part of their religion and was called Narmedhayagna. He discloses that most elaborate descriptions of the rite are found in the *Yajur-Veda Samhita*, the *Yajur-Veda Brahmanas,* the *Sankyana* and *Vaitana Sutras*. About worship of phallus, he maintains:

The worship of genitals or what is called Phallus worship was quite prevalent among the ancient Aryans. The cult of the Phallus came to be known as Skambh and was recognised as part of Aryan religion as may be seen in the hymns in Atharva-Veda X.7. Another instance of obscenity, which disfigured the religion of the Ancient Aryans, is connected with the Asvamedha-Yajna or the horse sacrifice. A necessary part of the Asvamedha was the introduction of the Sepas [penis] of the Medha [dead horse] into the Yoni [vagina] of the chief wife of the Yajamana [the sacrificer] accompanied by the recital of long series of Mantras by the Brahmin priests.

Ambedkar on Marriage Ritual of Saptapadi

Then Ambedkar comes to *Saptapadi*, which is the most essential ceremony in a Hindu marriage and without which there is no marriage, in Law. Ambedkar goes on to why of this rite and reaches the followinmg conclusion:

The reason is quite obvious. It is a test whether the Deva who had his right of prelibation over the bride was satisfied with the Avadana and was prepared to release her. If the Deva allowed the bridegroom to take the bride away with him up to a distance covered by Sapatapadi it raised an irrefutable presumption that the Deva was satisfied with the compensation and that his right was extinguished and the girl was free to be the wife of another. The Saptapadi cannot have any other meaning. The fact that Saptapadi is necessary in very marriage shows how universally prevalent this kind of immorality had been among the Devas and the Aryans.

Ambedkar on Morals in Ancient India

Ambedkar believes that this survey cannot be complete without separate reference to the morals of Krishna. Since the beginning of Kali Yuga, which is the same thing, which is associated with his death, his morals became of considerable importance. Ambedkar raises a question and himself answers that:

How do the morals of Krishna compare with those of the others? Full details are given in another place about the sort of life Krishna led. To that I will add a few. Krishna belonged to the Vrisni [Yadava family]. The Yadavas were polygamous. The Yadava Kings are reported to have innumerable wives and innumerable sons—a stain from which Krishna himself was not free. But this Yadava family and Krishna's own house was not free from the stain of parental incest. The case of a father marrying daughter is reported by the Matsya Purana to have occurred in the Yadava family. According to Matsya Purana, King

Taittiri an ancestor of Krishna married his own daughter and begot on her a son named Nala. The case of a son cohabiting with his mother is found in the conduct of Samba the son of Krishna. The Matsya Purana tells how Samba lived an illicit life with the wives of Krishna, his father, and how Krishna got angry and cursed Samba and the guilty wives on that account. There is a reference to this in the Mahabharata, also. Satyabhama asked Draupadi the secret of her power over her five husbands. According to the Mahabharata, Draupadi warned her against talking or staying in private with her stepsons. This corroborates what the Matsya Purana has to say about Samba. Samba's is not the only case. His brother Pradyumna married his foster mother Mayavati, the wife of Sambara.

Ambedkar declares that it is not possible to divide this history into definite *Yugas* and to say that what state of morals existed in *Krita*, what in *Treta* and what in *Dwapara*, which closed at the death of Krishna. But he argues that in *Krita* age, the state of morality could be the worst:

If however, we allow the ancient Aryans a spirit of progressive reform it is possible to say that the worst cases of immorality occurred in earliest age, i.e., the Krita age, the less revolting in the Treta and the least revolting in Dwapara and the best in Kali age.

Ambedkar's inquiry into the ancient moralities takes him to the Devas and the rishis, the top ranking individuals in Arayn history and mythology, in which connection. he makes the followinmg observations:

Devas and rishis occupy a very high place in the eyes of the common Aryan and, as is usual, the inferior always imitates their superior. What the superior class does forms a standard for the inferior. The immoralities which were prevalent in the Aryan Society were largely the result of the imitation by the common man of the immoral acts and deeds of the devas and the rishis. To stop the spread of immoralities in society, the leaders of the Aryan Society introduced a reform of the greatest significance. They declared that the acts and deeds of the devas and the rishis are not to be cited or treated as precedents. In this way one cause and source was removed by a bold and courageous stroke."

Ambedkar seems to have erred in reaching this conclusion because it is not to be expected from the *Devas [Bhusuras]* that they would do something to curtail their rights and privileges. Rather there can be another explanation, which seems to be more plausible. The

Pauranika Brahmans had naturally departed from their more ancient practices, not because they were interested in reforming their society. Rather it appears more reasonable to assume that the process of Aryanisation had to be accelerated for reasons of bringing an end to the Buddhist and Jain religions. For that purpose, the Vedikas had to adjust their preaching to the prevalent practices in the population, which was sought to be converted to their own neo-religion. They had also to attract greater number of women to their fold on the pattern of Buddhism and Jainism. There is no doubt that the standard of the women of non-Aryans was of a higher order and, therefore, the converts to the new religion would not like to permit the corruption of their own women on the lines of the morals of the ancient Aryans. Accordingly, the Aryans felt forced to put the above-said stipulation, in order to serve a different kind of selfish purpose.

20

Ambedkar's Search for Alternatives

Shourie has criticised Ambedkarism but not defined it. Therefore, we shall have to attempt a definition of Ambedkarism. Dr. Ambedkar's starting point was to expose Brahminism. As such, **Ambedkarism can be described to be anti-Brahminism**. If so, Ambedkarism is not as old as Ambedkar; **it is one of the modern alternatives to Varnasrama Dharma**. In the past there have been other alternatives, which were tried at different times.

Varnasrama was representing *Deva-Sanskriti,* which favoured the social divisions. *Danava-sanskriti* represented social unity. In ancient times, religion was all-pervasive. Therefore, even political questions were treated as religious questions. In such a situation, the religious upheavals led to provide even political alternatives. The reaction to excessive religious exploitation under the protection of state forced the victims to tread carefully, so that they carved a way out by following the middle path, which provided them facility to survive even in extremely hostile situations and yet make them steadily progress with their mission. Their predicament did not leave any room for any violent reaction.

The ancient-most alternative to *Vrnavyvastha* was found in Buddhism. The same Buddhism is unable to solve the present day problem, which has been caused by a new kind of *Varnavyastha*, which has further degenerated into much worse caste system. Thus, old Buddhism had to be adjusted by Ambedkar. He reached the very root of the problem quite early and hit it directly and suggested the surgical operation of mutilation of the affected part. As such, he led a relentless struggle for annihilation of caste.

Those who had been progressing and surviving because of the caste divisions natually argued that their religion could not exist without caste. They were right since their religion was based on organised exploitation, which had been given a seemingly innocent name of caste. The like of Hindu argument in favour of caste could be advanced by the British imperialists also, otherwise it would not have been possible for them and the Hindu leadership to collaborate with each other so easily and for so long.

Had all Indians sympathised with the British imperialists, the latter would not have left Indian colony of slaves at all. Similarly, if Ambedkar had appreciated the argument of Gandhi, he would not have been able to write the destiny of the Depressed Classes and the OBCs, through landmarks between Poona Pact and the Constitution of India. Dalit emancipation from Varna Vyavastha is directly comparable with India's securing freedom from British rulers. Since the British came from a distant land and were clearly distinguishable from Indians because of their belonging to the white race, they could leave and be made to leave the country. But the problem of Dalits is more complex. Their exploitative masters belong to the same blood and by now to the same mixed race and belong to the same country, namely, India. Like masters or slaves or like equal partners of the same company, both the parties have to perforce exist side by side. As long as the caste system survives, the gain of one is to be treated as loss of the other and vice versa. They can come to have a permanent understanding only on the demise of caste system. If the Hindus continue to ignore this fact, there is no alternative to the inevitability of their mutual doom and destruction.

Ambedkar's solution was simple. He had to take the obvious hint from the ancient Indian history of rise of Buddhism as an alternative to *varna* system. Since the shape of the said varna system has undergone a sea change by evolving into more pernicious caste system, the old remedy of old Buddhism, could not be sufficient to the malady of modern India. Hence Ambedkar's formulations of Neo-Buddhism, his, new Buddhahood, or new Bodhistvvahood, which can legitmately be described with the help of his own name, Ambedkar, from which the name Ambedkarism has been derived.

Ambedkarism and Neo-Buddhism

The Buddhists on account of his reviving Buddhism in the twentieth century might like to call Dr. Ambedkar as the 23rd Buddha. But those Ambedkarites, who follow his policies and accept him as the true ideal, may regard him as the first Ambedkar in the sense of being the propounder of new idea, which has come to stay as Ambedkarism. They may also trace earlier personalities in the line of providing such an inspiration and place Ambedkar at the end of such a line, on the analogy of Buddhism, Jainism and Sikhism.

Buddhism Answers Marxism Regarding Exploitation

In "Buddha and Karl Marx," Ambedkar posed Buddhism against Marxism. He saw Buddhism as a solution to the problems of exploitation posed by Marxism. He seemed to believe that Buddhism answers "Marxist" questions. *The Buddha and his Dhamma* radically challenges some of the basic tenets of Buddhism existing in Theravada or Mahayana or Vajrayana forms. Ambedkar, first, rejects the traditional version of Siddhartha's *Parivraja* or "going forth". He argued that the story of being moved by the sight of a dead person, a sick person, and an old person was impossible to believe.

Then, he claims that the "four Aryan truths" purported to be of Buddhism are not part of the original teaching of the Buddha. According to him, The four Aryan Truths are a great stumbling block in the way of non-Buddhists accepting the gospel of Buddhism.

Bhikhu Should be Social Servant, Not Perfect Man

Further, Ambedkar asserts a "a terrible contradiction" between the doctrines of *karma* and rebirth**,** and the Buddha's denial of the existence of the soul. Finally, he claims that the Bhikhu can only be the "hope of Buddhism" if he is a social servant and not a "perfect man." Gail Omvedt thinks that Ambedkar's project in *The Buddha and His Dhamma* is to resolve these problems.

Ambedkar gives his own interpretation of Buddhism in the way of almost any charismatic religious leader. He feels free to claim that every value he approves of is in Buddhism. He seems to have developed an argument that any contrary interpretation of Buddhism that seems to be in the texts was a Brahmanical insertion. Here a question arises, "Would Ambedkar's Buddhism be acceptable to others, particularly Buddhist believers?" Whether they accept or not, one thing is clear that Ambedkar continues to guide the aspirations of millions of ex-Untouchables and other converts. This is especially so because, the Indian Buddhists are the ardent followers of Ambedkar, who have already started giving him the status of God, irrespective of the fact whether traditional Buddhism believes in God or not.

Weaker Sections: United They Stand

There is a definite need for basing its theoretical thinking on contemporary principles of Ambedkarism. At present, all those working in the name of Dr. Ambedkar are basically interested in selling the name of Ambedkar or in selling themselves or pawning the Ambedkarites with the enemies of Ambedkarism. There is an utter need for all such bodies and individuals to unite themselves and then to unite the broad masses of the people around the definite practical tasks of the present epoch.

The present Indian situation is marred by the retreat of revolution that had been ushered in by Dr. Ambedkar. The retreat has been caused by a great offensive against Ambedkarism of the type exhibited by Shourie, which is in fact an all-round anti-social offensive against the broad masses of the people. Simultaneously, there is a conciliatory programme of the type mentioned above, which consists in luring some of the important persons to its own side. The methods of the fundamentalists can be broadly compared with the peacekeeping programme of the United States, in relation to many developing countries.

It has been said by CGPI, *"In India, as in many other countries, the situation is complicated by the deformation of the very notion of communist political work. Communist politics has been reduced to the level of either participating in the running of the state apparatus or directly contributing to the cult of violence, which the ruling classes are consolidating in India."*

Applying this observation to the Dalit problem, it can be said that many of their leaders have been reduced to the level participating in the programmes dear to the fundamentalists. These fundamentalists are directly giving rise to a new cult of violence through the cinema and the TV serials, in the name of informing the masses about the hidden philosophy of the mythology.

All such programmes are directly anti-*Asuras*. All of them preach the constant use of violence and deceit against the Asuras. And the *Jaagrans*, the *Ramayana*, the *Mahabharata* epics and the *Saptaah-Yajnas* of *Srimad-Bhaagavata-Purana* as also the solar and lunar eclipses occurring every year do remind all concerned about the present day representations of gods and demons. According to them, the Brahmanas are the present day representations of the gods and that the present day Dalits are the representations of the *Asuras* like Raahu and Ketu. Some particular castes of the Dalits are encouraged by the

Brahmanas to collect Dana or gifts in the name of *Raahu* and *Sani* or planet Saturn, whose effect in astrology is as destructive as that of Raahu.

Concept of Rights for Masses and Ambedkar

Incidentally, how many persons realise that the concept of rights for the Dalits and the masses was introduced mainly through the efforts of Dr. Ambedkar through the Poona Pact in 1932? The Dalits and others placed in their position cannot afford to confine themselves to merely reaffirming their belief in Ambedkarism. Their leaders have to lead them and others to eliminate all harmful notions of society being peddled in India, by the western capitalists. Merely making offerings to the writings and speeches of Dr. Ambedkar is not going to console the oppressed and exploited.

The Dalits have to guard against their collaboration and role in the fundamentalistic organisations, which feel forced to approach them through various elementary educational and health programmes in slums. Such programmes are designed to keep them at the same level of deprivation and to stop them from trying to solve their own problems themselves.

According to the communists, after the success of the Soviet Union after the Second World War, the western Imperialists had launched a direct attack on the revolutionary theory of Marxism-Leninism. It was done by denying its constant need for enrichment through applying it to the concrete problems of ongoing revolution and the construction of socialism. The same can be said of Ambedkarism. It was first sought to be killed through sheer neglect. But when Ambedkarism got resurrected with the centenary celebrations of Dr. Ambedkar, the fundamentalists woke up from slumber and decided to attack Ambedkarism on the pattern of Western imperialism.

Need to Check Attacks on Ambedkar

Shourie's endeavour is the first organised attack in this behalf. If not checked, others are likely to follow him. Such endeavours are likely to develop into euphoria about Ambedkarism. But that cannot be helped. The fundamentalists compare every dissent with darkness of the night. If so, they are forgetting that their day is bound to be followed by a long night. That will be the night for the fundamentalists but it would usher in an era of beaming progress of enlightenment for the weaker sections.

The strife can be avoided not by such sections but by the fundamentalists themselves. They have give rise to the problems for the weaker sections and consequently for themselves through their divisive philosophy. The problems can come to an end by ending the philosophy of division and that of exploitation of man by man and so on.

Dr. Ambedkar had compared Hindu fundamentalism with Nazism of Adolph Hitler. But Hitler himself had failed and got finished. The same has to be the fate of all fascism and Nazism. Hindu Fundamentalists must take this warning of history. They must take measures to deal with the real problems that confront the masses, especially in the sphere of the economy and politics. They must not continue to refuse to establish any connection between theory and the definite practical tasks of the epoch. They must realise that they had already lost the war 2500 years ago.

Hindu Fundamentalists are now trying to create an impression on their small minority of hardcore followers that they are alive and kicking. Actually they had died a notional death long back when they created the myth of *Dvijas*, or of those taking a second birth through *yajnopaveeta* ceremony and incorporated in their scripture of the scriptures, Manu-Smriti. They must know that they cannot reverse the wheel of time through the Mandir [temple] gossips and the half-truths spread therefrom.

It is correct that communism died a sudden death through its own people beginning with Khruschchev, who made the people believe that attacking the personality of an individual is a legitimate way of assessing behaviour, especially after the death of that person. "Without analysing the objective and subjective conditions and finding solutions to the problems being faced by the Soviet Union and Marxism-Leninism, Khruschchev filled the entire atmosphere with slander, innuendo and the most backward methods of bourgeois politics.

Shourie is attempting the same thing. If such an action boomerangs, it can be the beginning of an end to the Hindu fundamentalism, since it cannot exist in the void. It is daily annoying the opinion of the Christians, of the Muslims and of the Buddhists. It aspires to establish the Hindu theocratic state but by separating the bulk of its blind followers constituting the masses. This action can be suicidal. It must follow the advice of Confucius to take care of their house first before going out to reform others. The doctor is advised to heal himself before healing others.

Dangerous Habit of Character Assassination

Shourie has introduced in India the cult of character assassination into the movement in place of dealing with the problems of the Upper Castes and the Lower Castes. Mahatma Gandhi had also committed the same mistake but that remained buried in the layers of the so-called freedom movement. And, Shourie has made the same Mahatma Gandhi as his ideal and hero. Ambedkar cannot be killed so long as the pitiable condition of the Dalits and other weaker sections and un-cared for segments of population continue to exist. If there remain no Dalits etc. as the exploited classes, Ambedkarism will automatically die having lost its relevance. But by relegating the Dalits to still lower depths Ambedkarism is being kept alive not by the Dalits but by their enemies, the Upper Castes, operating the obsolete and already repealed Hindu scriptures, to the detriment of the already famished Dalits etc.

So long as the master is alive the slave has to remain alive. Many people believe that communism has died with Gorbachove and Yeltsin. No. The workers in Russia and elsewhere in the world continue to live along with the capitalist masters. If so, the struggle must continue. The fall of USSR can be compared with losing of the first match between two rival teams. The Indian mythology of constant wars between gods and the demons has already attributed a permanent character to such wars. It is another matter that the Hindus, in spite of being the authors of the concerned mythological story have themselves forgotten the message. Similarly, the attacks on Ambedkar cannot kill him for all times to come.

Need to Revolutionise Political Mechanism

In fact, there is a need to revolutionise the political mechanism so that the people, the masses, including the Dalits and the minorities could directly participate in governing themselves. And, there is a need to revise the Hindu scriptures so as to bring them to a level which makes them caring for all on the basis of equality of opportunity and common welfare without any kind of prejudice.

Still, there is no doubt that just like the attacks on the life and work of Stalin, those on Dr. Ambedkar did infect for a time the entire movement with this disease of gossip and slander. But it is also a fact that the act of AS himself has become instrumental in renewed interest in Ambedkar and his thought. Swami Vivekananda had said 'the Reason is the helper, the reason is the bar'. Shourie had invented reasons to kill Ambedkar. The same reasons are now resulting in making Ambedkar resurrect with a renewed force.

The mood of the likes of AS is indicative of a bad dream which has shaken them out of hallucination, which was even worse than that had been haunting them for millennia. Sudden memory of their deeds of commission and omission at times leaves them in a dazed condition, which prompts them to engage them in renewed suicidal pursuits. They suffer from a strange sickness, which makes them dread the physician.

Part VII
Ambedkar and Hindu Traditionalists

21

Mind of Ambedkar

Ambedkar is the first man in history of India to analyse the Hindu *shastras* and philosophy and to prove that they utterly lack in the message of humanity, ethics, morality, and sense of social responsibility and social justice. He became the first man in history to correctly diagnose the ills of Indian society in the context of Hindu religion. Instead of suggesting to others, he himself raised the banner of social, political, economic and religious revolution. Before we proceed further in this regard, it would be worthwhile to have a look at th the important events in the life of Babasaheb Dr. B R Ambedkar, who was born on 14 April 1991.

- Witness in South Barrow Commission, 1917
- Untouchables' conference, Nagpur, 1918
- Bahishkrit Hitkarini Sabha Formed 20th July 1924
- Nominated as MLC, Bombay Province, 1926
- Mahad Satyagraha, December 1927
- Witness in Simon Commission, May 1928
- Nashik Kala Ram temple Satyagraha, 2nd March 1930
- Representative at Round Table Conference, 1930-32
- British Communal Award, 20th August 1932
- Poona Pact, 20th September 1932
- Yewale District, Nasik Conference, 23rd October 1935
- Mahar Parishad, Bombay Province, 31st May 1936
- Independent Labout Party Formed , August 1936
- Elected MLA, Bombay Province, January 1937
- All India Scheduled Caste Federation Formed at Nagpur, April 1942

- Appointed as Labour Minister in the Viceroy's Executive Council, July 1942
- People's Education Society Formed, July 1945
- Elected to Constituent Assembly from Bengal, November 1946
- Law Minister in Independent India, 15th August 1947
- Appointed as Chairman, Drafting Committee of the Constitution of India, 29th August 1947
- Resigned from Union Cabinet, September 1951
- Elected to Rajya Sabha, March 1952
- Buddhist Society of India Formed, May 1955
- Embraced Buddhism, 14th October 1956
- Parinirvan (Death), 6th December 1956

Exposed Tiny Minority Masquerading as Leader of Exploited Majority

Dr. Ambedkar rose to prove that a small lamp of knowledge was enough to discard the dense darkness and courage was enough to subdue the biggest typhoon of oppression, suppression and exploitation of the vast masses let loose by a tiny minority masquerading as the leader of the same exploited masses. He challenged in a forthright manner and directly both the indomitable Hindu religious leadership and the rulers of the mighty British Empire. and in presence of the British rulers, Indian leaders of all Religions and about six hundred slavish Indian princes.

Gave Unprecedented Hope of Emancipation to Downtrodden

Dr. Ambedkar gave the unprecedented hope to the downtrodden people of India that they could be emancipated in their own lifetime through their own effort and without intervention of God, tailored by their oppressors and made an accomplice in their game of oppression.

Proved Most Saints Being Partners in Exploitation

Dr. Ambedkar proved that the best of the yogis, were the concealed partners of the exploiters. who prevented all inquiry into the ills of humanity. He showed that such yogis had been mute witnesses to the woes deliberately caused to the masses, who were made to suffer the organised ignorance, illiteracy, poverty and the dogma. He proved beyond any shadow of doubt that political rights were the best means of redressing any kind of problems _ political, social, economic or religious.

Taught Aggrieved Person How to Represent His Case

Dr. Ambedkar had first emerged on the political scene of India in 1925. When in the year 1927, the British Government appointed an Indian Statutory Commission under the Chairmanship of Sir John Simon to re-examine and revise the 1919 Act, Dr. Ambedkar expressed his dissatisfaction with the composition of the Commission. The Congress party had also boycotted it. However, an all party conference was held in Bombay on 19 May, 1928, which appointed a Committee under the Chairmanship of Pandit Motilal Nehru to consider and determine the principles of the Constitution for India. The committee enumerated 19 fundamental rights to be embodied in the statue. Dr. Ambedkar noted that not only there was no specific reference to the abolition of untouchability, but the same religious form was also to be maintained after country became free.

Illustrated How to Embarrass One's Opponent

The report had proposed joint electorates with reservation of seats for minorities on population-basis, with the right to contest additional seats. The report did not recognise the Depressed Classes as a minority, and did not contemplate any specific safeguards for them. The Nehru Report had, of course, made the following observations:

1. *The solicitude of government had so far brought little relief to these classes. It has resulted in giving them some nominated seats in the legislature and some minor condition for special schools.*
2. *In our suggestion for the Constitution we have not made any special position for the representation of the 'Depressed' classes in legislatures. This could only be done by way of special electorates or by nomination. We are not prepared to extend this unsound and harmful principle if we can help it, nor do we think that we will do any good to these classes by ensuring some seats for them in this way. We are still more opposed to nomination."*

Dr. Ambedkar submitted on 29 May 1928 a Memorandum to the Simon Commission in order to counter-act the mischief done by the Nehru Committee (consisting of the Hindus, Muslims and Sikhs), stressing the need for safeguards for the Depressed Classes. He forcefully pleaded for due representation of the Depressed Classes in the Legislatures in his Note of Dissent to the Commission's Report. He said:

"All these classes do in fact begin and often complete their lives under a weight of inherited vices and social difficulties for

the existence of which society is responsible, and of the mitigation of which much can be done by legislation. The effect of legislation to alter the conditions under which the lives of individuals are spent has been recognised elsewhere in the world. But this duty to social progress will not be recognised unless those like the Depressed Classes find a place in the Cabinet of the Country".

It is to be noted with adequate sensitivity and sensibility that the analysis that had gone behind coming to the above-said conclusion had never been exhibited by anyone in the recorded history of India. To ensure the general human welfare is considered the main responsibility of the state. Religion and God are supposed to be superior to the state which and who are approached as the last resort in a sort of appeal against the state injustice.

State, Religion and God Had Been Failing

But in India, all the three, the state, the religion and God had been failing for centuries and millennia, in their duty to save and protect the masses from the combined tyranny of the state and religion. The state under the Varna scheme had been operating under an exploitative, oppressive, inhuman, immoral, unethical and arbitrary *Varna* system, which had further degenerated into more dangerous caste system. Finding that the state had been acting as a mere robotic tool of the Vedic religion, the more sensitive young princes like Mahavira and Gautam Buddha, had to voluntarily abdicate the throne and torpedo the pernicious system from within, more than 2500 years ago.

Their efforts had led to giving birth to new religions, known as Jainism and Buddhism, which gave the message of equality, fellow feeling, compassion, peace and non-killing. The state that had been operating up to that time almost at a village level, came to progress rapidly and enormously so that India produced the formidable yet humane empires under the dynasties known as Nanda dynasty and Maurya dynasty, which continued to serve their respective citizens for a full millennia.

Taught the Victims to be Courageous in Telling Truth

Dr. Ambedkar was the first person after that period to seek and suggest to the rulers in their face and in most forceful manner, at the first opportunity that had knocked at the Indian door through the agency of Simon Commission. Anyhow, the Brtish Government did not accept the Simon Commission's recommendations and convened a Round

Table Conference to settle the framework of the future constitutional set up for India. The tripartite Round Table Conference comprised of the representatives of India, the British Government and the British Political Parties. Ambedkar, along with Rao Bahadur Srinivasan, was invited to participate in this historic Conference on behalf of the Depressed Classes.

Taught the Oppressed to Graphically Narrate Sufferings

Strangely, barring the Indian National Congress, all Indian parties and other interests participated in the first Round Table Conference, which opened in London on 12 November 1930. Ambedkar speaking on behalf of and for the Untouchables, gave a graphic picture of the sufferings of the Depressed Classes in India in these words :

> *Mr. Chairman, my purpose in rising to address this conference in principle is to place before it the point of view of the depressed classes, whom I and my colleague, Rao Bahadour Srinivasan, have the honour to represent, regarding the question of constitutional reform.*

Proved Dalits were No Integral Part of Community

Ambedkar stressed that it was the point of view of 43,000,000 people, or one-fifth of the total population of British India. He emphasied:

> *Although the depressed classes, are included among the Hindus, they in no sense form an integral part of that community. Not only have they a separate existence, but they have also assigned to them a statute which is individually distinct from the status occupied by any other community in India.*

Proved Dalits were Midway Between Serf and Slave

Ambedkar conceded, "There are communities in India which occupy a lower and subordinate position; but the position assigned to the depressed classes is totally different. It is one which is midway between that of the serf and the slave, and which may for convenience, be called servile with this difference, that the serf and the slave were permitted to have physical contact, from which the Depressed Classes are debarred. What is worse is that this enforced servility and bar to human intercourse, due to their untouchability, involves, not merely the possibility of discrimination in public life, but actually works out as a positive denial of all equality of opportunity and the denial of those most elementary of civic rights on which all human existence depends."

Right Solution of Political Problem Intended

Ambedkar expressed the hope that the point of view of such a community, as large as the population of England or of France, and so heavily handicapped in the struggle for existence, could not but have some bearing on the right sort of solution of the political problem.

No Other Great Man Had Taken Note of Problem

The political scientists and practitioners of today have to ask themselves whether any other contemporary of Dr. Ambedkar, wearing the cloak of greatness, had realisation of this state of affairs and the courage to articulate the reality faced by so large a section of population, that equals that of England and France. India boasts of many swamis, yogis and Mahatmas, but let us ask ourselves, who among them had exhibited the sensibility and sensitivity to think or imagine about the infliction of that part of humanity, privately or publicly. The reason for theri lack of concern was that since only the wearer knows where the shoe pinches, they could not experience the pain becuase they had not personally suffered the concwertned inflictions and indignities.

No Stooge can be Expected to Talk so Harsh

Let the readers ask themselves, out of those who are given the epithet of the best of the freedom fighters, who became successors to power after the British had left India, had embarrassed the rulers in such a forthright manner, on the platform shared by the rulers and their subjects. Dr. Ambedkar had told the rulers that they had been good-for-nothing fellows in so far as the plight of the Depressed Classes is concerned. Such classes were poor, weak, illiterate and exploited, before coming of the said rulers and they (such classes) continue to be in the same wretched position, in which they were existing at the time they (rulers) had come. This means that such rulers have been useless for such people for more than 150 years. He had shocked the audience by his remarks that such rulers must leave the country as soon as possible, and leave all the Indians to themselves.

The question that has been asked in the above paragraph about the so-called leaders deserves to be repeated in this connection also. Ambedkar's following words throw better light on his personality and put the faces of other stalwarts into realm of darkness.

Safeguards against Tyrannies and Injustices Needed

Dr. Ambedkar insisted to have certain safeguards for his people in an unequivocal manner as follows:

We know that political power is passing from the British into the hands of those who wield such tremendous economic, social and religious sway over our existence. We are willing that it may happen, though the idea of Swaraj recalls to the mind of many of us the tyrannies, oppressions and injustices practised upon us in the past and the fear of their recurring under Swaraj. We are prepared to take the inevitable risk of the situation in the hope that we shall be installed, in adequate proportion, as the political sovereign of the country along with our fellow countrymen.

Only the naives among his critics can question the loyalty of Ambedkar to the nation and his fellow citizens. His above words are misinterpreted by those who are not bestowed by nature with any power of reason to falsely show that Ambedkar was interested in perpetration of the British power.

Do Not Leave Settlement of Problem to Time

What Ambedkar had pointed out was that in the absence of the suggested safeguards, the depressed classes would land themselves in the worse den, and, therefore, those in whose hands the power as expected to slip should be bound to remain humane in respect of their attitude towards the deprived sections of Indian population. Ambedkar had clarified the position in the following words:

But we will consent to that on one condition and that is that the settlement of our problem is not left to time. I am afraid the depressed classes have waited too long for time to work its miracle. At every successive step taken by the British Government to widen the scope of representative government the depressed classes have been systematically left out. No thought has been given to their claim for political power. I protest with all the emphasis I can that we will not stand this any longer.

Dr. Ambedkar was further prompted to comment at the Round Table Conference like this:

"A patriot and a nationalist in India is one who sees with open eyes his fellowmen treated as being less than man. But his humanity does not rise in protest. He knows that men the women for no cause are denied their human rights. But it does not prick his civic sense to helpful action. He finds whole classes of people shut out from public employment. But it does not rouse his sense of justice and fair play. Hundreds of evil practices that injure man and society are perceived by him. But they do not sicken him

with disgust. I am glad I do not belong to that class of patriots. I belong to that class which takes its stand on democracy and which seeks to destroy monopoly in every shape and from."

Dig At Pseudo Religious Swamis and Mahatmas

Dr. Ambedkar had a dig at the pseudo religious leaders of India, who falsely posed to be spiritualists and, in no mistaken words and manner:

Our religious leaders under the cloak of false spirituality, go on harping day in and day out on the necessity of appreciating the real greatness. And, in their endeavour, they turn all thinking minds into robot-like followers of the anti-human dogma under the false promise of the ultimate redemption of the soul, which, of course, stands already killed under the weight of the cleverly administered anti-human poison.

Those who wish to go into the recesses of the mind of Dr. Ambedkar and his being the only one to fight for the real social justice for the entire population rather humanity, are advised to refer to Ambedkar's Annihilation of Caste, his Riddles in Hinduism, his Buddha and His Dhamma, and his speeches delivered in Parliament and the Constituent Assembly.

Power Behind Force of Thoughts and Courage

A question may occur to one's mind, as to how Ambedkar could talk so fearlessly, so courageously and so convincingly. In this connection, the mind automatically goes to the quality of sincerity of purpose, which Ambedkar possessed, in good measure. Next point is the serious preparation and study that must have remained behind all that. The first important manifestation of such preparation and courage had come to the notice of the nation on 25 September of 1927, when Ambedkar had publicly burnt a copy of Manu Smriti. The second instance was provided by the publication of his masterpiece *Annihilation of Caste,* which had invited spontaneous criticism of Mahatma Gandhi. The third occasion was provided by the Round Table Conference just mentioned above. Another occasion was provided by the publication of his book Riddles in Hinduism which presented the essence of his studies.

22

Unexplained Silence over Ambedkar's Analysis of Scriptures

After carrying out a serious survey of the entire religious literature of the Hindus, Ambedkar had put quite a few questions, which were very logical for a rationalist, but quite embarrassing for such of the Hindu fundamentalists, who had been blinded by self-afflicted selfishness. They included:

> Is it not a question for every Hindu to consider why in the matter of his own religion his position is so embarrassing and so puzzling?
>
> Why is he not able to answer so simple a question, which every Parsi, every Christian, and every Muslim can answer?
>
> Is it not the time that he should ask himself what are the causes that have brought about this religious chaos?"

However, he also realised the extent of ignorance of an average Hindu, about the philosphical content of his religion. Therefore, he helped them by providing simple reason, which was, accordingto him, the blind faith caused by the preachers, who had a vested interest in such ignorance of the masses.

Further, Ambedkar had analysed all the basic scriptures of Hindusim with a view to educate at least the Dalits about certain facts which were being used to keep them as community slaves, in the belief that their good lay in being willing and good slaves of the Upper Castes in the hope of being rewarded by God in future births, by promoting them to a caste enjoying good status and privileges. He had also in mind the idea of helping the religious leaders in bringing some much-needed reforms so that Hindu religion could compete with other religions, which gave their followers a better sense of equality and brotherhood.

His views about the caste are avaialbale in his Annhilation of Caste. But his more important work is titled Riddles in Hinduism, which centres round the Hindu mythoogy, with particular reference to the Vedas. In this chapter, wer are going to discuss some of these riddles.

Beginning of the Veda

Dr. Ambedkar had expressed himself on the question of the beginning of the Veda as follows:

> *What Kalluka Bhatt says is that the Vedas were reproduced from memory. The real question is who made them and not who reproduced them. Even if one accepts the theory of reproduction at the beginning of each (creation), the question still remains who made the Vedas when the first Kalpa began. The Vedas could not have come into being ex nihilo. They must have a beginning though they may have no end. Why don't the Brahmins say openly? Why this circumlocution?*

Dr. Ambedkar had come to this conclusion after devoting three pages to finding out an answer. Later on, he conducted another survey, which is contained in 24 page long Appendix attached to his book under reference. The riddle became even more serious even after the said survey. Final paragraph of the Appendix is as follows:

> *This survey discloses a number of riddles in regard to the Vedas. In addition to the three riddles namely why did the Brahmins insist that the Vedas were eternally pre-existing, that they were non-man non-God made, that they were infallible. There are other riddles regarding the Vedas, which are equally puzzling. —The Vedas at one time did not have any precedence or infallibility. Why did the Brahmins feel it necessary to give the Vedas this infallibility. Why did the Brahmins exclude the Sutras from the term Sruti and why did the Brahmins give up the infallibility of the Vedas and sought to give infallibility of the Puranas?*

Multiplicity of Answers to Simple Question

Ambedkar takes special note of multiplicity of answers to the question regarding the origin of the *Vedas*. The answers differ, according to him, in respect of their

(1) originating from the mystical sacrifice of *Purusha*;

(2) resting on *Skambha*;

(3) having been cut or scraped off from him, as being his hair and his mouth;

(4) springing from *Indra*;
(5) having been produced from Time;
(6) having been produced from Agni, Vayu, and Surya;
(7) springing from *Prajapati*, and the Waters,
(8) being the breath of Brahma;
(9) being dug by Gods out of mind-ocean,
(10) being the hair of *Prajapati's* beard; and
(11) being the off-spring of *Vach*.

Ambedkar finds that strangely,the writers who have come forward to furnish these answers are all Brahmins. They belong to the same Vaidik school of thought. They alone were the guardians of the ancient religious lore. Why should they have given such incoherent and chaotic answers to a simple question? Dr. Ambedkar had wondered.

Infallibility of Vedas?

Dr. Ambedkar had argued that to say that the *Vedas* occupy a very high position in the religious literature of the Hindus is to make understatement. To say that the *Vedas* form the sacred literature of the Hindus will also be an inadequate statement. For the Vedas besides being a sacred literature of the Hindus are books whose authority cannot be questioned. The *Vedas* are infallible. Any argument based on the *Vedas* is final and conclusive. There is no appeal against it. This is the theory of the *Vedic* Brahmins and is accepted by the generality of the Hindus, he maintained.

Dr. Ambedkar went on "The view of the Dharma Sutras shows that the [1] Veda, [2] Tradition [Smriti], [3] Practice of *Shishta* and [4] Agreement in an assembly were the four different authorities which were required to be refered to in the decision of an issue which was in controversy. It also shows that there was the time when the *Vedas* were not the sole infallible authorities. That was the time represented by the *Dharma Sutras* of Wasishtha and Baudhaayana. *Aapastambha* does not invest the *Vedas* with any authority at all. He makes knowledge of the Vedas as an electoral qualification for membership of the Assembly whose agreed decision is the law and the only law. The *Veda* was not at all regarded as a book of authority and the only recognised source of authority was an agreement arrived at in the assembly of the learned. It is only in the time of Gautama that the *Vedas* came to be regarded as the only authority. There was a time when an agreed decision of the Assembly was admitted as one source of authority. That is the period represented by Baudhayana."

Dr. Ambedkar asks, "What was the purpose, what was the motive of the Brahmins who concocted this theory? The authors of the Hindu scriptures had established eternal connection between the 'Word' and its meaning? But he finds it difficult to accept this proposition. Dr. Ambedkar discloses that Brahmins are steadfast neither in their regard to *Vedas* nor in respect of their sacred character. Elsewhere, they fought to maintain the thesis that the Vedas were not only sacred but that they were infallible. Even they spent their ingenuity to invent strange arguments to support the doctrine of infallibility. He finds that subsequently they had not the slightest compunction to overthrow the position of the *Vedas* and to subordinate them first to the *Smriti*, then to the *Puranas* and lastly to the *Tantras*. He wonders what made the Brahmins thus degrade the *Vedas*.

Creation of Varnas?

The position regarding the creation of the Varnas was also found by Dr. Ambedkar as puzzling as it was with reference to the infallibility of the Vedas. He had observed:

> *"On the issue of who created them [Varnas], there is no uniformity. The Rig-Veda says Prajapati created the four Varnas. It does not mention which Prajapati. One would like to know which Prajapati it was who created the four Varnas. There are so many Prajapatis. But even on the point of creation by Prajapati there is no agreement. One says they were created by Brahman. Another says they were created by Kassyapa. The third says they were created by Manu.*

Thus, about the *Varnas also*, he found that there was no uniformity. The *Rig-Veda* says four *Varnas* were created. But other authorities say only two *Varnas* were created, some say Brahmans and Kshatriyas and some say Brahmans and Sudras. According to him, *Rig-Veda* lays down the rule of graded inequality based on the importance of the part of the creation from which particular *Varna* was born. But the white *Yajur-Veda* denies this theory of the *Rig-Veda*. *Upanishads*, *Ramayana*, Mahabharata, and *Puranas* are in agreement with *Yajur-Veda*. *Harivansha* goes to the length of saying that the Shudras were twice born, observes Dr. Ambedkar. He concluded that this chaos seems to be the result of concoction of the theory of *Chaturvarna*.

Morality in Vedas?

Similarly, Dr. Ambedkar did not find anything in the *Vedas* that could be said to be spiritually or morally elevating. He had come to the following conclusion in this behalf:

Enough has been extracted from the Vedas to show that they contain nothing that can be said to be spiritually or morally elevating. Neither the subject matter nor the contents of the Vedas justify the infallibility with which they have been invested. Why then did the Brahmins struggle so hard to clothe them with sanctity and infallibility?

Upanishads Declaring War on Vedas?

Dr. Ambedkar has given a scholarly analysis of certain excerpts of the *Upanishads* and other religious literature to show that *they* are generally described as the *Vedanta* or the concluding portions. This could mean that they were in consonance with the *Vedas*. But he has concluded that the *Upanishads* had actually declared war on the *Vedas*. Dr. Ambedkar has quoted *Gautama Dharma Sutras* to indicate that the *Upanishads* have been mentioned as independent set of books and that the confusion of regarding them as being one and the same, has been caused by a faulty interpretation of a particular passage of the said *Sutras*. He quotes Chapter XIX Verse 12 in which Gautama speaks of the purification and says:.

The purificatory [texts are] the Upanishads, the Vedantas, the Samhitas — text of all the Vedas.... from this it is clear that at the date of Gautama the Upanishads were distinguished from Vedantas and were not acknowledged as a part of the Arnyakas and were not acknowledged as a part of the Vedic literature. Hardatta in his commentaries says " those parts of the Arnyakas which are not [Upanishads] are called Vedantas". This is unimpeachable proof that the Upanishads did not come within the range of the Vedic literature and were outside the canons. He has also quoted the Gita to prove that it also does not include the Upanishads in the term Vedic literature. One of the reasons advanced in support of the point is that the subject matter of the Vedas and the Upanishads is also not the same.

Anuloma and Pratiloma of Vedas?

Dr. Ambedkar has provided with another insight into the Hindu religious literature. So far the words *Anuloma* and *Pratiloma* have been understood to be used only in the sense of inter-*Varna* marriages. But Dr. Ambedkar has stated that "the words initially referred to the question of seeking religious instruction by Kshatriyas from Brahmanas which position was regarded as unapproved, since the Vedas had given the monopoly of instruction to the Brahmanas. If the Kshatriya instructed a Brahmana it was against the practice and therefore it was called *Pratiloma*. On the other hand, seeking of instructions by Kshatriya from a Brahman was in keeping with the prescription and as such it was called *Anuloma*." He says "reading the observations of Mr. Kane in the light of the definition of the word *Pratiloma* it is obvious that the *Upanishads* far from being acknowledged as part of the *Vedic* literature were, if not despised, held in low esteem by the *Vedic* Brahmins." He further observes:

> *This is an additional piece of evidence, which shows that there was a time when the relation between the Vedas and the Upanishads was of antagonism.*

Thus, the belief that the *Vedas* and the *Upanishads* are complimentary came into being is really a riddle, argued Dr. Ambedkar.

Baadaraayana and Upanishads

Dr. Ambedkar's conclusion in this behalf was that 'this thesis of Baadaraayana — which underlines his *Vedanta Sutras* and according to which the *Upanishads* are a part of the *Veda* and there is no antagonism between the *Vedas* and *Upanishads* — is quiet to the tenor of the *Upanishads* and their relation to the *Vedas*. Badarayana's attitude is not easy to understand. But it is quite obvious that Badarayana's is a queer and a pathetic case of an opponent, which begins his battle by admitting the validity of premises of his adversary. Why did Baadaraayana concede to Jaimini on the question of infallibility of the *Vedas*, which were opposed to the Upanishads? Why did he not stand for truth, the whole truth and nothing but the truth as expounded by the *Upanishads*? The Baadaraayana has in his *Vedanta Sutras* betrayed the *Upanishads*. Why did he do so?

Mutual Fight Between Hindu Gods themselves?

Dr. Ambedkar also felt intrigued over the question of the Hindu gods fighting amongst themselves. If they had been doing so what message they could give to the Hindus excepting that of going on fighting among themselves in imitation of their gods? He had been led to conclude:

> *Consequently the existence of many gods among the Hindus is quite understandable because the Hindu society has been formed by the conglomeration of many tribes and many communities each of whom had their own separate*

Gods. What strikes one as a strange phenomenon is the sight of the Hindu gods, struggling one against the other, their combats and feuds and ascriptions by one god to the other, all things that are a shame and disgrace to common mortals. This is what requires explanation.

Hindu Idols as Living Organisms?

Ambedkar did not find anything wrong in idolatory of Hindus. According to him, making an idol is nothing more than having a photograph of the deity and if there can be no objection to keeping a photograph what objection can there be to having an image. He expressed his objection, however, about the idolatory of the Hindus as under:

Real objection to Hindu idolatry is that it is not mere photography, mere production of an image. It is more than that. The Hindu idol is a living being and is endowed with the functions of a human being. Hindu Idol is given life by means of a ceremony called Pranapratishtha. The Buddhists also are idolatrous in as much as they too worship Buddha's idol. But the idol they worship is only a photograph, a mere image."

Similarly, he had no objection to the fact that the Hindus are are polytheists, i.e., they worship many Gods. He disclosed that the Hindus are not the only people who are guilty of the practice of Polytheism. Other communities have also been known to have polytheism. He pointed out that the Romans and the Greeks were essentially polytheists. They too worshipped many gods. Therefore, the Hindus can console themselves at least by noting that Ambedkar did not find fault with the idea of their being polytheists.

Brahmin Lack of Loyalty to and Faith in Their Gods?

Ambedkar, however, found that real charge which can be leveled against the Hindus was that they are never steadfast in their devotion to their Gods. He observed in this behalf as under:

There is no such thing as loyalty or faith in one God. In the history of Hindu Gods one finds it a very common experience that some Gods have been worshipped for a time and subsequently their worship has been abandoned and the Gods themselves have been thrown on the scrap-heap. Quite new Gods are adopted and their worship goes with an ingenuity of devotion, which is full and overflowing. Again the new Gods are abandoned and are replaced by a fresh crop of new Gods. So the cycle goes on. In this way, the

> *Hindu Gods are always undergoing rise and fall — a phenomenon which is unknown in the history of any other community in the world. Poor creatures they became nothing more than mere toys in the hands of the Brahmins. Why did the Brahmins treat the gods with so scant a respect?*

Any rationalist will find the researches of Dr. Ambedkar revealing, logical and even interesting. A piece of research is always a tentative hypothesis whose conclutions can always be called to question by another researcher. If any other researcher does so, the former is not entitled to take any objection or offence to that. The above findings of Dr. Ambedkar could be questioned by any one after the publication of the concerned book or books. The same course is still open to any Hindu fundamentalist, including Arun Shourie. But Shourie instead of controverting the findings of Dr. Ambedkar, mischievously has only charged the latter that he brought shame upon Hindus. Even Shourie himself has maintained studied silence over the findings of Ambedkar for decades. Similarly, all Hindus have been silent for over 60 years in this behalf. This is not the way of intellectuals.

23

Kaamdhenu : Permanent Bone of Contention

Kaamadhenu, literally, wish-granting cow, was no cow in the ordinary sense. It stood for the *Brahma*nical monopoly over educational and religious matters, which resulted in an unending and automatic flow of wealth in the form of *daana, dakshinaa* and *bhikshaa*, from all the non-*Brahmanas* [cf. A-Suras]. The said non-*Brahmanas* were converted into *Kshatriyas* [or guards to be used as the tools using arms for protection of the *Brahmanas*] and the *Vaisyas* [the tools providing the needed wealth for all *Brahma*nical pursuits].

Dana consisted in the wealth that came to *Brahmanas*, without being demanded, like the offerings in a temple. *Dakshinaa* consisted in fees being charged by individual *Brahmanas*, for performing the ritual of wagging their tongues, through muttering of unintelligible *mantras* on any ordinary or extraordinary occasion. The *dakshinaa* was as per schedule, depending on the time consumed in uttering the mantras. More the time spent, the higher was the *dakshinaa*. The *dakshinaa* was not negotiable and it could not be left in arrears. *Bhikshaa* consisted in whatever that was specifically demanded by a *Brahma*na under any pretext of meeting any expenditure as per his whims. None could refuse the *bhikshaa* demanded by a *Brahma*na. Anyone saying no was liable to be prosecuted by the State, as it amounted to a cognisable offence.

All these conclusions are as per the analysis of *Manu-Smriti*, attempted by this author in his book *Hindu Scheme of Things: Socio-political Analysis of Manu-Smriti.* Incidentally, the said book had been reviewed, *inter alia*, in *The Tribune* of Chandigarh in 1987. As a consequence of that, it had been debated for four months in the same newspaper, between April and July 1988, when V.N. Narayanan was the Editor-in-Chief of The Tribune Group of Papers.

Mythological Wars between Brahmanas and Kshatriyas

Kshatriya Viswamitra had used Kshatriya Rama to humble *Brahma*na Parsurama and to dethrone the latter from the position of being the Vishnu-Incarnate, when he had challenged Rama for the fault of breaking the bow of Lord *Shiva*. Significantly, Parsurama and Wasishtha are the only two persons in the entire Hindu mythology owning the *Kaamadhenu*, and both of them are *Brahmanas*, having a common ancestor in Lord *Brahma*. Not less interesting is the fact that the same Lord *Brahma* is the ancestor of even Ravana, yet another *Brahma*na, humbled by the same Kshatriya Rama. To this sequence, may be added the fact of other *Kshatriyas* being the Gautam Buddha and Lord Mahavira, who had not only similarly humbled the *Brahmanas* but had also finished Brahminism itself from the face of the earth.

Wasishtha had retaliated to his repeated humiliations. He engineered palace intrigue so that Kshatriya Rama, Lakshmana and Sita, the daughter of Janaka were, sent to exile for 14 years.

Significantly, Kshatriya Rama and Lakshmana had become the disciples of Kshatriya Sage Vishwamitra and Sita was the daughter of Kshatriya Janaka, who had usurped the Brahamnical function of preaching the Dharma. Thus, Brahmana Washistha had torpedoed the strategy of Kshatriya Vishawamitra in one stroke. This period of 14 years is very significant judged in the light of the present day life imprisonment under the Indian Penal Code. Life imprisonment means in practical terms imprisonment for 14 years. By this one stroke, *Brahma*na Wasishtha was able to avenge his humiliation and defeat of *Brahmanas* at the hands of the *Kshatriyas*. Such a defeat is against the spirit of the *Manu-Smriti* and all other Hindu *Granthas*, including *Srimad-Bhagavad-Gita*. Anyway, Wasishtha was able to hit back all the concerned *Kshatriyas*—Viswamitra, Rama, and Janaka. But in this longstanding war, the ultimate victory lay with Kshatriya Rama and Kshatriya Visvamitra.

Plight of Rama

Rama had been made an outcast among the *Kshatriyas* or rulers of North India, apparently by a *Brahmanical* decree for the sin of helping Vishwamitra, the sworn enemy of the Brahaman Guru Sage Washishtha. However, Rama was in a position to befriend the *Vaanaras* or animal like aborigines in control of the Deccan and thus regain his lost status, in a far off region, which had not yet been aryanised and, thus, had remained free from being contaminated by *Brahma*nical religion of varnasrama.

Beyond the Indian peninsula, Ravana was in control of vast ocean power with headquarters in Ceylon. This Ravana was a nephew of Wasishtha can be presumed to have as per the Pauranic genealogy, which connected both of them with Lord *Brahma*. With a view to taking revenge on Viswamitra and Rams, and with a view to check the progress of Rama turning into a formidable power with the help of the non-Aryans or aborigines, Wasishtha can be presumed to have instructed Ravana to deviate Rama from his expansive designs and the path of genuine virtue. Accordingly, Ravana took the first step by way of abducting Sita, so that Rama could feel dejected and lose his self respect among the forest tribes [then headed by Bali] by being unable to protect his own wife.

As a consequence, there was a war, in which the *Kshatriyas* from India, being under the influence of the *Brahmanas*, did not come to the rescue of Rama, since he had ceased to be Kshatriya by virtue of having been exiled by his father. But, since Rama came victorious, he could return to Ayodhya like a real hero. Now, his brother Bharata had no option but to return the throne to Rama.

With Rama's return, Wasishtha had to presumably retire to forest yielding his place of kula-guru (the family priest) to Viswamitra. In the forest also, there was no peace for Wasishtha. There was long drawn war between him and Kshatriya Viswamitra and between their respective hundreds of sons, who could be logically speaking their respective disciples, over the question of possession of *Kaamadhenu*, the all-giving cow. Kshatriya Viswamitra snatched the said cow also from Washishtha, and forcibly became a Brahmarishi.

Brahminical Supremacy and Humiliation

The so-called Brahminical supremacy is a long story of *Brahma*nical humiliation. First, they conceded Godhead or the position of Vishnu Incarnation to Kshatriya Rama. Secondly, they subsequently accepted Krishana, a Yadava, as Vishnu Incarnate, after the honey-moon with *Kshatriyas* was over. Thirdly, they compromised with the *Vaisyas*, by siding with Jainism, as against Buddhism. They had been accepting the over lordship of the Nandas and Maurya, the Sudra Empires. In Rajput age, they compromised their position even with the tribals, who had thus far been treated as being outside the Varna System.

In modern India, the *Brahmanas* have been repeatedly compromising their positions with the Dalit leaders like Dr. Ambedkar Babu Jaggiwas Ram, Chand Ram, B.P. Maurya, Kanshi Ram and Kumari Mayawati, Bangaru Laxman, Balayogi, Ram Bilas Paswan and others. By now, The *Brahmans* and other upper castes have created a strange mess for themselves. They find it extremely impossible to extricate themselves therefrom. Every new step they take to solve the problem tends to create newer and more serious problems for them. The Urdu saying *marz* barhtaa gayaa jyun jyun dawaa kee, that is, the disease went on becoming more and more serious with every dose of medicine) aptly explains their predicament. This has been their lot since the ancient days of Charvaks, the predecessors of Buddhists.

Rajputs are Tribals

In fact, the Rajputs are the remote ancestors of the present day Scheduled Tribes. Some of them were also the ancestors of the present day Dalits. The fact of Guru Ravidas, following the traditional occupation of a cobbler having been invited from a far of place, Varanasi, to be the preceptor of the Rajputs of Chittorgarh, who also remained the guru of Meeraa Baai is a proof in this behalf.

This story has been reconstructed on the basis of the bits scattered in the Hindu tradition and scriptures themselves, over which the *Brahmanas* cleverly assumed the monopoly rights. Mr. "S" is now engaged in exposing others, the so-called left historians, for distorting history. If his love for objectivity is itching, there is a better scope for re-writing history of ancient India, by purging it of the *Brahma*nical influence and mischief. Does he have a heart to engage in that task? Will his so-called *Brahma*nical origin and his pledge to work for Sangh Parivar and for strengthening Caste Hindu vested interests permit him to undertake a work demanding supreme sense of objectivity ?

There is a *saastric* rule that the *saastric* or scriptural knowledge has to be kept secret from non-*Brahmanas*, and each of them can be told only about the particular rules relevant to the performance of their *Varna* 'duties', and that too in the discretion of the *Brahmanas*. Fortunately, 'the print media and electronic media' have robbed the Hindu fundamentalists of that privilege.

***Brahma-Loka* near Manasarovar and Visvamitra**

Having finished the *Brahmanical* monopoly in the regions to the east of Delhi, present Delhi was renamed Indraprastha, which suggested the **departure of Indra**, the Lord of the Devas or *Brahma*nas to the Himalaya. Viswamitra now concentrated his activities in extreme North and northwestern regions. Vishawamitra made his headquarters at Mount Abu, from where, he planned to lead a major offensive against *Brahma-loka (the land of Brahmanas)*, around Mansarovar, [cf. *Manu-sarovara*, or the lake of Manu] extending up to Himachal, which is known as the valley of gods *(Brahmanas)*. The correct significance of this term, the valley of gods, is that it was being ruled directly by the gods on earth or the Bhu-*suras* or the *Brahmanas*, as distinguished from non-Brahmanas or non-gods or a-suras or false gods.

Mount Everest as Headquarter of *Brahmanical* Kingdom

The *Brahma*nical Kingdom had its headquarters near Mount Everest. The said mountain and the areas around the Mansarovar Lake were nicknamed as *Brahma*. The term *Brahma* was comparable with soul of *Brahma-loka*. Later on, the whole cosmos was also named after the *Brahma*-loka, as *Brahmaanda*. Alternatively, the Mansarovar Lake itself was called *Brahma*, from which many big and perennial rivers issued. The main river issuing from Mansarovara or *Brahma*, therefore, came to be known as *Brahma*-putra, literally, the son of *Brahma*. The other rivers issuing from Mansarovar, being comparatively smaller, were called as daughters of *Brahma*, which include Ganga, Saraswati and Yamuna.

The said *Brahma*nical empire was initially controlled by King Indra, who arrogated to himself the position of being a brother to Lord Vishnu, the most important of the Hindu Gods, dear to Kshatriyas. Lord Indra, therefore, became a permanent reference point for the *Brahmanas*. Henceforth, they looked to him either for support or for protection. *Brahma-loka*, the headquarters of the Kingdom of *Brahmanas*, became unapproachable or out of bounds for non-*Brahmanas* for various reasons. The enemies could not go there in any case. But the chosen individuals could be taken there through the recommendation of individual *Brahmanas*. The *Manu-Smriti* mentions the following geographical divisions of Indian sub-continent:

> ***Brahma*avartta**, covering the areas to the north and upwards of Kurukshetra;
>
> **Aryavartta**, covering the areas between Kurukshetra and the Vindhyachal mountains in the South; and Dakshinaa (Deccan), covering the areas beyond Vindhyachal, in the South.

Kshatriya Viswamitra, in due course, brought the entire Aryavartta under his control. When he was engaged in the task of consolidating his power, the *Brahma*nical kingdom at that time was ruled by Indra, who deputed a nymph, known as Menakaa with instructions to make Viswamitra give up his dangerous pursuit, dangerous for the *Brahma*nical kingdom of *Brahma*-loka. This mission failed as Menakaa got sexually entangled with Viswamitra, giving birth to a daughter, named Sakuntalaa. Menakaa had abandoned Sakuntalaa in jungle, which formed part of an ashram of a *Brahma*na sage, Kanava, in Kurukshetra region. Sakuntalaa grew up into a woman of great beauty.

Once the Kshatriya King Dushyanta happened to visit the said Ashram and to stealthily unite with Sakuntalaa in a groove. The king went back to his capital and chose to forget all about the said incident. But Sakuntalaa had conceived. When she was in advanced stage of pregnancy, she was sent by the sage Kanava to the King's court. Dushyanta, for any reason, good or bad, turned her out by charging her of trying to malign a great King. Ultimately, she gave birth to a male child, in the ashram itself. King Dushyanta became old but he had no son, who could be the heir to his vast kingdom. He suddenly remembered Sakuntalaa and tried to find out whether she had given birth to a male child. On being informed by his spies that she had given birth to a son, who had no equal of his prowess, he invited Sakuntalaa and her son and owned up both the son and the mother. Poet Kalidas had constructed a Sanskrit drama known as *Abhjnanashaakuntalam*, which has enabled us to reconstruct the history, narrated above.

India, that is, Bhaarata : *Brahma*nic Humiliation

The son of Sakuntalaa was named Bharata. He became so famous as a king that his reputation excelled that of all the past emperors. He brought even *Brahma-loka* under his control, and gave the Indian sub-continent a new name after his own name, Bharata. The word *Bhaarata*, means 'of Bharata'. This is the current name of India. The Constitution of India also describes this country as India, that is, Bharat.

So far, *Brahmin-Bania* combine has failed to realise that the name Bharat reminds them of the defeat of Brahminism in political sense, which does not have another parallel in Indian history. But they do know that the real analysis of their mythological history can invite their doom. This is why the *Brahma*na priests keep themselves engaged in spreading blind faith about their religion and shun debates with non-*Brahmanas*. Whenever reason has acquired an upper hand, the Brahminism has lost the hold over the entire Indian population. It lost religious battle against Bharat, Rama, Krishna, the Buddha, Mahavira, Nanak and Ambedkar, precisely because all of them employed reason against blind faith. In the face of these facts, it shall never be possible for Shouries to defeat Ambedkars.

Fight between Rama Kshatriya and Ravana Brahmana

Kshatriya Rama had to wage a fierce war with Ravana, an emperor of South India, who was again related to both Washishtha and Parasurama as per Hindu mythology. After Rama coming victorious in the said war, Sage Vishvamitra had decided to carry on his mission of finishing the supremacy of the *Brahmanas* from the entire country. Therefore, he had shifted his area of operation to modern Rajasthan, Haryana, Punjab and Himachal Pradesh etc.

To racapitulate, Vishvamitra had first concentrated in the then fertile area of Mount Abu and later shifted his attention to Kurukshetra region. In the latter region, he had to initially fall a prey to *Brahma*nical strategy of getting sexually involved with Menaka, a *Brahma*na girl, who was described as Apsara or heavenly nymph. Indra [king of gods or *Brahmanas* had deputed her] at the bidding of Lord *Brahma*. It was here that the *Brahmanas* lost their final battle against the *Kshatriyas*, after which they had been left with no option but to retreat to Himalayas where they established their exclusive kingdom which was given the name of *Brahma-loka*. They also started calling the Kangra Valley as the valley of gods.

Planning of Mahabharata War

When it became impossible for the *Brahmanas* to contain the Kshatriya onslaughts for ages, the *Brahmanas* had to decide to plan the Mahabharata war in order to finish all shades of *Kshatriyas*, by designating non-Kshatriya Yadavas and using them as means to finish all the existing *Kshatriyas*. The *Mahabharata* war had to be planned when the earlier expeditions of *Brahma*na Parasurama to annihilate the *Kshatriyas* even after leading 21 expeditions against them had failed.

For correct appreciation of the mythological history of India, it will be inevitable to study the roles of Visvamitra, Rama, Gautam Buddha, Vardhaman Mahavira, Bharat, Shaantanu, Dhritraashtra and Duryodhana in one sequence. That sequence tells the story of the steady erosion of all kinds of *Brahma*nical monopoly and superiority otherwise enshrined in the Hindu scriptures.

Every Varna other than *Brahma*na Varna, has been making its positive contribution to the downfall of Brahminism from time immemorial. The *Kshatriyas* have made their contribution through the above personalities. The *Vaisyas* have done so through Jainism and Gupta dynastic rule, and through exercising political power through Harsha Vardhan and Rajya-Vardhan up to the 7th century AD. After that for the sake of their own survival, the *Brahmanas* felt forced to declare the Rajputs as *Kshatriyas* through a fake ceremony at Mount Abu.

_Brahma_vartta to Bharata

The story of the *Mahabharata* war could be enacted over any strife between two groups of cousins. The actual author of the *Gita* can be said to have utilised the same story for his own purpose. This could be done by showing that, *pima facie*, the work was an epic, given the name Bharata, but its concealed purpose was to make available to the favoured party, an already prepared manual, suggesting the ways and means of ensuring success against an adversary, in argument or a wordy *duel*. The fact that there is a very strong opinion for the *Gita* having been interpolated in the exiting Mahabharata goes to lend the needed credibility to the above-said hypothesis.

Bharata and Mahabharata

Here, we may pause for a while to consider the justification of the name Bharata to the Maha-Bharata Epic, in the initial stages. Both the Kauravas and the Pandavas had a common ancestor in Shantanu, who might have adopted Vyasa the son of his wife, Satyavati, born to her before her marriage to himself. This Shantanu belonged to the line of king Dushyanta, who was in turn the son-in-law of Vishvamitra, the staunch enemy of the *Brahmanas* under the leadership of Sage Washishtha. Bharata was the son of Dushyanta from his union with Shakuntala, the daughter of Vishvamitra and Menaka, from the court of Indra, the king of gods or the *Brahmanas*. Menaka, in turn, was a *Deva-kanya* (a Brahmin girl), deputed to accomplish a job given by Indra, the King of Gods, the Brahamanas.

As already said, this Bharata had become so powerful that he lent his own name to the Indian sub-continent by replacing the name of *Brahma*vartta, literally, the Land of the *Brahmanas*. Thus, he had taken an important step to further the war between the *Brahmanas* and the *Kshatriyas,* which had earlier taken serious turn with Karttaveerya's fight with Parasurama and, later on, with Parasurama's fight with Rama.

The *Brahmana-Kshatriya* war had continued between sage Wasishtha and the sage Vishwamitra on the question of recognition of Vishvamitra as a *Brahmarishi*. This claim had been opposed tooth and nail by sage Washishtha and it was after a very severe war between the *Brahmanas* and the *Kshatriyas* that the Brahamanas had only reluctantly accepted the sage Vishvamitra's claim to *Brahma*nahead.

In the time of Rama, the said struggle seems to have raised its head because of *Kshatriyas*' re-establishing their supremacy with the humiliation of Parasurama, a close but estranged relative of Washishtha. Of course, Rama had to pay the price by way of having been exiled through the machinations of the family priest of kings of Ayodhya, traditionally called as Washishtha.

Hindu Mythology centres round the eternal war between *Suras* and *Asuras* or between gods and non-gods. We know that in so far as the earth is concerned, Hindu mythology has named Brahmans as Bhu-suras or the *suras* (gods) on earth. Analytically speaking, in India there has been constant struggle between Brahmins and Non-Brahmins. This fight has been going on even in Independent India in political field. It is because of this fact that so far no non-Brahmin Prime Minister has been able to complete 5 years of rule. In the light of this trend, it will be a miracle if Manmohan Singh the present non-Brahmin and non-Hindu Prime Minister, completes 5 years of existence as Prime Minister.

It is pertinent to note that the above discussions proves Brahmanas to be bhu-suras, or gods-on-earth, or to be simply gods or suras. *It follows that all others even those who are termed as Kshatriyas and Vaisyas are non-gods or asuras.* Since the entire Hindu mythology and the festivals centre round the victory of *suras* and fall of *asuras*, the secret purpose of the mythology was to remind the suras ar Brahmanas to annihilate the *asuras*. And, the *asuras* signify not only the aborigines or Dalits, or Sudras, but also the Kshatriyas and the Vaisyas. Judged in this light, the Kshatriyas have been reaching the level of Prime Minister, but the said position continues to be forbidden to Vaisyas, for the simple reason that the latter have allowed themselves to be most reliable tools of the Brahmanas. The day they cease to be such tools, they would be in a legitimate positionn to aspire for the office of the Prime Minister, on the analogy of Ms. Mayawati, a Dalit woman who has today proved herself to be the only man among the politicians of women.

Part VIII
Ambedkar and Social Justice

24

Social Justice in India and Plight of Weaker Sections

We have discussed that in Indian context, there is a tie between Mahatma Gandhi and Dr. B.R. Ambedkar for being declared to be the Man of Millennium. In this world, there has been a perennial fight between might and right. Often the mighty have suppressed the weak and made them deprived in every sense and exploited them in every possible way. In other words, the weak have been repeatedly demand social justice. Similarly, the weak have been repeatedly toppling the mighty with a view to ensuring social Justice for themselves. The Imperialism, the Colonialism, the capitalism, the class system and caste system have been the biggest damages for social justice.

Foresight of Ambedkar Regarding Social Injustice

Dr. Ambedkar was the only man in the long history of so-called fight for independence of India, who had foreseen the perpetration of the same social injustice in India, which had been prevailing from times immemorial. In his efforts, he was not supported even by Mahatma Gandhi, who is credited by his admirers, as being the greatest man of the millennium, for reasons of service to humanity.

Dr. Ambedkar had worked very hard to have enshrined the provisions concerning the justice, fraternity, equality etc. in the Constitution, which was ably fathered by him. But since its promulgation, it has been amended numerous times and some of the amendments have been responsible for diluting the most laudatory provisions of the Constitution aimed at ensuring the social justice and fair play in public life.

Dr Ambedkar had the worst adversary in the form of Mahatma Gandhi. The vice versa is also true. Though both of them stood for values, which were diametrically opposed to those held dear by each of them, yet both of them have been allowed by the Indian society and the government to be officially accepted as the ideals for masses. This is a great contradiction in itself. It is well nigh impossible to reconcile the idea of allotting equal place to each of the said personalities in history. But it is true that if not for the same set of people, they were the respected ideals for different sets of people, who have traditionally stood at loggerheads throughout the major part of recorded history.

Weight of Slavery

Indians had suffered a very long period the assault on their sense of social justice throughout the recorded history. When Mahatma Gandhi and Dr. Ambedkar emerged on the political scene of India, the country was reeling under the unbearable weight of slavery, imposed on it by the British Empire. Mahatma Gandhi rose to be the greatest nationalist in the sense that it made the Indians conscious of the need to throw away the yoke of slavery.

The efforts of Mahatma Gandhi are believed by many to have been responsible for putting up a united attempt to the British rulers by the adherents of various religions and by most of the people divided on caste and class lines. But there are many in India and abroad who would like to question this assumption.

Controversy over Question of Social Justice

It is a matter of common knowledge that, initially, Gandhi and his Congress had decided to leave the social question out of the purview of the Congress struggle for freedom. In other words, Congress under his leadership had been ignoring the question of social justice altogether. Rather, it had once resolved that such questions would be kept out of its purview in future.

Dr. Ambedkar was the first and the only person in India to realise and point out to both the imperialist rulers and the Congress managers that inclusion of social question in the struggle for freedom was of paramount importance. Therefore, he championed the cause of the weakest of the weak, the Depressed Classes, and impressed upon all concerned to grant social rights particularly to the Untouchables. He also emphasised that adequate safeguards should be kept for them so that in Independent India, they do not remain slaves of the upper castes as before and forever.

Communal Award Having Bearing on Social Justice

When Indians failed to have a common viewpoint on the issues, they had left the matter for arbitration of the then British Prime Minister. Accordingly, he announced the Communal Award, which, *inter alia*, meant granting separate electorates for the Depressed Classes. Mahatma Gandhi had resorted to fast unto death.

Impressing upon the British rulers the need to withdraw the Communal Award. Analytically speaking, the Mahatma was working for denying the Social Justice not only to the Depressed Classes but also to Weaker Sections, known as Sudras, condemned to be poor, ignorant and shelterless by the Hindu Scriptures and Hindu Law Code, the Manu Smriti.

Poona Pact and Harijan Sewak Sangh

The matter was finally resolved by the Poona Pact of 1932 between Madan Mohan Malviya on behalf of the Caste Hindus and Dr. Ambedkar on behalf of the Depressed Classes. It was after this Pact, that the Mahatma endeavoured to play his part for his brand of the amelioration of the Depressed Classes, then known as Untouchables. In other words, only after the signing of the Poona Pact, the Mahatma started working in the direction of "ensuring social justice" to the Untouchables. He established *Harijan Sewak Sangh* and even named his Journal as Harijan, after giving to the Untouchables, a new name of *"Harijans"*.

Dalits Giving Credit to Ambedkar, Not to Gandhi

The Dalits as a class have been giving the entire credit to Dr. Ambedkar for granting them the Social Justice. But Arun Shourie, in his book already mentioned above has denied to Dr. Ambedkar and given all credit to Mahatma Gandhi in connection with emancipation of the Dalits or conferring of human rights and social justice upon them. Both these extraordinary claims cannot be true. The matter can be sorted out only through objective examination of the lot of the Dalits, through the ages, their position at the time of the formation of the Congress, during the Gandhi's fight for freedom, and after gaining of freedom by India and their position under the governments of the Congress and its opponents from time to time.

Caste System: Worst Enemy of Social Justice

One thing has to be realised by all concerned that there is no enemy like caste system of humanity, and still we have had witnessed the roles of the admirers of this pernicious system through millennia. There have been undoubtedly great critics of the system some of whom have become known to be the founders of great religions. We have also known many of the thinkers who had been criticising caste but while remaining within the fold of Hinduism. They were mostly the saints of medieval India.

The perpetrators of the system later on were able to merge such critics within their own system of thought and they have been using the thoughts of such great men as their own and trying to pat themselves on their own backs by vainly exhibiting their greatness, which, of course, has always been eluding them. History has never known a critic of caste system like that of Ambedkar. The history does not know any objective critic of his calibre.

Politicians' Double Standard regarding Social Justice

Politicians do try to harp on the evils of the caste system at the time of elections, but since they have to woo also the staunch supporters of the caste system, including their own family members at home, they feel duty-bound to themselves dilute their own criticism so that it turns out to be a mere whisper, which remains practically inaudible to those who are chronicle perpetrators or sufferers of the system.

Such critics also do not want to make any dent on their caste men for obvious reasons. Their non-serious views, therefore, cannot be expected to have any sobering effect on their audience, since an overwhelming proportion of them belongs to higher castes. Such higher castes do realise that the caste system is the chief hindrance to progress of the country, but each one of the Indians unfortunately is in the habit of first being loyal to his caste or religion and not to country.

Inevitability of Loyalty to Caste

The impact of such a practice is so great that everyone who wants to defend himself and his community from the rigours of the caste system is forced to appeal to his caste men or people belonging to a group of castes and in the name of caste. History of caste system shows that the first beneficiary of the system was Brahmin. Kshatriyas first imitated his actions and thoughts first, then the Vaisyas and subsequently some of the intermediary caste like Jats, Ahirs and Gurjars also followed suit.

This can be illustrated by the establishment of educational institutions with a view to educate their own children on the pattern of

Brahmins and Baniyas. Swami Vivekanada had said, *reason is the helper, reason is the bar*. This applies even to the caste. The people have been suffering because of caste and yet they have been organising themselves on the basis of caste and have been deriving some benefits. Even Dr. Ambedkar was no exception to that.

Dalits Still Lack Basic Needs like Drinking Water

India got Independence in 1947. Still Dalits (the erstwhile Untouchables) lack basic needs including drinking water, food, shelter and the right to live as human beings in society, although they are indispensable for their survival. In villages, a Dalit is not allowed to draw water from public wells. In certain pockets, his shadow is still supposed to pollute the so-called upper castes. All this is because of Hindu social order, sanctioned by Hindu *Dharmashastras*. That order means the evil caste system and the practice of untouchability that has made life of Dalits miserable in every sense of the term.

Indian Democracy Run on Lines of Dictatorship

Although the leadership of all the political parties has the moral responsibility to aggressively make and implement policies for the uplift of the all including the Dalits, under the Constitution of India, yet the Indian democracy is being operated as dictatorship of the ruling party on the pre-independent feudal lines. Babasaheb Dr. B R Ambedkar was the first person in history of India who was able to wrest from the Hindu Upper castes the first instalment of human rights. It was done in the form of Communal Award, which had been granted in 1932 by the then Prime Minister of British Empire, Ramsay Macdonald.

The Award had granted separate electorates to the Dalits, who were being referred to in government records as the Depressed Classes those days. However, such classes that are today refered to as Dalits were described as *asprisyas* or untouchables by Hindu scriptures. The Communal Award signified that the Dalits could elect their own leaders to the Parliament and the state legislatures.

The advantage that had come to the Dalits was diluted through Poona Pact of 1932, between the Hindu Leaders and Dr. Ambedkar because Mahatma Gandhi had resorted to fast unto death against the said Award, on the ostensible ground that it would bring an end to Hindu religion. The provisions of Poona Pact were incorporated first in Government of India Act of 1935 and later on in the Constitution of India, whose Chief Architect came to be Dr. Ambedkar himself.

Lame Reservations Misrepresnted as Privileges

One of the practical advantages for Dalits came to be in the form of reservations in Parliament, state legislatures and local bodies and the services under Government of India, union territories, and state governments. It was vainly hoped by the Constitution-makers that in ten years period, Dalits would be able to rise to the level of upper castes and would be able to join the main stream of Hindu population, and as such, there would not remain any need for continuing the reservations.

But the reservations alone could not help all the Dalits. Focus partly shifted to problems of land reforms, right to work and credit. But even those measures have not helped the Dalits substantially mainly for the reason that in spite of certain rules and regulations, there has been total lack of political will of all the parties which have been rising to become ruling parties from time to time. Even the opposition parties have been continuously failing in their duty of embarrassing the ruling government for its failure in this behalf.

Dalit Leadership being Co-opted one is Ineffective

The Dalit leadership has failed to provide real leadership to the Dalits and satisfy their aspirations obviously on account of the fact that under the joint electorates that came to be substituted for separate electorates, Dalits have been unable to send their true representatives to any of the elected bodies. The so-called Dalit representatives in the elected bodies are practically nominated by those who have been responsible in the past for forcing them to remain below subsistence level and to live a life, which was sub human. As a result, the old prejudices against Dalits have not only continued in most cases, but they have also become more pronounced. Some individuals from among Dalits could, of course, enjoy some sympathy from the enlightened individuals among the upper castes in pre-independence days. Now, open hostility and jealousy have substituted that sympathy. In practice, the spirit of Manu Smriti that had been "repealed" by the Constitution of India seems to have revived. Some good is coming to Dalits only because of the fact that at the time of elections, the upper caste candidates, who have to compete with each other, need Dalit votes and, therefore, to appease them by making false promises to do something for them.

Gandhi's Removal of Untouchability No Substitute for Social Justice

Mahatma Gandhi had dreamt of abolishing untouchability, although he had not been able to chalk out any specific and effective programme to that end. But Dr. Babasaheb Ambedkar became the liberator of millions of Dalits and other weaker and downtrodden sections of Indian population, in his capacity as the Chief Architect of Constitution of India. But that credit has to be rightly shared by Mahatma Gandhi and Jwaharlal Nehru, who had entrusted the duty of Constitution-making to Dr. Ambedkar. The credit must also be shared by members of the Constituent Assembly and other members of the then Parliament and other legislatures who became instrumental in passing of the Constitution.

Dalits Being Scattered Cannot Elect Single Legislator

Unfortunately, Dalits are scattered all over India in towns and villages in such a manner that they cannot elect a single representative of their choice since they carry minimal electoral influence in any constituency. For most of them little has changed in independent India. Dr. Ambedkar had taken vow not to die a Hindu. He had examined some religions in order to pick up one of them for conversion. But he found only Buddhism, which according to him was the Buddha's vision of a casteless society. Dr. Ambedkar's grievance against Mahatma Gandhi was that the latter never went on fast on the question of Dalit uplift or for removal of untouchability. Dr. Ambedkar complained that Gandhi vainly tried to treat the symptoms, not the cause of the disease. He was of the firm view that untouchability cannot be abolished without annihilating caste. Mahatma Gandhi, on the other hand, had opined that if caste was abolished the Hinduism could not survive. About Buddhism Ambedkar had told his men as under:

> *Buddhism can serve not only this country, India, but the whole world at this juncture in the world affairs; Buddhism is indispensable for world peace (and so) you must pledge today that you, the followers of Buddha, will not only work to liberate yourself, but will try to elevate your country and the world in general.*

Gandhi wanted the higher castes to change their hearts; Dr. Ambedkar felt suffering of untouchables has continued for over 2000 years, with many Hindu saints having come and gone, without any change in their social status. Ambedkar wanted to legally empower Dalits.

Nishikant Waghmare has said with reference to Article 17 of the Indian Constitution and the Untouchability Abolition Act as under:

> *With caste stratification spread wide and routinely accepted, if implemented, half of India's population could be in jail.*

Constitution Proving Impediment Because of Spirit of Poona Pact

Undoubtedly, Constitution of India has given some identity to Dalits. But now the same Constitution is proving an impediment in the matter of their total emancipation, because Dalits would never be able to elect a single MP or MLA on their own, since the Constitution provides for joint electorate. If the nation wants to make Dalits and other weaker sections to join the main stream, then it is essential that while preserving their gains from reservations, efforts are made to suitably amend the Constitution. At present, not only a true representative of the Dalits cannot be elected, the Party discipline and whips also restrict their representatives from opening their mouth. It is because of the fact that they are interested in keeping their party leadership in good humour so that they could get the party ticket (nomination) in the next election. It was in realisation of this fact that Dr. Ambedkar had once commented:

> *Dalit representatives elected from reserved seats open their mouths in the Parliament only when they have to yawn.*

The Poona Pact made Dalit leadership toothless but saved Gandhi from a sure death. However, Dr. Ambedkar transcends time and he will continue to mould future generations. Nishikant Waghmare has expressed the following opinion about Dr. Ambedkar:

> *He might not be the media's man of the second millennium. He may yet be the man of the third millennium. Watch him!*

Dr. Ambedkar had addressed the following inspiring words to Dalits, which will go on proving as their path finder:

> *"Noble is your aim and sublime and glorious is your mission. Blessed are those who are awakened to their duty to those among whom they are born. Glory to those who devote their time, talents and their all to the amelioration of slavery. Glory to those who would reap their struggle for the liberation of the enslaved in spite of heavy odds, ... humiliation, storms and dangers till the downtrodden secure their Human Rights."*

25

First Organised Attempt for Restoring Social Justice

The Bolshevik experience was probably the first one to claim that revolution could win freedom for the masses. That experience gave rise to the following types of complaints from writers like Emma Goldman as back as 1922:

> Soviet Russia, had become the modern socialist deliverer, to which the blind and the lame, the deaf and the dumb felt attracted for miraculous cures to approach. The Russian Revolution provided the first occasion when decades of revolutionary ideas could be applied to real life. "What was theory was now practice. The struggle between the two concepts of revolution - the statist-centralist and the libertarian federalist - moved from the realm of the abstract to the concrete."

The October Revolution of Russia threw up certain fundamental questions as a consequence of which Communism was conceived as an inevitable alternative to capitalism, in case the latter failed. And, the October Revolution of 1917 did prove for some decades that the capitalism had certainly failed in Russia and that its place had been taken by Communism or the Dictatorship of the Proletariat.

The word Proletariat signified the lower class or common people, or working class and plebian, nay, the masses. The word plebian, meant farm worker, labourer, farmer, peasant, serf or kulak. Freedom and democracy were regarded necessary for the growth of communism. Communism was regarded as a stage prior to and leading to Socialism.

According to a website on the internet, at that time, the communist movement was described as being an anarchist one, since the words 'communists' and 'anarchists' were being used by certain scholars interchangeably. Material equality and freedom were the dimensions to socialism.

According to socialism, the society was to run according to the dictum "from each according to his/her ability, to each according to his/her needs." It was also to give the communists the power to control their own lives. It was believed then that the world had enough of wealth to provide for all their material comforts. In this sense, Socialism sought to liberate people from the constant worries about mortgages, the rising cost of living and the numerous other problems that were grinding the masses down in their daily life. It had been their experience that their entire lives were forced to obey somebody else's orders, and that they were treated like children or bits of machinery. It was considered possible that since human beings had great potential, that could be realised only in a socialist society.

Socialism is believed to be concerned about both material equality and freedom. It believed that as long as power is distributed unequally, a section of society will continue to have privileges leading to material advantage, and through some chance, if it was distributed equally, the society will ultimately again be divided into classes of haves and have-nots.

Revolution was considered to be the only alternative that was believed to be capable of defeating the ruling class, and of removing it from their economic and political dominance. As such, it was considered necessary that the working class must in every sphere of activity make the decisions affecting them irrespective of the fact whether they were to be taken in factories, communities, universities, newspapers or film studios and so on. Many questions were raised and answered. Such questions included the following:

What does revolution mean?

Once capitalism has been overthrown how is society to be run?

Who will control the factories, how will production be managed?

How will the population be fed, how will the economy be organised?

How will the revolution be defended against opposition and its survival ensured?

Correct answers to such questions were to be found and insisted upon if communism was to become a reality. Different brands of

Communism were established in USSR, China and many East European countries.

By now the USSR has disintegrated. The communism in other countries has partially given way to capitalist practices. China has practically said good bye to communism, although it continues to retain the name.

Right type of communism could possibly promise heaven to the Indian masses, who had been suffering the consequences of the pernicious caste system, which divided the society into thousands of bits and at the same time, which clubbed them in two main parts, known as Dvijas and non-Dvijas. Non-Dvijas were further divided into Sudras and Ati-Sudras or modern Dalits. The Hindu Dharma was made to keep the leadership with the leaders of the *Dvijas*, the Brahmanas, through the scriptures, which were declared to have been issued from "God" directly. Even Lord Krishna was made to utter the words *Chaturvarnyam mayaasrishtam,* that is, the four Varnas were created by me.

Anyhow, communism did enter India, but it was appropriated by the Hindu religious leadership in such a way that the leadership remained with the same upper castes. Yet the so-called communist governments were formed in West Bengal and Kerala, where the things are managed in the same old fashion, where communism continues the masses deprived of power, riches, and higher education as before. For example, the communists have been ruling in West Bengal for more than two decades by keeping the Varna system intact and by continuing to deny the power to the masses. The same thing has been happening in Kerala. Thus, Communism in India has never graduated to the dectatorship of the proletariat.

Ambedkar had the foresight to visualise the plight of the masses under communism. Accordingly, he never showed interest in communism, in spite of being the greatest protagonist for all sorts of equality for the lowest of the lowly, the Dalits. There was another reason for his distaste for communism. He did not believe, unlike the communists, in violence, still he was keen to have the basic safeguards for Dalits, so that they were not permanently condemned to a life of untouchability and slavery of the Upper castes.

Ambedkar never grudged the freedom of the Upper castes. He only wanted the Dalits to have them assimilated with the ruling classes. He wanted the Hindu society to reform itself by discarding the anti-masses practices and philosophies of Hinduism. It is well known that he had declared decades before his death, his intention of giving up

Hinduism. Still, he had waited till the last year of his life to see whether Hindus had any intention of reforming themselves and their religion and to sadly find that they had none.

Ambedkar believed that the Upper Caste Hindus had been suffering from the chronic disease of untouchability and wanted them to cure themselves, by becoming conscious of the said disease. Finding that his hopes had been totally denied, he had no option but to walk into another religion of his own choice and own making. He decided to convert to Buddhism, but he ensured that he and his people should not be uprooted from the roots of Indian tradition. Therefore, he chose Buddhism, a religion of Indian religion, which had the history of providing for equality and of defeating the Vedic religion, which had been appropriated by the modern Hindus.

Ambedkar had realised that in the sort of revolution visualised and practised by Bolsheviks, there will be no "force capable of directing the chaotic mass movements into one channel towards the correct aim."

To the communists, the crucial difference between 'representative' democracy and 'direct' democracy was that under the former, voters had no part in deciding policy and were unable to recall their representatives, although they had the illusion that by voting they were in some way able to control the political process. Dr. Ambedkar wished that the workers, in a time of social revolution, could organise their new life themselves, from the bottom, and with the help of their immediate economic organisations, and not from above. To that extent he favoured communism but did not approve their methods, which regarded `violence as the necessary tool to come to power.

Ambedkar had realised from the outset that the Congress leadership did not believe in real freedom to masses, since it was interested in having Ram Rajya, in which Rama was no more than a tool in the hands of Brahmanas, who were practically the authors, interpreters and implementers of the Smriti rules, which had divided the population into tiny bits with a view to facilitate their organised and systematic exploitation in every possible sense. As such, Ambedkar was in no doubt that the Congress did not want the social set up to change for the better so that the masses, the Sudras and other deprived sections could go out of the clutches of the Upper three Varnas.

According to him, being the ardent follower of Hindu scriptures and its pernicious caste system, the Congress wanted to maintain the social, political and economic status quo mainly on the pattern of Manu-

According to him, being the ardent follower of Hindu scriptures and its pernicious caste system, the Congress wanted to maintain the social, political and economic status quo mainly on the pattern of Manu-Smriti.

He believed that it was precisely for this reason that it was always keen to have social questions kept out of the purview of the discussions in its working committee. The social questions were allowed by the Congress to be raised after some agitation. But in due course, such questions were excluded from the discussions of the Congress working committee. In this sense, the Congress was averse even to the communistic concept of freedom.

The Congress policy suited the British rulers because under its leadership, the masses were bound to be kept suppressed. And, to that extent the British rulers were free to have a dialogue only with a handful of the leaders of the Upper Caste Hindus in an atmosphere of give and take. This policy could be of mutual benefit to the British rulers and the Hindu leadership because it was thus possible to keep the Muslim hopes of regaining power from the British.

Significantly, the British rulers and the Upper Caste leadership of Hindus regarded Muslim insurgency as their common enemy. Mahatma Gandhi had been repeatedly emphasising that he was a Varnasrami Hindu, apparently with a view to ensure the British that he did not mind the division of Hindu society on caste lines. That policy was apparently in keeping with the declared state policy of the British, that is, the policy of divide and rule. At the same time, Gandhi had directly assured the Hindu fundamentalists that he was, like them, averse to giving any share in political power to the Sudras and Ati-Sudras on the pattern enshrined in the Hindu *Sastras*.

The revolutionaries of India were a category apart. They had taken inspiration from the western democracies, where all matters were managed by the people themselves through representative democracy. They had a common programme of ousting the British from India. In view of their being dis-organised, they had not been able to think about the manner of the affairs being managed by the Indians in the event of the British leaving India.

Naturally, the revolutionaries had kept the consideration of such questions deferred until the time of departure of the British from India. Like communists, the revolutionaries also believed in the cult of violence, which militated against the Congress policy of non-violence. But there was one significant difference between the communists and the revolutionaries. This was over the question of their respective ideologies.

The communists circulated that they did not believe in any religion, whereas, the revolutionaries came out of generally the Hindu families which were neck-deep in divisive religion and superstition. So far as the communists were concerned, in practice, they were anti-religion on political platform but the moment they entered their own respective houses, they were equal prisoners of Hindu religion and superstition. For this reason, Ambedkar had no hopes in either of them.

Anyhow, the revolutionaries were in a position to regularly disturb peace in India, even though the British were keen to have peace in the country, since they could continue ruling over India only when there was otherwise calm and peace.

In view of their keenness to go on ruling over India, the British devised a method of ascertaining the points giving rise to distrust between the rulers and the ruled. The Congress was formed under a government initiative with this end in view. The rulers were initially monitoring the membership of the Congress so that only the loyalists found representations on it. Such chosen members lost no time in expressing their gratitude to the British at the first available opportunity. The oft-quoted views of Ranade regarding the need of the Indians being grateful to the British could, therefore, be expected to be a rule rather than exception.

Ambedkar, on the other hand, had to find a way out of this tricky situation, since he was not in a mood to pin his hopes on any of the warring factions, who were, of course, fighting among themselves also. Ambedkar's philosophy and actions are to be appreciated in the background of the above-said confusing position, in which none was coming to the expectations of Ambedkar, in so far as the emancipation of the lowliest of the lowly was concerned.

Since the Congress was the only body which was ostensibly engaged in the so-called fight for freedom, which was also likely to succeed the British rulers in the event of their ultimate departure from the country, Ambedkar had no option but to address the Hindus about his views and aspirations on behalf of his community, through his writings and speeches. Obviously, he had his own platform since he had no access to Congress platform, in the absence of Congress membership, his views happened to percolate to the Congress leadership and finally to the Life-time dictator thereof, Mahatma Gandhi.

Ambedkar's first masterpiece was obviously, his *Annihilation of Caste*, to which Gandhi volunteered to respond. *Annihilation of Caste* was apparently addressed to Hindu religious leadership. Similarly, he addressed his writings even to the Congress leadership and general readership, the most prominent among which was *What Congress and Gandhi have Done to Untouchables.* Thus, some sort of dialogue had been going on between Ambedkar on one side and the Congress and Hindu leadership on the other. The two parties had been coming also face to face in their discussions with the government representatives, the most important among which was that which took place in the Round Table Conferences.

Ambedkar always talked logically and in a language that was printable, to which the aggrieved party was free to reply in similar fashion. The Hindu and Congress leadership did avail of the opportunities to reply back to the extent it was possible for them. But they showed no courage to reply to the fundamental questions raised by him.

A weak and illogical endeavour had been made on the occasion of the celebration of his centenary in 1997, by Shourie and his associates, whosoever they may be. That endeavour has also failed in its mission since it has given rise to renewed interest in Ambedkar and his thought. This is evident from the appearance of numerous publications on and about Ambedkar since the release of Shourie's book of vilification by Arun Shourie, taken from the Internet. Obviously, there should be hundreds of other books in different languages from lesser beings that on account of lack of resources cannot take the advantage of putting their writings on the Internet.

Although Gandhi began by starting a non-serious attempt to bring some change in the deplorable conditions of the Dalits under the ostensible programme of abolition of untouchability, yet since his entire emphasis seemed to be centred round the self-cleaning of one's latrines, his efforts can be said to have been targeted to only one community of scavengers out of the hundreds of Dalit communities. Even in that respect his efforts remained confined to making feeble appeals to the uppercaste Hindus to change their outlook. In this connection, he had also been offering arguments which were not backed by actual dictates of Hindu scriptures, which could appear to be simply unconvincing to the knowledgeable Hindus.

Unlike Gandhi, Ambedkar had come out with direct suggestion to ensure genuine uplift of all the Dalits, through his suggestion to annihilate caste or to end the varna-vyvastha. Gandhi volunteered to oppose this remedy and came out openly in defemce of indefencible caste.

Then, Ambedkar tried political solutions of the problems of Dalits and through his able advocacy at the Round Table Conferences was able to secure the well-known Communal Award from the then Prime Minsiter of Great Britain, which granted separate electorates to Dalits, who were then called the Depressed Classes. Gandhi opposed that also by resorting to faast unto death, which was interpreted by the rationalists to be an attempt to blackmail Ambedkar so that the latter felt forced to accept the joint electorates for the classes, which meant that the Dalit represntatives for legislatures etcetra could be elected through joint electoraes in which the majority votes would be of those who had been tormenting the Dalits for millennia.

It appears that Gandhi felt great remorse for being instrumental to the perpetration of injustice to the Dalits. Consequently, he entertained a secret wish to give Ambedkar free hand in the matter of shaping the destiny of his people at the appropriate occasion. That occasion came after independence, when the question of giving a Constitution to Independent India became pertinent. Now it is a matter of history that Gandhi volunteered to suggest to the first Prime Minsiter of free India, Jawharlal Nehru the name of Ambedkar, his life time opponent of Gandhi, for making the Chief Architect of Constitution of India. And this wish of Gandhi was duly honoured in letter and spirit by Nehru so that Ambedkar was invited to become the first Law Minsiter of Independent India as also the Chairman of the Drafting Committee of Constitution of India. Gandhi's change of heart manifested not suddenly but over a period of time, when he continued to watch the impact of Ambedkar's thought and the sincerity of his sense of purpose over a very long period of time.

26

Gandhi and Social Justice

There is GAG's Homepage on the Internet. It has a write up titled Gandhism-Doom and Gloom available on domain = name Htp:// www.Periyar.org/8mr15.htm. It is concluded like this: "*The declaration of Mr. Gandhi cannot be taken to mean any fundamental change in Gandhism. It cannot make Gandhism acceptable to the Untouchables. The untouchables will still have ground to say: "Good God! Is this man Gandhi our Saviour?"*

The write-up is by Dr. Ambedkar on the subject of *Gandhism* and it answers the following questions:

> *What is Gandhism? What does it stand for? What are its teachings about economic problem? What are its teachings about social problem?*

At the outset it is necessary to state that some Gandhists have conjured up a conception of Gandhism which is purely imaginary. According to this conception, Gandhism means return to the village and making the village self-sufficient. It makes Gandhism a mere matter of regionalism. Gandhism, I am sure, is neither so simple nor so innocent as regionalism is. Dr. Ambedkar proceeds to define the scope of Gandhism as under:

> Gandhism has a much bigger content than regionalism. Regionalism is a small insignificant part of it. It has a social philosophy and it has an economic philosophy. To omit to take into account the economic and social philosophy of Gandhism is to present deliberately a false picture of Gandhism. The first and foremost requisite is to present a true picture of Gandhism.

Gandhi's Social Philosophy

According to Dr. Ambedkar, "Mr. Gandhi's views on the caste system - which constitutes the main social problem in India - were fully elaborated by him in 1921-22 in a Gujarathi Journal called *Nava-Jivan*." He had translated the Gujrati article into English as near as possible in his own words. Says Mr. Gandhi:

1. I believe that if Hindu Society has been able to stand it is because it is founded on the caste system.
2. The seeds of Swaraj are to be found in the caste system. Different castes are like different sections of military division. Each division is working for good of the whole....
3. A community which can create the caste system must be said to possess unique power of organisation.
4. Caste has a ready made means for spreading primary education. Every caste can take the responsibility for the education of the children of the Caste. Caste has a political basis. It can work as an electorate for a representative body. Caste can perform judicial functions by electing persons to act as judges to decide disputes among members of the same caste. With castes it is easy to raise a defence force by requiring each caste to raise a brigade.
5. I believe that interdining and intermarriage are not necessary for promoting national unity. That dining together creates friendship is contrary to experience. If this was true there would have been no war in Europe... Taking food is as dirty an act as answering the call of nature. The only difference is that after answering call of nature we get peace while after eating food we get discomfort. Just as we perform the act of answering the call of nature in seclusion so act of taking food must also be done in seclusion.
6. In India children of brothers do not intermarry. Do they cease to love because they do not intermarry? Among the Vaishnavas many women are so orthodox that they will not eat with the members of the family nor will they drink water from a common water pot. Have they no love? The Caste system cannot be said to be bad because it does not allow interdining or intermarriage between different Castes.
7 Caste is another name for control. Caste puts a limit on enjoyment. Caste does not allow a person to transgress caste limits in pursuit of his enjoyment. That is the meaning of such caste restrictions as interdining and intermarriage.

8. To destroy caste system and adopt Western European social system means that Hindus must give up the principle of hereditary occupation which is the soul of the caste system. Hereditary principle is an eternal principle. To change it is to create disorder. I have no use for a Brahmin if I cannot call him a Brahmin for my life. It will be a chaos if every day a Brahmin is to be changed into a Shudra and a Shudra is to be changed into a Brahmin.
9. The Caste System is a natural order of society. In India it has been given a religious coating. Other countries not having understood the utility of the Caste System it existed only in a loose condition and consequently those countries have not derived from Caste system the same degree of advantage, which India has derived.

Gandhi's Conclusion

"These being my views I am opposed to all those who are out to destroy the Caste System," Gandhi had pointed out. In 1922, Gandhi was a defender of the caste system. Pursuing the inquiry, one comes across a somewhat critical view of the caste system by Gandhi in the year 1925. This is what Mr. Gandhi said on 3rd February 1925:

> *I gave support to caste because it stands for restraint. But at present caste does not mean restraint, it means limitations. Restraint is glorious and helps to achieve freedom. But limitation is like chain. It binds. There is nothing commendable in castes as they exist today. They are contrary to the tenets of the shastras. The number of castes is infinite and there is a bar against intermarriage. This is not a condition of elevation. It is a state of fall.*

In reply to a question, Mahatma Gandhi had said: *"The best remedy is that small castes should fuse themselves into one big caste. There should be four such big castes so that we may reproduce the old system of four Varnas."* Dr. Ambedkar had declared, "In short, in 1925 Gandhi became an upholder of the Varna system." Ambedkar disclosed that Gandhi explained his Varna system in the following terms:

1. I believe that the divisions into Varna is based on birth.
2. There is nothing in the Varna system which stands in the way of the Shudra acquiring learning or studying military art of offence or defence. It is open to a Kshatriya to serve. The Varna system enjoins that a Shudra will not make learning a way of earning a living. Nor will a Kshatriya adopt service as a way of earning a

living. Similarly a Brahmin may learn the art of war or trade. But he must not make them a way of earning his living. A Vaishya may acquire learning or may cultivate the art of war. But he must not make them a way of earning his living.

3. The Varna system is connected with the way of earning a living. There is no harm if a person belonging to one Varna acquires the knowledge or science and art specialised in by persons belonging to other Varna. But as far as the way of earning his livings is concerned he must follow the occupation of the Varna to which he belongs which means he must follow the hereditary profession of his forefathers.

As to the object of Varna syatem. Gandhi had clarifed that it was to prevent competition. Not only this, he mentioned that yet another object was to avoid class struggle, since it determined the occupations of all individuals. Gandhi articulated these ideas in his own words, as follows:

4. The object of the Varna system is to prevent competition and class struggle and class war. I believe in the Varna system because it fixes the duties and occupations of persons.
5. Varna means the determination of man's occupation before he is born.
6. In the Varna system no man has any liberty to choose his occupation. His occupation is determined for him by heredity."

Gandhi's Economic Philosophy

As early as 1921 Mr. Gandhi gave vent to his dislike for machinery. Writing in the Young India of 19th January 1921, Gandhi said:

> "Do I want to put back the hand of the clock of progress? Do I want to replace the mills by hand-spinning and hand-weaving? Do I want to replace the railway by the country-cart? Do I want to destroy machinery altogether? These questions have been asked by some journalists and public men. My answer is: I would not weep over the disappearance of machinery or consider it a calamity."

His opposition to machinery is well evidenced by his idolisation of *charkha* (the spinning wheel) and by insistence upon hand-spinning and hand weaving. This opposition to machinery and his love for charkha is not a matter of accident. It is a matter of philosophy. Gandhi took special occasion to propound this philosophy in his presidential address at the Kathiawad Political Conference held on 8th January 1925. This is what Gandhi said:

> "Nations are tired of the worship of lifeless machines multiplied ad infinitum. We are destroying the matchless living machines viz., our own bodies by leaving them to rust and trying to substitute lifeless machinery for them. It is a law of God that the body must be fully worked and utilised."

He continued, "we dare not ignore it. The spinning wheel is the auspicious symbol of *Sharir Yajna*-body labour. He who eats his food without offering this sacrifice, steals it. By giving up this sacrifice we became traitors to the country, and banged the door in the face of the Goddess of Fortune."

It was stated, "Anyone who has read Mr. Gandhi's booklet on Hind Swaraj (Indian Home Rule) will know that Mr. Gandhi is against modern Civilization. The book was first published in 1908. But there has been no change in his ideology." Writing in 1921 Mr. Gandhi said:

> "The booklet is a severe condemnation of `modern Civilization'. It was written in 1908. My conviction is deeper today than ever. I feel that, if India would discard `Modern Civilization' she can only gain by doing so."

In Gandhi's view "Western civilisation is the creation of Satan." There is another Home Page on the NeT, which is titled *Welcome to Sergeant-Major Gandhi Page*. It can be traced on the Internet through domain name http://members,aol.com/Gandhi7495/gag3.html. It starts with these words:

> "As opposed to the popular perceptions, here you will see Gandhi's image from the eyes of a very famous untouchable leader, named Dr. B.R. Ambedkar (1893-1956)".

In the said Website, Ambedkar has been further quoted thus: "The social life of Gandhism is either caste or Varna. Though it may be difficult to say which, there can be no doubt that the social ideal of Gandhism is not democracy. For, whether one takes for comparison caste or Varna both are fundamentally opposed to democracy...." It has been clarified by Ambedkar, "That Mr. Gandhi changed over from the caste system to the Varna system does not make the slightest difference to the charge that Gandhism is opposed to democracy. In the first place, the idea of Varna is the parent of the idea of caste. If the idea of caste is a pernicious idea it is entirely because of the viciousness of the idea of Varna. Both are evil ideas and it matters very little whether one believes in Varna or in caste."

According to Ambedkar, the second ideal of Mr. Gandhi mentioned therein is the elimination of class war and even class struggle in the relationship between employers and employees and between landlords and tenants. With reference to this Dr Ambedkar had said that Mr. Gandhi did not wish to hurt the propertied class and that he was even opposed to a campaign against them.

Referring to the propertied class Mr. Gandhi said that he does not wish to destroy the hen that lays the golden egg. Dr. Ambedkar went on that Gandhi's solution for the economic conflict between the owners and the workers, between the rich and the poor, between the landlords and the tenants and between the employers and the employees is very simple. The owners need not deprive themselves of their property. All they need do is to declare themselves trustees for the poor. Of course, the trust is to be a voluntary one carrying only a spiritual obligation. In this connection, Ambedkar had asked:

> *"Does it promise him (the common man) a better life, a life of joy and culture, a life of freedom, not merely freedom from want but freedom to rise, to grow to the full stature which his capacities can reach?*

Ambedkar had himself calrified, "There is nothing new in the Gandhian analysis of economic ills, insofar as it attributes them to machinery and the civilisation that is built upon it. That machinery and modern civilisation help to concentrate management and control into relatively few hands, and with the aid of banking and credit facilitate the transfer into still fewer hands of all materials and factories and mills in which millions are bled white in order to support huge industries thousands of miles away from their cottages, maimings and cripplings far in excess of the corresponding injuries by war, and are responsible for disease and physical deterioration due directly and indirectly to the development of large cities with their smoke, dirt, noise, foul air, lack of sunshine and outdoor life, slums, prostitution and unnatural living which they bring about, are all old and worn-out arguments. There is nothing new in them. Gandhism is merely repeating the views of Rousseau, Ruskin, Tolstoy and their school".

Ambedkar's response to this was as under :

> *According to Ambedkar, "The ideas, which go to make up Gandhism, are just primitive. It is a return to nature, to animal life. The only merit is their simplicity. As there is always a large corps of simple people who are attracted by them, such simple ideas do not die, and there is always some simpleton to preach*

them. There is, however, no doubt that the practical instincts of men—which seldom go wrong—have found them unfruitful and which society in search of progress has thought it best to reject." Ambedkar continued that the economics of Gandhism are hopelessly fallacious., that thew evils of machinery pointed out by Gandhi may be admitted these evils are no argument against them For the evils are not due to machinery and modern civilisation but they are due to wrong social organisation, which has made private property and pursuit of personal gain and matters of absolute sanctity. He said that the remedy is to alter the organisation of society so that the benefits will not be usurped by the few but will accrue to all.

Ambedkar maintained that in Gandhism, the common man has no hope. It treats man as an animal and no more. Ambedkar stressed that the distinctively human function is reason, the purpose of which is to enable man to observe, meditate, cogitate, study and discover the beauties of the Universe and enrich his life and control the animal elements in his life.

Ambedkar described that Gandhism suited to a society, which does not accept democracy. Only a society that doea not believe in democarcy, can affored to be indifferent to machinery and the civilisation based upon it. An undemocratic society may well content itself with a life of leisure and culture for the few and a life of toil and drudgery for the many. But a democratic society must assure a life of leisure and culture to each one of its citizens, maintained Dr. Ambedkar. He emphasised that the slogan of a democratic society must be machinery, and more machinery, civilisation and more civilisation. In short, Ambedkar declared that Gandhism with its call of back to nature, means back to nakedness, back to squalor, back to poverty and back to ignorance for the vast mass of the people.

As to the class structure upon which Gandhism insists upon, Ambedkar opined that it regards the class structure of society and also the income structure as sacrosanct with the consequent distinctions of rich and poor, high and low, owners and workers, as permanent parts of social organisation, which annot be acceptable to modern man.

Ambedkar said that the idea of trusteeship, which Gandhism proposes as a panacea and by which the moneyed classes will hold their properties in trust for the poor. It is the most ridiculous part of Gandhism. Ambedkar burst out regarding this in the following words:

> All that one can say about it is that if anybody else had propounded it the author would have been laughed at as a silly

fool, who had not known the hard realities of life and was deceiving the servile classes by telling them that a little dose of moral rearmament to the propertied classes—those who by their insatiable cupidity and indomitable arrogance have made and will always make this world a vale of tears for the toiling millions—will recondition them to such an extent that they will be able to withstand the temptation to misuse the tremendous powers which the class structure gives them over servile classes.

Finally Ambedkar concluded that "Gandhism is a paradox. It stands for freedom from foreign domination, which means the destruction of the existing political structure of the country. At the same time, it seeks to maintain intact a social structure, which permits the domination of one class by another on a hereditary basis, which means a perpetual domination of one class by another.

According to Ambedkar the philosophy of Gandhism helps those who want to keep what they have and to prevent those who have not from getting what they have a right to get. Ambedkar is emphatic in saying that the fact remains that Gandhism is the philosophy of the well-to-do and the leisure class, that Gandhism wants to delude people into accepting their misfortunes. Ambedkar clarified this aspect by giving some examples as under:

> "The Hindu sacred law penalised the Shudras (Hindus of the fourth class) from acquiring wealth. It is a law of enforced poverty unknown in any other part of the world. What does Gandhism do? It does not lift the ban. It blesses the Shudra for his moral courage to give up property."

Ambedkar says that : It is well worth quoting Mr. Gandhi's own words:

> The Shudra who only serves (the higher caste) as a matter of religious duty, and who will never own any property, who indeed has not even the ambition to own anything, is deserving of thousand obeisance...The very Gods will shower flowers on him."

Another illustration in support is the attitude of Gandhism :

> "The sacred law of the Hindus lays down that a scavenger's progeny shall live by scavenging. Under Hinduism scavenging was not a matter of choice, it was a matter of force. What does Gandhism do? It seeks to perpetuate this system by praising scavenging as the noblest service to society!"

As a President of a Conference of the Untouchables, Mr. Gandhi said:

'I do not want to attain Moksha. I do not want to be reborn. But if I have to be reborn, I should be born an untouchable, so that I may share their sorrows, sufferings and the affronts levelled at them, in order that I endeavour to free myself and them from that miserable condition. I therefore prayed that if I should be born again, I should do so not as a Brahmin, Kshatriya, Vaishya, or Shudra, but as an Ati-Shudra.... I love scavenging.

'In my ashram, an eighteen-years-old Brahmin lad is doing the scavenger's work in order to teach the ashram scavenger cleanliness. The lad is no reformer. He was born and bred in orthodoxy....But he felt that his accomplishments were incomplete until he had become also a perfect sweeper, and that, if he wanted the ashram sweeper to do his work well, he must do it himself and set an example.' You should realise that you are cleaning Hindu Society."

In view of such utterings of Gandhi, Ambedkar asks in exasperation : "Can there be a worse example of false propaganda than this attempt of Gandhism to perpetuate evils, which have been deliberately imposed by one class over another? If Gandhism preached the rule of poverty for all and not merely for the Shudra the worst that could be said about it is that it is mistaken idea. But why preach it as good for one class only?... In India a man is not a scavenger because of his work. He is a scavenger because of his birth irrespective of the question whether he does scavenging or not. If Gandhism preached that scavenging is a noble profession with the object of inducing those who refuse to engage in it, one could understand it. But why appeal to the scavenger's pride and vanity in order to induce him and him only to keep on to scavenging by telling him that scavenging is a noble profession and that he need not be ashamed of it? To preach that poverty is good for the Shudra and for none else, to preach that scavenging is good for the Untouchables and for none else and to make them accept these onerous impositions as voluntary purposes of life, by appeal to their failings is an outrage and a cruel joke on the helpless classes which none but Mr. Gandhi can perpetrate with equanimity and impunity."

In the end, Ambedkar puts some pertinent questions about Gandhism.

"Should Gandhism become the law of the land what would be the lot of the Untouchables under it?" cannot require much scratching of the brain.... In India even the lowest man among the caste Hindus—why even the aboriginal and the Hill Tribe man—though educationally and economically not very much above the Untouchables. The Hindu society accepts him claim to superiority over the Untouchables. The Untouchable will therefore continue to suffer the worst fate as he does now namely, in prosperity he will be the last to be employed and in depression the first to be fired.

"What does Gandhism do to relieve the Untouchables from this fate? Gandhism professes to abolish Untouchability. That is hailed as the greatest virtue of Gandhism.

Ambedkar feels intrigued to think as to what does this virtue amount to in actual life? He clarifies that to assess the value of this anti-Untouchability, which is regarded as a very big element in Gandhism, it is necessary to understand fully the scope of Mr. Gandhi's programme for the removal of Untouchability. Does it mean anything more than that the Hindus will not mind touching the Untouchables? Does it mean the removal of the ban on the right of the Untouchables to education?

Ambedkar volunteers to say in reply as under :

"To start with the first question. Mr. Gandhi does not say that a Hindu should not take a bath after touching the Untouchables. If Mr. Gandhi does not object to it as a purification of pollution then it is difficult to see how Untouchability can be said to vanish by touching the Untouchables. Untouchability centres round the idea of pollution by contact and purification by bath to remove the pollution.

Then Ambedkar raises other pertinent questions about Gandhism : Does it mean social assimilation of the Untouchables with the Hindus? Mr. Gandhi has most categorically stated that removal of Untouchability does not mean interdining or intermarriage between the Hindus and the Untouchables. Mr. Gandhi's anti-Untouchability means that the Untouchables will be classed as Shudras instead of being classed as Ati-Shudras [i.e., "beyond Shudras"]. There is nothing more in it.

Gandhi Names Untouchables as Harijans

Ambedkar continues that Mr. Gandhi has not considered whether the old Shudras will accept the new Shudras into their fold. If they don't then the removal of Untouchability is a senseless proposition for it will still keep the Untouchables as a separate social category. Mr. Gandhi probably knows that the abolition of Untouchability will not bring about the assimilation of the Untouchables by the Shudras. That seems to be the reason why Mr. Gandhi himself has given a new and a different name to the Untouchables. The new name registers by anticipation what is likely to be the fact. By calling the Untouchables Harijans, Mr. Gandhi has killed two birds with one stone. He has shown that assimilation of the Untouchables by the Shudras is not possible. He has also by his new name counteracted assimilation and made it impossible.

Regarding the second question, it is true that Gandhism is prepared to remove the old ban placed by the Hindu Shastras on the right of the Untouchables to education and permit them to acquire knowledge and learning. Under Gandhism the Untouchables may study law, they may study medicine, they may study engineering or anything else they may fancy. So far so good. But Ambedkar asks?

> Will the Untouchables be free to make use of their knowledge and learning?
>
> Will they have the right to choose their profession?
>
> Can they adopt the career of lawyer, doctor or engineer?

To these questions the answer which Gandhism gives is an emphatic "no." The untouchables must follow their hereditary professions. That those occupations are unclean is no excuse. That before the occupation became hereditary it was the result of force and not volition, does not matter. This will be so because the argument of Gandhism is that what is once settled is settled forever even it was wrongly settled. Under Gandhism the Untouchables are to be eternal scavengers. There is no doubt that the Untouchables would much prefer the orthodox system of Untouchability. A compulsory state of ignorance imposed upon the Untouchables by the Hindu Shastras made scavenging bearable. But Gandhism, which compels an educated Untouchable to do scavenging, is nothing short of cruelty. The grace in Gandhism is a curse in its worst form. The virtue of the anti-Untouchability plant in Gandhism is quite illusory. There is no substance in it. And finally Ambedkar asks:

> "What else is there in Gandhism, which the Untouchables can accept as opening a way for their ultimate salvation?

Gandhism is Simply Another form of Sanatanism

Barring this illusory campaign against Untouchability, Gandhism is simply another form of Sanatanism, which is the ancient name for militant orthodox Hinduism. Ambedkar puts anoher more pertinent question:

> What is there in Gandhism which is not to be found in orthodox Hinduism?
>
> And, he replies as under:
>
> There is caste in Hinduism; there is caste in Gandhism.
>
> Hinduism believes in the law of hereditary profession, so does Gandhism.
>
> Hinduism enjoins cow-worship. So does Gandhism.
>
> Hinduism upholds the law of karma, predestination of man's condition in this world, so does Gandhism.
>
> Hinduism accepts the authority of the Shastras. So does Gandhism.
>
> Hinduism believes in idols. So does Gandhism.

All that Gandhism has done is to find a philosophic justification for Hinduism and its dogmas. Hinduism is bald in the sense that it is just a set of rules, which bear on their face the appearance of a crude and cruel system. Gandhism supplies the philosophy, which smoothens its surface and gives it the appearance of decency and respectability and so alters it and embellishes it as to make it even more attractive.

What hope can Gandhism offer to the Untouchables? Ambedkar still wants to know. And, he comes with the similar disappointing answer:

> *To the Untouchables, Hinduism is a veritable chamber of horrors. The sanctity and infallibility of the Vedas, Smritis and Shastras, the iron law of caste, the heartless law of karma and the senseless law of status by birth are to the Untouchables veritable instruments of torture, which Hinduism has forged against the Untouchables. These very instruments which have mutilated, blasted and blighted the life of the Untouchables are to be found intact and untarnished in the bosom of Gandhism. How can the Untouchables say that Gandhism is a heaven and not a chamber of horrors as Hinduism has been? The only reaction and a very natural reaction of the Untouchables would be to run away from Gandhism.*

Ambedkar's conclusion that Gandhism is another form of Sanatanism is patently correct. This can be directly confirmed by a historical fact. Initially, Gandhi had strong association with Arya Samaj leader Swami Shraddhananda. Arya Samaj had propounded that Varnas were to determined on the basis of Guna, Karma and Svabhava, on that of qualities, actions and mental dispositions. This declaration and *Shuddhi* programme of Samaj had annoyed both the Sanatanist (orthodox) Hindu and the Muslims. Since Gandhi was essentially a political leader, he could not afford to lose his following. Accordingly, he said good-bye to Swami in 1922, and tried to placate the orthodox Hindus. Gandhi's articulations of 1925 can be best appreciated in the above said background, which forced him to disown the Harijans.

27

Communism and Social Justice

Communism rose with Marx and Engels. It came to be attributed basically to Marx and, thus, it came to be called Marxism. Lenin added new dimension to their philosophy. His dimension came to be known as Leninism. Stalin added a new idea to that Philosophy, which came to be called as Stalinism. In China, Mao gave new impetus to Marxism-Leninism-Stalinism and his philosophy came to be named as Maoism. Thus, Mao was the first man to give birth to Maoism, yet he regarded Marx and Lenin as his ideals. In the light of the analogy of Buddhism, he may be called as umpteenth Mao. The same can be true of Lenin or Stalin.

Rise of Communism

Ambedkar who rejuvenated the Sudras, and Ati-Sudras of Hinduism, came to be compared with Sukracharya of Hindu Mythology. Sudras and Ati-Sudras are comparable with the workers of Communism. Communism and Ambedkarism can be said to be having somewhat parallel philosophy so far as the welfare of the workers, Sudras, and Ati-Sudras is concerned. But communism took birth in Eastern Europe and in the background of Industrial labour. As the industrialisation ushered in India, the relevance eof Marxism or communism was felt in India also. Therefore, the first Communist Party of India was formed in 1920, not long after the end of the First World War and the October Revolution of 1917 in Russia.

Since the communism believed in violent revolution, the Indian industry as also the British rulers then thought of countering that revolution through an idea, which could be called as revolution of non-violence. The British rulers and the Indian industrialists had both vested interests in that new kind of revolution. The British rulers had also their problem with Indian revolutionaries believing in violence. Such revolutionaries were naturally emerging as a political movement. It was in the interest of British imperial interests to introduce the non-violent character to the Indian politics through its own baby, the Indian National Congress. The British did not have such problems only in India. They had a very vast empire and the whole Empire was to be insulated against violence and new inspiration for those believing in violence in the form of communism.

The communism rose to be a big power as being an anti-religion force. In Indian conditions, the British rulers had already been using Hindu religion and Hindu fundamentalism to their best advantage. They were thus rightly using Hindu religion as the opium of the Indian masses. As such, they needed someone who could pose as the opponent of the British Empire, who could said to represent the Hindu masses, who could similarly represent the Indian farmers, the Indian poor, the Indian industrial workers and as Indian politician. Mahatma Gandhi was already being groomed as the non-violent political worker since 1908. He had graduated in non-violence and as the most outstanding servant of the British Empire in 1915. He was being introduced to the Indian masses through Gopal Krishan Gokhale and Bal Gangadhar Tilak, through his rural tours.

The success of October revolution of 1917, and consequent overthrow of equally mighty Empire of the Tsar, was bound to send shivers to the British Empire. The fact of founding of the Communist Party of India in 1920 was another big challenge for the British rulers in India that required to be met without any loss of time. The top Industrialists like Birla and Tata were also feeling equally shaky with the rise of Communism in India. Therefore, their choice naturally fell on Mahatma Gandhi who was already on British probation along with Motilal Nehru in another pocket and in another sense discussed elsewhere in this book.

Sudras and Industrial Labour

Communism was very appealing to the Indian industrial labour. Therefore, the industrialists and the British rulers jointly approached the Congress leaders to take charge of the conspicuous leadership of the Industrial labour under the full patronage of both of them. Accordingly, the bodies like Indian Trade Union Congress came into being in due course. Their job was also to keep the labour non-violent. Since the Indian National Congress had become the main political party through the connivance of the Upper Hindu Caste leadership, the Industrialists and the British rulers, the Communist party had no option but to remain a sort of trade union in the absence of co-operation from the Hindu religious leadership.

Rather, it would be more appropriate to regard them as another branch of the Congress, which had taken a vow not to fight the British for securing freedom of the country. It was indulging in sporadic violent activities in order to provide Mahatma Gandhi the justification of showing that his *Ahimsa* was a valid principle and in order to provide the British to pose as being threatened by the non-violent programme of Mahatma Gandhi. In that event, their gestures were sought to have great propaganda value for all concerned in relation to the efficacy of the non-violence movement. Thus, the Communism had to operate in the given area of Industrial labour. It could not make any inroads into farm workers for the same reason. The Hindu religion was prevalent in more virulent form in rural areas, where anti religion organisation like the Communist party of India could not take firm roots.

Failure of Communism in India

Communism in India has failed because its leadership having remained confined to the Upper castes, never wished it to succeed, by virtue of regarding the *Varnasrama* as sanctified principle of Dharma, like the Hindu fundamentalists. Viewed in this background, Indian Communism cannot be said to be anti-religion or anti-Hinduism. The role of the Communists has been to practically ensure the defeat of Communism so that the orthodox Hinduism might survive. It was their more than ordinary involvement with the *Varnasrama* Dharma that the Communism did not attract Dr. Ambedkar or that Dr. Ambedkar did not feel attracted to Communism. Independent India has produced many chief ministers like Bhagvat Dayal Sharma of Haryana, who had the trade union background and who had at the same time the great reputation of being the really orthodox Hindus. Thus, the labour of Trade Union Congress was doomed to failure from the very start, since it has continuously failed to appreciate the role of historical factor of *Varnasrama* Dharma to influence its activities. As such, the entire leadership of Indian labour has been indulging in an organised sabotage of labour. At best, it has been bartering away its cherished goals in exchange for some petty gains from its hidden collaborators within the ranks of orthodox Hinduism.

For similar reasons, Communism could not become a world force since it could not include within its ambit the segments of population which did not belong to the industrial labour. Moreover, the industrial countries of Europe stalled the communist progress and America through their conscious highjacking pro-labour legislation and other welfare measures. Under the circumstances, the Communists were not left with any real work in the political field.

Indian Communists and Varna-vyavastha

Indian communists also suffered from the same weakness as discussed above. But their problem was more serious judged in the background of the Hindu Varna system, which was directly under the thumb of the religion. The Sudras, the Dalits and other weaker sections could cover the labour of communistic interpretation. They were totally submerged under the ocean of religion, from where it was not easy to extricate them for an irreligious body like that of Communists. Besides, the Upper Caste Hindus through the channel of the Indian National Congress also provided the Leadership to the Communists.

In the light of the above situation, it can be assumed that the problems of the workers in Indian context remained un-tackled until the time of coming of Dr. Ambedkar on the Indian political scene. And Dr. Ambedkar treated the problem of the oppressed people not as those of industrial labour. He viewed the problem from overall social, religious, economic and political angle. The traditional Hindu labour could not fall in the definition of labour as given by the Communists.

The industrial labour in India was contributed by all the castes. Thus, the labour remained divided on the pattern of Hindu Varna system. Within the labour, there were Brahmanas, Kshatriyas, Vaisyas and the Sudras. As such, they could never take up any issue jointly. Here, the appeal of Ambedkar was also minimal, since he **had risen to be the champion of the oppressed in the religious sense, and not of the labour in industrial, sense.**

Communist Assessment of Indian Conditions

In spite of the facts being so, we can derive some benefit from the assessment of Indian conditions by the Communists. Lal Singh, General Secretary of the *Communist Ghadar Party of India* [CGPI], had presented a Draft Report on behalf of its Central Committee at the

Third Consultative Conference of CGPI held in New Delhi on December 23-24, 1995. The said report had been published in March 1996 and distributed for The *Communist Ghadar Party of India* by *Lok Awaz* Publishers and Distributors 8/251, DDA Flats, Kalkaji, New Delhi. The published report was titled as *Wither India*? The introduction thereof had began like this:

> We recognised in 1977 that the entire communist movement was being fragmented under the pressure of the bipolar division of the world. Different varieties of modern revisionism were playing their counter-revolutionary disruptive role by adhering to parliamentary democracy, and uniting with the state to eliminate any challenge to the existing status quo. Capitalism was flourishing and utilising the remnants of feudalism,, colonial domination and increasing imperialist penetration against the people. This flourishing capitalism, in turn, was protecting these feudal remnants, colonial domination and imperialist penetration. It was this that was responsible for the worsening conditions of the masses. A variety of revisionism called such capitalist growth and expansion as the path of "non-capitalist development".

The division between Capitalism and communism can be said to be partialy valid since the whole world can never be said to be divided between the industrialists and their industrial workers. It could, of course, be divided between their masters and the slaves on the pattern of Hindu *Varnavyvastha*. Judged in the context of the Hindu Varna system, the Sudras and the Dalits etc. had been condemned for all times to come as the workers, bifurcated into touchable Sudras and untouchable Sudras. Significantly, the Upper Caste Hindus were the masters and the Sudras were their slaves. At least, in Indian conditions this division is valid even today in practical terms, in spite of the provisions of the Constitution of India to the contrary.

The CGPI, however, took notice of an important fact. It was observed that *"This variety of revisionism openly conciliated with the Congress Party in India and with Soviet social-imperialism internationally. We made the decision, under those conditions, to establish a vanguard party of the Indian working class in which all the Indian communists would militate; a party that would build the political unity of the working class and broad masses of the people and open a path for the progress of society; a party based on the theoretical thinking of Marxism-Leninism in opposition to revisionism and opportunism of all hues."*

Incidentally, since the communists believe in violence, their revolution also presupposes violent revolution. It was declared "Our strategic aim remains the overthrow of capitalism and building of socialism through revolution."

While quoting Engels the CGPI said that it must continue to *"sum up the entire experience within this epoch of imperialism and proletarian revolution by starting from the present, as it continues to do at this time. CGPI must not succumb to the lure of the liquidationist who seeks perfect and final knowledge before anything revolutionary can be achieved. We must continue the summation in the course of organising the working class for the victory of revolution and socialism."* Their programme can be said to compare with what can be indicated by the phrase 'on the job training'. Instead of making the perfect planning in advance, they would like to make a start with the current ideas and to steadily go on adjusting their programmes in the light of the new experience and in that of the changing circumstances, on which nobody can have full control.

In Light of Hindu Social Organisation

In view of what has been said about the *Varna-Vyvastha*, the fate of all the brands of socialist parties stands already sealed. Indian politics cannot be run without the power of brain, money and muscle. All these three had been traditionally under the control of Brahmanas, Kshatriyas and the Vaisyas respectively to be worked under the overall direction of the Brahmanas. The Upper castes have perfected a system, which keeps them united, and the Labour force of the Sudras and the Dalits etc. divided as also unarmed, and non-violent. This philosophy had been enshrined in the *Manu-Smriti* long ago.

The said Smriti had declared that so long as the *Brahmana* and the Kshatriyas stand united the empire of the whole world is theirs. It had also declared that if the Vaisyas and the Sudras happened to join, it would mean the end of the Brahminical supremacy. The class of Kshatriyas in demographic sense has been a misnomer. Only those in formal bureaucratic positions or in armed forces of various hues have been practically treated Kshatriyas and those left out were always treated as the Sudras. Thus, there was normally a question whether the Vaisyas and Sudras could join or not. Whenever they joined together, they brought a downfall to the Brahmanas and the Kshatriyas. In modern times, also this fact has been demonstrated a number of times from the time of rise of Charan Singh, to the time of VP Singh, Chandra Shekhar, Devilal, Mulayam Singh Yadava, Kanshi Ram and Miss Mayawati.

Criminalisation of Politics

About Criminalisation of politics, CGPI thought as under: ***"The broad-scale criminalisation of the polity and the use of state terrorism as a matter of course, has deprived hundreds and thousands of people of their lives and liberties. This activity has restricted the scope of political action to the narrowest focus, even putting it in the hands of criminal elements. Increasing offers of positions and responsibilities within the state have broadened the role of some communists in justifying the criminalisation of the polity in India."***

The principle contained in the above excerpt can be said to be a direct reminder to the events that took place in Maharashtra and elsewhere consequent upon the desecration of the statues of Dr. Ambedkar in July 1997. A dozen of the Dalits were reported to have been killed by the police on the pretext of saving a petrol pump. It has been shown that the police had fired to kill the Dalits rather than to disperse them. The statements made by the then Chief Minister of Maharashtra and of the Shiv Sena chief also went to instigate the Shiv Sainiks and other die-hard Hindu fundamentalists to suppress the Dalits in a new kind of offensive. The treatment of the Dalits in the manner discussed above can be the direct result of state terrorism engineered by the BJP-Shiv-Sena combine.

The communist experience is relevant for the Dalits in the sense that theirs is the fight against capitalism and that the Hindu Varna-Vyvastha is also nothing but capitalism in its worst form. It differs from the capitalism of the west in as much as that brand of communism does not prevent the state from taking substantial welfare measures in favour of the industrial workers. But the capitalism of the Varna-*Vyvastha* does prohibit the Upper Castes to improve the lot of the Sudras and Dalits etc. The co-operation between the international capitalism and the Indian capitalism is also going to work against all the interests of the Dalits and the weaker sections in India.

The international co-operation between the two types of Capitalists gives rise to the notion that social leadership has no obligation towards anyone except itself. Its logic declares that there is no choice but to reform the capitalist system in order to intensify exploitation to the extreme. It seems to suggest that there is no alternative to intensifying the exploitation of the working class as the only path to prosperity. The capitalists further seem to equate their own prosperity with the well being of all. CGPI rightly believes that.

The big capitalists and big landlords of India have launched a broad anti-social offensive. They are also promoting the use of communal violence and other diversions to divide the people so that they are not be able to resist their offensive.

28

Ambedkar and Social Justice

There is an article on the internet titled as *Ambedkarism and Republic of Rage* authored by the editor-in-chief of CNN-IBN and IBN, which makes a significant observation that Ambedkarism is seen as a **genuine vehicle of social mobility**. It has been said therein with reference to recent desecration of one of the statues of Ambedkar in Kanpur (Uttar Pradesh) that there are more statues of Bhimrao Ramji Ambedkar in India than any other historical person of the last millennium. This fact of the statues was acknowledged even by AS whose reaction thereto led him to write a very long book of vilification against Ambedkar already mentioned. AS had felt particular pain from the said fact when he found that the number of statues of Ambedkar far exceeded those of Gandhi.

It has been further remarked by quoting Gail Omvedt from her book *Ambedkar: Towards an Enlightened India*, that the statues have played a major role in political assertion in contemporary India. She writes: "The raising of the statues has represented a claim to pride and public space. Their opponents also take them as such and express their hostility to Dalit assertion by putting 'garlands' of chappals around such statues – actions which have often led to severe rioting and police firing..." The author of the said article surmises, and rightly so, that ironically, Ambedkar himself would have hated being a statue. He finds support from Ambedkar's following remarks made in 1943:

> *"India is still par excellence a land of idolatry. There is idolatry in religion and in politics. Heroes and hero-worship is a hard if unfortunate fact in India's political life. Hero worship is demoralising for the devotee and dangerous for the country."*

AS in his said book already referred to finds Ambedkar statues aesthetically repugnant and symbolic of the bankruptcy of the Dalit leadership, as if all the statues all over the country and abroad, had been installed and funded by Dalit leadership. The fact of the matter is that most of the statues of Ambedkar have been installed as a consequence of regular resolutions of elected bodies at different levels, with the help of public funds. It can, of course, be conceded that the demand could have originated with certain groups of Dalits.

As such, if the demand is ultimately accepted by different elected bodies, it has to be presumed that the decisions in this behalf have been taken and implemented by the entire population of the administrative bodies with the help of public money. All such bodies are obviously controlled by the majority of non-Dalit representatives. As such, critics like AS fail to realise that Ambedkar today is an enduring symbol of the most potent weapon in electoral politics. It is evident that no party can dare oppose the raising of an Ambedkar statue. An opinion has been given therein that when a statue of Gandhi is garlanded with chappals in Gujarat, there is no major flare-up, but when an Ambedkar statue is desecrated, there is a near-spontaneous eruption.

Politics of identity shows that Ambedkar is invoked at the time of elections not only by the Dalits but by all the political parties, communalist or secular, leftist or rightist or even centrist. Moreover, every political party exhibits unmistakable pride in appropriating Ambedkar for the purpose of using his name in order to improve its chances of winning inn elections. This is equally true of the parties like the Congress, the BJP, the BSP or any of the brands of Janata Parties. It is also true that though Ambedkar had been national leader from every angle yet all concerned have been reducing multi-faceted personality to a caste leader, wittingly or unwittingly

The philosophy of Ambedkar has come to be regarded as Ambedkarism, although we have already seen earlier that most people fail to articulate what Ambedkarism actually implies. Still, Ambedkarism is seen as a genuine vehicle of social mobility. The above-said article holds that the demand for an equitable society – as exemplified in the clamour for reservations – is seen to be far more 'real' and 'achievable' at an individual and collective level than even Gandhi's battle for a humane society.

It has also been noted therein that by invoking Ambedkar, his followers are seen to be asserting a more basic desire for a more 'inclusive' society, a demand that is fundamental to any social or economic change in contemporary India and that it's a demand, which is universal enough to ensure that no political party can afford to ignore it.

The author of the said article goes to trace the origin of such an anger of Dalits. It finds that an average angry Dalit feels that he has been left out of development. To that extent, it has been stressed that the mob violence that follows the damage to an Ambedkar statue is not simply Dalit anger at having their icon humiliated. It is also an attempt at 'revenge' by all those groups who feel alienated from a socio-economic system that still benefits only a limited few. Thus, it not surprising then that the violence has spread to those towns in Maharashtra where the pace of growth has been the most uneven, and where Dalits and other social groups feel they are being left behind by the newly dominant caste and class interests.

Ambedkar's assertion was that simply exercising the vote was meaningless unless caste was totally eradicated. His message consisted in acquiring power to change society and not acquiring power simply to rule. This message has undoubtedly given the Dalits and even other weaker sections, a peculiar sense of identity. This fact tends to give rise to a reaction in certain die-hard upper caste Hindus, which leads to repeated bestial attacks against Dalits like the one that recently happened in Khairlanji.

In the light of the above background information, it is important to take an over view of Ambedkar's vision of new social order, which will be obviously helpful in understanding as to what Ambedkarism implies. This is so vast and controversial subject in India that no view advanced by any body, irrespective of its being logical or illogical, is likely to be wholly acceptable by all the experts. We have, therefore, considered it sufficient to take the advantage of one who is accepted as a celebrity among the authors on Ambedkar, and to give a summary of the views of hers, who is Gail Omvedt. The credentials Gail Omvedt as being one of the greatest authority on Ambedkar and as being one of the most objective writers already stand widely accepted. We hope to be excused for making the use of her labours for the purpose of the book in hand.

Gail Omvedt, while delivering 5th Dr. Ambedkar Memorial Annual Lecture for the Year 1999, which had been postponed to the year 2000!, began by saying that It would not be an exaggeration to say that Ambedkar is here India's most significant figure. She made very significant observation as under:

> *Dr. Bhimrao Ramji Ambedkar's vision and life truly stands at the junction of the old and the new; coming from the depths of the society marked by hierarchies of inequality and involved complexities of fixed exploitation to a leading role in the formation of a new order, symbolised by his role in the drafting of India's Constitution, symbol of a new order, Ambedkar was indeed a man marking the beginning of an era, a man whose life and thought encompassed both analysis of, rage about and struggle against the old exploitation and the visions of the new society.*

Gail Omvedt, was among the first intellectuals to suggest that Ambedklar was the real man of millennium as compared to rather bewildering collection of Indians. She had declared in unequivocal terms as follows:

> *While Indira Gandhi and Mahatma Gandhi's names have been taken around the world as important figures of the millennium, it is not they nor any other of the rather bewildering collection of Indians mentioned (including Godse and Bacchan!) but Dr. Bhimrao Ramji Ambedkar who has to be considered India's man of the millennium.*

Ambedkar Regarded Gandhi Age as Dark Age of India

Even in the matter of Dalits making contribution to global society, made a forceful observation that "It is Babasaheb who best represents the global-Indian heritage. Nehru was a national figure at most; his daughter Indira was also a national figure." Coming to Mahatma Gandhi, Gail Omvedt agreed that he was indeed a global figure, who is recognised throughout the world today as a forerunner of the ecological movement."

But she reminded the world of Babasaheb's harsh judgement in 1939 in which he had lamented, "this Gandhi age is the dark age of India" (Vol I: 352) and continued, "I think will stand: the values that Gandhi represented, the proclamation of Hinduism and the glorification of a village society, in whatever idealised form, were ultimately backward values, the values of a pre-modern society."

Gail Omvedt clarified, "It was Babasaheb who stood within the Indian tradition of modernism, justice, freedom and equality and who gave the ideals of the French revolution local form and shape. I am using strong words here because the debate over these values is raging sharp and fierce today in India, because Babasaheb Ambedkar himself used strong words and took sharp positions on the issues involved, issues of development, freedom and equality".

Evolution of Ambedkar's Thinking

The evolution of Ambedkar's thinking can be seen through his own periodicals, namely, *Janata, Bahishkrut Bharat* and *Prabuddh Bharat*. The last mentioned one was obviously the end result of his social philsophy. *Prabuddh Bharat,* literally means the Enlightened India, which apparently signifies India of rationality and science that would link her with the most developed nations Europe, of America, and of Japan and China.

Ambedkar's vision of a new social order can be summed up in three words taken from the great slogan of the French revolution, "liberty, equality, fraternity." Gail Omvedt prefers to change the final term to "community" as according to these "Liberty, equality and community" are the three most important components of a human vision for the new millennium.

Ambedkar's New Social Order in Contrast to Gandhian View

Dr. Ambedkar's vision of a new social order is obviously in contrast to the Gandhian and eco-romanticist position. His vision is more in conformity with Marx who had conviction that the history brought with it an advance in human welfare. Marxist believed that the forces of production bring with them an advance in human capacities and in freedom. The Indian traditionalists believe that all advancement is simply a phase in endless cycles or final degeneration. On the other hand, Ambedkar believed that human history is a history of progress, a forward movement. Further Ambedkar believed in a form of social liberalism, expressed mainly in his essay *"Buddha and Karl Marx."*

Against Preaching Gospel of Poverty

Gail Omvedt mentions Maria Mies argueing that the French revolution is finished; its ideals cannot be extended to Dalits, women or other sections of the marginalised in the world, and we must turn away from this vain effort to achieve "growth" to acceptance of a society based on limited needs, subsistence production. Gail Omvedt discloses that Ambedkar himself gave a very early answer to the romanticisation of a pre-industrial life and to the morality of "simple needs" in a 1918 essay reviewing a book by Bertrand Russell as under:

> *"This time-honoured complaint of the moralists against `love of money' is only a part of their general complaint against the goods of the world and finds its justification in the economic circumstances which gave rise to this particular belief....At a time when the whole world was living in `pain economy' as did the*

ancient world and when the productivity of human labour was extremely low and when no efforts could augment its return, in short, when the whole world was living in poverty it is but natural that moralists should have preached the gospel of poverty and renunciation of worldly pleasures only because they were not to be had."

No Condemnation of Property

But Ambedkar also distances himself from the condemnation of property so common to radicals and romanticists and came out with the observation, "The trouble therefore one might say is not with property but with the unequal distribution of it". And, he retained this position lifelong. However, he has been against the glorification of poverty either in Hindu tradition or in Christian tradition.

Ambedkar is against exploitation while not being against development and accumulation, he gives legitimation to the honest and energetic efforts of "householders" to work and earn.

No Acceptance of Economic Interpretation of History

While settling his accounts with Marx he declares, "Nobody now accepts the economic interpretation of history as the only explanation of history" (Vol 3: 444). According to Gail Omvedt, in *The Buddha and His Dhamma* Ambedkar gives the clear priority to "mind" as determinant. He includes "recognition of the mind as the centre of everything. Mind precedes things, dominates them, creates them. If mind is comprehended all things are comprehended. Mind is the leader of all its faculties. Mind is the chief of all its faculties. The very mind is made up of those faculties. The first thing to attend to is the culture of the mind" (Vol 11: 104)

Apparently, Ambedkar has moved from a form of economic materialism to idealism as the main force in history. His life work concludes with his religious and spiritual concerns, and much of his writing on Indian history emphasises the ideal-ideological factors. In his *Revolution and Counter-Revolution,* he classifies its stages in religious terms: *Brahminism, Buddhism and Hinduism.*

His writings show that Ambedkar was seriously concerned to have a rigorous scientific method and his orientation is very much towards the material world. He never denies the role of material factors and economic impulses as a necessary part of any overall historical and social explanation. According to Gail Omvedt Ambedkar's specific economic thinking can be said to have gone through three major stages (see also Omvedt, 1999).

First Phase: Classical Economics

It is represented by his writings of the 1920s, which include two major books - The Problem of the Rupee and The Evolution of Provincial Finance in British India - and a number of articles. Ambedkar was trained in classical economics (i.e., in the economics of the earlier twentieth century which was already moving into Keynesianism). These show him as a liberal economist, though with significant influence of Keynesian.

His economic theory, it has been recently and convincingly argued, was a liberal one, with concerns for responsible government financing that would be welcomed by liberalizers today. He retained, of course, an important concern for the role of the state, but he certainly believed in the potential of the market and trade for increasing individual and national wealth.

Second Phase: Equates Brahminism and Capitalism

According to Gail Omvedt, the 1930s did usher in a second phase of Ambedkar's economic thinking. By then he had become heavily involved in social movements not only of Dalits but also of workers and peasants generally, and with this he came into contact with Indian communists and in many ways came under the influence of Marxism. This never really left him. It was during this period that his weekly *Janata* was filled with articles urging the unity of "peasants and workers" against "capitalists and landlords", when he made his famous Mahad statement characterising the enemies of Dalits as "capitalism and Brahminism."

Now Ambedkar seems to equates Brahminism with capitalism. He says, by Brahminism, I mean the negation of the spirit of Liberty, Equality and Fraternity. In that sense it is rampant in all classes and is not confined to the Brahmans alone, though they have been the originators of it" (reported in Times of India, February 14, 1938). In taking these Brahminism and capitalism as the focus of struggle, Ambedkar was inclined to accept a Marxist explanation of social-economic exploitation with only the necessity of adding an appreciation for the role of caste as an autonomous, exploitative and oppressive social structure. This meant, in effect, taking Marxism as the theory with which to analyse capitalism and supplementing it with an analysis of caste focusing on religion and ideology. This period climaxed with the proclamation of the need for "state socialism" in *States and Minorities*. It is the Ambedkar of *States and Minorities* who is usually cited today by various types of socialists and Marxists as justification for their own position.

Third Phase: Wants State to Remove Poverty

Towards the end, he rejected the Marxist approach to economic issues. He was, of course, continuing to lead Dalit struggles for equality and liberation. This shift in his policy led to his this third and final period, which can be described as "Buddhist economics."

Ambedkar returns in "Buddha or Karl Marx," to an appreciation of the role of the private accumulation of wealth gives a reinterpretation of state, market, and community through a Buddhist parable. The householder striving to increase his wealth honestly provides the foundation of the economy. The state's role is of ensuring against the poverty of the most oppressed, in order to avoid the chaos or revolution. And, the Bhikku Sangh represents community, the ideal communist society.

Stands for Enlightenment Values

However, Ambedkar's political-economic philosophy remains a form of liberalism. Being an individualist and a rationalist, he always returned to the basic Enlightenment values that are central to Indian tradition. He thought that while **in "antique society" the moral code laid down by religion was based on utility, in "modern society" it is based on justice,** which according to him is equivalent to the values of liberty, equality and fraternity.

He focused on state policy, including state welfare policy, with its role in reducing poverty and compensating for conditions of social injustice. Ambedkar was critical of Indian leftists not only for their attitude towards caste, but also for their unwillingness to accept constitutional democracy.

In his speech presenting the Constitution, he makes several important points. For example, he agreed with Thomas Jefferson that every generation has inherent right to change Constitution or create new. Otherwise, in view of Jefferson, to refuse this right would mean that "the earth belongs to the dead and not to the living." However, Ambedkar says, there will never be a need to reject India's Constitution as such, because of its flexible scope for amendment. (Vol. 13: 1211).

Against Agitation and *Satyagrahas*

Referring to the danger to democracy in India, he suggested that agitation and *satyagrahas* should be given up in favour of parliamentary methods of trying to achieve change. He believes that the main dangers to the existence of India as a democratic nation comes from inequality or casteism and from the tendency to worship "mahatmas", who make the population yield to authoritarianism. He warned that **"those who suffer from inequality will blow up the structure of political democracy."**

He emphasises that we must make our political democracy a social democracy, which means a way of life, which recognises liberty, equality and fraternity as the principles of life. Ambedkar believed that problems of inequality and exploitation could be resolved without recourse to class warfare. He maintained:

> *"Down-trodden classes are tired of being governed, they are impatient to govern themselves. This urge for self-realisation in the down-trodden classes must not be allowed to develop into a class struggle or a class war."*

Regards Hinduism Unfit for Transcendental Morality

Ambedkar was **single-handedly responsible for the revival of Buddhism as a mass religion in the land of its birth. This is nothing short of a miracle.** He did not simply "revive" a traditional form of Buddhism. Rather, he reinterpreted and rejuvenated Buddhism and in a way recommended it as a religion for the contemporary world. He believes that **religion, in the broadest sense of a transcendental morality, is necessary for ordered social existence.** He regarded Hinduism as a form of "Brahminism" as being unfit for the purpose, because of its involvement with deliberate exploitation of not only masses, but also its junior partners, namely, Kshatriyas and the Vaisyas. His "The Philosophy of Hinduism" had already condemned Brahminism. He was aware almost from the very beginning that Dalits needed a new religion. But there was a time when he argued in his challenge to Gandhi that Hinduism could be acceptable if "all the Shastras and Puranas were given up." But he did know that the said was simply unacceptable.

Ambedkarism: Living Guide to Action

The Communists have tried to justify their thinking by quoting V I Lenin, who wrote: *"It is precisely because Marxism is not a lifeless dogma, not a final, finished and ready-made immutable doctrine, but a living guide to action, that it was bound to reflect the astonishingly abrupt change in the conditions of social life."* This communistic thinking can be applied in equal measure and with equal emphasis on Ambedkarism.

Ambedkarism has a much sounder basis and logic to stand on its own as compared to Communism of Indian brand. Ambedkarism represents much better defined segments of population already divide by the *Varnasrama Dharma*. The orthodox opposition of Ambedkar would go on giving further leases of life to Ambedkarism. **Orthodox Hinduism can kill Ambedkarism only after committing suicide. If it does that there is no need for Ambedkarism also to exist in a vacuum.**

Ambedkarism is like an opposition in the parliamentary form of government. If there is a ruling party, the opposition is bound to be there to cause a constant headache to it. And the mere fact of its existence as opposition, one day enables to it overthrow the rue of the ruling party. In that case, the erstwhile ruling party becomes the opposition to play the same role. At present, the *Varna-Dharma* is ruling. Ambedkarism is in opposition. No ruling party can retain its position for all times to come. Some day it must tire itself to give way to the opposition, that is, Ambedkarism.

All the opposition parties at present are relying in varying degree on Ambedkar's followers and Ambedkarism, which is steadily turning into a dogma, capable of demolishing the dogma of the varnasrama Dharma, which is not merely a religious ides. It encompasses every aspect of life and politics is its main favourite. Therefore the greatest danger to the *Varnasrama Dharma* comes from politics and Ambedkarism has itself taken birth in politics. It is here that the thinking of AS has some relevance. *Varnasrama Dharma* represents the true gods of the said *Dharma*.

Ambedkarism represents the *Asuras* of the Hindu Mythology. The gods have never been able to annihilate the *Asuras* permanently. Rather, the latter have been engaging their permanent attention just as it is being reflected in the T V serials heavily burdened by the Hindu mythological scenes ever since the beginning of the eighties of the last century.

Need for Steadily Re-writing Ambedkarism

If the believers in Ambedkarism commit the mistake of treating Ambedkar as having written the final word, it can be erased by the efforts of men like AS. But, if they steadily continue enriching and developing Ambedkarism in their own way, even hundreds of Shouries would not be able to cause a single dent in the body structure of Ambedkarism.

According to this author, the concerned classes can draw some lessons only from the communistic philosophy with certain important modifications, chief among them being not to follow the violent methods thereof. CGPI has said:

> *The historical destiny of the working class is to end this period of pre-history, this history of fate, dogmas and things and phenomena without causes. It is the destiny of ushering in history - a conscious, material, human history - which is the very act of the revolutionary class in creating the new society.*

Any party engaged in the welfare of the workers in India must not ignore the historical, mythological and religious factors. And, it must confine the definition of the workers so as to include the traditional Sudras, the Dalits etc. and the minorities and then investigate into the causes of their backwardness etc. Only the correct diagnosis can lead to correct cure. Even correct preventive measures cannot be taken up if the diagnosis is wrong. The method of the fundamentalists is to avoid correct analysis of the problems so that they remain beyond solution. They also dismiss the problems being the outcome of the sins of the actions committed by the persons concerned in their past births. Consequently, no living person can be held responsible for the ills caused by themselves for others.

Part IX
Dr. B.R. Ambedkar : Man of Millennium for Social Justice

29

Nation's Appreciation for Ambedkar

The real history is written not by the contemporaries of those who have ruled the roost. But it is done by the unconcerned future generations after assessing the pros and cons of the personalities, who had remained diametrically opposed to each other during their lifetime. The examples of Dr. Ambedkar and Netaji Subhash Chandra Bose are outstanding ones in this behalf. Another outstanding example is provided by Loknayak Jai Prakash Narayan, who had been imprisoned in his lifetime for opposing the Emergency imposed by Mrs. Indira Gandhi as Prime Minister in 1975. He had been similarly conferred the same highest honour in the last week of 1998, by others who have over-ruled the Narayan's assessment by Mrs. Indira Gandhi.

The nation as a whole, having an overwhelming majority of liberal Hindus has been rejoicing in raising befitting memorials to perpetuate the fond memory of Dr. Ambedkar. But Mr. 'S' and some other egg-headed individuals out of the narrow-minded Caste Hindus, the fundamentalists, have found it hard to stand the greatness of Dr. Ambedkar, on account of some deep-rooted jealousy and personal prejudices. Apparently, the recognition of Dr. Ambedkar, who belonged to the most deprived, underprivileged and exploited sections of the Indian population, had been found by more conservative leaders of Caste Hindus and the traditional exploiters of the deprived classes, impossible to placate. This is why they seem to have chosen certain hirelings to unsuccessfully demolish the greatness of Dr. Ambedkar?

Publication of Ambedkar's Complete Works Means Appreciation by Whole Nation

The writings and speeches of Dr. Ambedkar have been published by the Government of the same party, which claims the credit of winning the freedom for the country. The same party was the one of Mahatma Gandhi, who had been regularly opposed by Dr. Ambedkar, during the currency of the said fight for freedom. Moreover Dr. Ambedkar had thoroughly exposed the Hindu religion and its 'true Gods', who were the gods in whom the Mahatma had ardently believed. As such, the differences between Mahatma Gandhi and DR. Ambedkar concerned the very fundamentals of religion, of faith and of the real objectives of fight for freedom of the nation.

Dr. Ambedkar had proved with the help of the authority of the Hindu scriptures themselves that Hindu gods discriminated between men and men. Mr. 'S' has come out as a champion of the Mahatma and the Hindu religion, and has come out with a hypothesis that Dr. Ambedkar was a false God. When compared with those gods and their followers, Dr Ambedkar being their opponent would not like to be accepted as a true God. If his opponents also do not consider him to be like their own gods, nobody should take exception to their said behaviour. To that extent the thesis of Mr. 'S', suffers from an apparent disability since any two persons differing from each other on the very fundamentals cannot be expected by any sane person to co-operate with each other, in relation to their respective pursuits, which are bound to be opposed to each other's pursuits.

In absolute sense, however, Dr. Ambedkar has proved himself to be far superior to gods who discriminate between man and man. Unlike such gods, Ambedkar had the courage and conviction of standing against every kind of organised injustice, exploitation, suppression and oppression, of the masses. Such tyrannies had been sold through the ages with the help of the imaginative examples of the said "true gods". In the light of this, Dr. Ambedkar himself would not like to stand in the queue of the said "true gods" and he himself would not have any objection in being dubbed as a false God in their comparison.

If Ambedkar's Recognition Surpasses that of Others?

The grouse of Mr. 'S' is the fact that the importance and the recognition of Dr. Ambedkar has surpassed even that of Mahatma Gandhi. He has credited Mahatma Gandhi to win the freedom to India.

The Mahatma is believed to have provided the unquestioned leadership to the Indian National Congress, which through a stroke of historical accident, has similarly got away with the entire credit for winning the freedom of India, as a party, 'fighting' for such freedom.

But by now the assumptions have been repeatedly questioned during the past 60 years of independence. The most prominent examples of such questioning can be provided by the fact that the very opponents of Mahatma Gandhi, like Dr. Ambedkar himself and Netaji Subhash Chandra Bose have already been conferred with the highest honours to which the best of the citizens of India can aspire for. The fact that those honours have been conferred on them posthumously speaks volumes so far as the proper history of appreciation of the actual role of the said individuals is concerned.

Contemporary Relevance

Shourie had probably thought of hastening the process of defeat of ultimate fundamentalism by trying to make Dr. Ambedkar appear totally irrelevant to the present times. But, he had forgotten that the truth must prevail in the end and that the truth is not the social division of the society preached by varnasrama, to which Mahatma Gandhi had remained wedded throughout his life. Such sastras, everyone knows, prescribed and preached the denials of human rights to vast masses of the nation. Shourie had forgotten that the truth consists in conferring the precious human rights on all the citizens and allowing equal opportunities to all in the matter of developing their careers and adopting any professions in their discretion, depending on their capabilities, choice and aptitudes.

Hindu Sastras and Denial of Rights to Masses

By declaring his adherence to the Hindu Sastras, Mahatma Gandhi had been directly working for denial of such rights to the entire masses. On the other hand, by repudiating the same sastras, Dr. Ambedkar had been trying to establish a just rule of law, which conferred equal rights on all the citizens irrespective of caste or creed. Through the Constitution, Dr. Ambedkar succeeded and Mahatma Gandhi failed.

By writing the book in question, Shourie has raised the important question of relevance of both Mahatma Gandhi and Dr. Ambedkar and their philosophies in the minds of all the citizens of India. Nobody need be criticised on that count, because such questions are in fact in the larger public interest. **But what is painful is the fact that such questions are answered, by the vested interests by twisting and misrepresenting the relevant facts. It is also unfortunate that a great man is wrongly compared with the measuring rod of a contemporary opponent, Mahatma Gandhi by investing the latter with excessive sense of nationalism, highlighted out of proportion**. More so, it has been done by assuming the latter as an infallible person, in spite of the fact that the said other person had represented throughout the organised exploitation of the people to which the former, his adversary, Dr. Ambedkar, belonged.

Gandhi and Ambedkar Represented Opposing Interests

The fact of the matter is that basically, the two stalwarts, so far as their politics was concerned, represented the mutually opposed interests of different sections of the Hindu population. Mahatma Gandhi represented the interests of the caste Hindus, who had been traditionally engaged in an organised game of exploitation of the masses, called as Sudras and the Untouchables. On the other hand, Dr. Ambedkar had devoted his life and entire energy to the matter of securing human rights to the most unfortunate sections of Indian population whereas Mahatma Gandhi stood for status quo and the former stood for social change and the upliftment of the entire masses.

Their meeting point was in the fact that both the groups represented by the two great personalities were the common slaves of the British. Their differences were based on the fact that the Untouchables were the slaves of the slaves, namely, the Caste Hindus. The slaves having the control over the body and spirit of other slaves, wanted freedom from the British, but were keenly interested in maintaining their own mastery over their slaves.

The two great personalities, in pursuit of their respective and mutually contradictory goals, had perforce to act in the same political field, some time strategically helping each other in overall national interest and some time opposing each other when the things pertained to the internal matters of Hindu social organisation. Any one, who had been engaged in the fight for freedom and against the prevalence of slavery of one kind, ought not to have legitimately supported the slavery of one particular set of population.

On Question of Compulsions

But, Mahatma Gandhi, on account of his being an orthodox Hindu, had no option but to play a strange tune, which was intended to sound different, to different parties to the fight for freedom. It was also intended to sound different to the British rulers, to the Caste Hindus and to the most deprived and oppressed sections of Indian population, the Untouchables.

Dr. Ambedkar had no such compulsions. His goal was simple. Since, he was interested in the freedom of the last individual, he could not be said to be interested in the slavery of even his opponents. But the Congress, a class that had been established by the British in order to help their own continuance in the country as masters, had set the role for Gandhi. The Congress and, therefore, Mahatma Gandhi could never shed the evil consequences of this background.

Congress was Bargaining Body, Not Fighting One

The Congress was established as a bargaining body, and it continued as such up to the end. If it had changed that stance, it could never have succeeded in being the beneficiary of the fact of transfer of power.

The Congress had never been a fighting body. Any one who took up a fighting stance found himself to be eased out of the Congress. The most glaring example in this behalf is that of Netaji Subhash Chandra Bose. In order to keep the Congress as a body of non-fighters, The Congresss and Maahtmna Gandhi never allowed the Kshatriya Castes to assume the leadership of the Congress. This endeavour of the Congress was very much to the liking of the British Government, since the lattter ahd earmraked the Kshatriyas for providing the recruits for the armed forces and the police.

Dr. Ambedkar had learnt the art of bargaining from the Congress and Mahatma Gandhi himself. Therefore, he had been able to secure a berth on the bargaining table, known as the Round Table Conferences. Bargain is after all a bargain, and the mutually warring parties had to be set for gaining as much as possible, for the sections respectively represented by each.

The givers in this case were the British rulers, and those interested in the receipts were the traditional elements of Indian population, namely, the Caste Hindus, Muslims, the Sikhs, Christians and Anglo-Indians. The Depressed Classes were made to join as independent elements in this behalf by able advoccy of cause of theirs by Dr. Ambedkar, much to the disssatisfaction of the Caste Hindus and their sole political leader, the Mahatma. Each element tried to get as much as possible. But traditional beneficiaries, frowned upon the efforts and success of Dr. Ambedkar and continue to frown upon him even after 60 years of India becoming free.

Distribution of Gains

Since Mahatma Gandhi represented the biggest chunk of Indian population, he got away with the largest share. Next in importance was Jinnah, who got away with Pakistan. Dr. Ambedkar had to be content with some reservations for his people in the legislatures and services etc. Mahatma Gandhi wanted the entire gains for himself and his own group. Since, his political adversaries foiled his attempts; he had every reason to feel bad about the whole game of transfer of power.

Unlike the Muslims, Dr. Ambedkar had not bargained for separate state for the Untouchables. Therefore, he had no option but to remain in India as a constant sore in the hearts of those, who wanted every thing for themselves, at the cost of the untouchables and other deprived castes and groups. The followers of the Mahatma and his Congress had no option but to lament over the loss they had sustained in the game of power. And they could not feel happy at losing whatever they had lost. They, of course, had no option but to be a consenting party to such a loss.

Gandhi's Greatness was not as Emancipator of Masses

In the light of the above presentation, the greatness of the Mahatma was not as an emancipator of the exploited sections of Indian society. It lay, if at all, in the field of politics and in the matter of means to seek ouster of the erstwhile British rulers. But that point continues to be debatable.

Still, it can be said that Mr. 'S' has done a commendable job for bringing some of the quotable quotes of Dr. Ambedkar all at one place. They are the quotes, which should be at the tip of the tongues of all those interested in a right type of social revolution. It cannot be denied that the revolution wished by Dr. Ambedkar is still far off and those interested therein will ever be in need of guidance from Dr. Ambedkar. The important quotations used by Mr. 'S' for the purpose of vilifying Dr. Ambedkar need to be reproduced, not only for the guidance of those interested but also as an aid to provide help in presenting the rebuttal to the misadventure of Mr. 'S' attempted in his book under reference. The same points will help in the comparative analysis of Mahatma Gandhi, who has been, unfortunately for Mr. 'S', used as the measuring rod for measuring the size of Dr. Ambedkar, as already pointed out.

30

Ambedkar in Eyes of Contemporary Celebrities

A book edited by B.K. Ahluwalia and Shashi Ahluwalia, titled *B.R. Ambedkar and Human Rights*, which had been published by Vivek Publishing Company, Delhi in1981. It contains independent chapters written by certain celebrities of India. For our purpose, it will be profitable to have a cursory look at certain extracts from some of the said chapters. These extracts have been given the titles after those of the concerned chapters for better facility of reaching straight away to the kernel of the considered opinions about the great man, Dr. Ambedkar.

Objective Assessment by Contemporaries and Others

Most of these opinions had been expressed at a time when the Hindu fundamentalists had not yet started feeling jealous of the upcoming Dalits and at the latter's growing sense of identity. The Dalits had been admirers of Dr. Ambedkar all right but he had not yet been deified by anyone. The Dalits and other weaker sections had acknowledged him a great source of inspiration but he had yet to be accepted as the Messiah of the Dalits.

The opinions expressed by the concerned celebrities were therefore not designed to win the favour of Dalits in any particular elections. They were in the nature of spontaneous expressions of certain human beings placed in high positions for another human being. As such, the opinions cannot be said to have been tainted by any kind of prejudice either for or against Dr. Ambedkar. Therefore, they can reasonably help clear the misunderstandings about him, deliberately created by Arun Shourie through his book in question.

Before taking a note of the assessment of Ambedkar by the Indian luminaries in various fields who had themselves played a special role in building modern India, it will be important to bear in mind the significant events of the life of Ambedkar, since they would form an important background for appreciating the select opinions about Babasaheb Dr. B R Ambedkar.

A True Patriot

Dr. S. Radhakrishnan, who was the Philosopher-President of India and an undisputed authority and exponent of Hinduism, and who had highlighted the positive side of Hinduism, had described Dr. Ambedkar as a true patriot. In his opinion Dr. Ambedkar had left a permanent impression both on our Constitution and on social life. He had said :

> *I have seen him at work, hammering out our Constitution and answering all sorts of problems.*
>
> *He was a patriot in the fullest sense of the term. He it was who said, "So long as we have these differences of Hindu, Muslim and others, or Sindhi, Madrasi, etc., we can never develop our nationality."*
>
> *He was much in revolt against social practices, humiliations to which large number of our people were subjected in the name of sastras, scriptures, etc.*
>
> *He revolted against all these. He was not so much of a reformer as a revolutionary was. He tried to overthrow the system of things and tried to establish a new order of society, a new social order, so to say:*

A Dedicated Life

This is what another President of India, V. V. Giri had said:

> *"The life history of Dr. Ambedkar epitomised the relentless struggle of down trodden community in our country against social ostracism and economic oppression. By his personal example, he showed how, by a total faith in self-reliance and indomitable courage and perseverance, one could raise himself to a life of purposive greatness and be a constant source of inspiration to his fellow men." "It has been my privilege to have known the late Dr. Ambedkar for more than four decades. From the beginning, I was deeply struck by his single-minded devotion to the cause of bringing up the under privileged and down trodden sections of*

the society and instilling in them a new hope for a better deal", maintained V.V. Giri.-

V.V. Giri's following remarks, if read in reply to the views of Mahatma Gandhi about the caste system, Varna-Vyavastha, and social justice, would be sufficient to indict Mr. 'S:

> *Dr. Ambedkar represented a dedicated spirit, an uncompromising faith in the justice of the cause he fought for. Whether one agreed with or not in his approach to problems or in his method of dealing with them, his power of appeal, his capacity for clear expression and the sincerity with which he put across his point of view always commanded respect and attention. The life of Dr. Ambedkar is a constant reminder to us how much we owe to society to rid it of its evils born of prejudice and customs, which had no sanction either of morality or of decent conduct. Social equality is not a creed for propagation; it has to be as fact of life.*

These observations of V V Giri would definitely tend to place Mahatma Gandhi in poorer light, since the latter being unmindful of the aspects of morality and decency, had emphasised the faith in the Hindu scriptures, which had deliberately sanctioned many of the evils in Hindu society, most of which issued from the philosophy of discrimination against man by man and that of exploitation of man by man.

What is important to note here is the fact that, unlike Gandhiji, V. V. Giri did not think it proper to talk of the sanction of Hindu scriptures, but he decided to refer to the sanction of morality and decent conduct. Mahatma Gandhi also lost to Dr. Ambedkar so far as the power of appeal, capacity for clear expression and sincerity were concerned. Similarly, the following words of V.V. Giri would place the Mahatma in the category of biggest sinners, his declared concern for the Untouchables, on account of untouchability, notwithstanding:

> *If Untouchability, or for that matter any disability, based on caste, creed, etc. is being practised in any part of our country by any one, the perpetrators of such practices should be branded the biggest enemy of society and dealt with as such. While Dr. Ambedkar will be remembered in history for his many-splendoured personality and his many sided contributions, as a jurist and Constitution-maker, as thinker, writer and debater, as great political organiser and a charismatic leader, he will be remembered most of all as great and compassionate social rebel, a militant reformer and a liberator of the down-trodden masses of the subcontinent.*

He was one of the brilliant intellectuals not only of Maharashtra but also of India and the world.

The Rebel

As early as 1930 Ambedkar had said, "to say that this country is divided by castes and creeds, and that it cannot be one united self-governing community unless adequate safe guards for protection of minorities are made a part of the Constitution, is a position to which there can be no objection. But the minorities must bear in mind that although we are today driven by sect and atomised by caste, our ideal is united India. That being so, it follows that every minority in formulating the safeguards it needs, must take care that they will not be incompatible with the realisation of that ideal".

K. R. Narayanan had expressed his opinion that "Ambedkar, Gandhi and Nehru—all had believed that India's social and economic problems, including those of the Scheduled Castes, could be solved through peaceful and democratic means. While none can deny the truth of this statement, Narayanan had erred in holding the view that "Gandhiji had launched a massive social movement to bring about reform through moral conversion". A close analytical examination of the views of Gandhiji leaves nobody in doubt that he was not at all serious in solving the problems of the Untouchables and the Sudras or the common masses. This much goes to his credit, however, that "he made caste Hindus ashamed of Untouchability and of the social and economic exploitation of the Harijans. While, this movement did not attack the root causes or solve the problems, it created a new temper and climate of social opinion which helped in the alleviation of social ills and paved the way for important legislations and executive actions by the Government."

The Visionary

Dr. Ambedkar was a social reformer. He stoically suffered the humiliation of his birth and was determined to redeem the Scheduled Castes by the sacrifice of his life. Poverty, misrepresentation, jealousy, scandals and even threats of violence had not deterred him from his chosen path. His whole life was a saga of sacrifice for the cause of the downtrodden. This is how K. Subbarao thought about Dr. Ambedkar. K. Subbarao had paid further glowing tributes to Dr. Ambedkar in the following words:

During his long career, he [Dr. Ambedkar] stood for the independence of the country. While he stood like a rock in the cause of the backward communities, he did not fall a prey to blandishments of power or manoeuvres of the enemies of the country.

He was a great patriot who fought for the Scheduled Castes without sacrificing the wider interests of the nation. Dr. Ambedkar's undoubted talents had not been fully utilised by the nation. The nation was poorer for this default. A nation which neglects brilliance and encourages mediocrity, discourages intellectual honesty and courage of conviction but favours courtiers and yesmen, is bound to go down. What a difference it would have made if a few men of his calibre had been in charge of the constructive activities of our country!

Every Hindu must learn a lesson from the life of Dr. Ambedkar. The blackest spot in Hindu religion is the action of the doctrine of Untouchability. It has become a hereditary sin of every Hindu. It is not enough that the Constitution has abolished it or the law has prohibited it. Every Hindu should redeem his sin by going all out to eradicate this stigma from Hinduism."

Dr. Ambedkar's "disillusionment with Hinduism made him a convert to Buddhism. What Hinduism had lost, Buddhism had gained, for he was one of those ardent reformers who tried his best to exorcise Hinduism of its abominations such as Untouchability etc." Believed K. Subbarao. His own well-considered conclusion was: Untouchability will disappear with the abolition of caste, for caste is the root cause of Untouchability.

The Democrat

"Ambedkar was a great humanist. His humanism was, to begin with, a sharp reaction to the inhumanity of man to man, of class to class in a society fissured by inequality of status and exploitation of the weak and the underprivileged. Ambedkar spared no pains to tell his countrymen that they must not be misled by the demand for the priority and primacy of the political democracy if that did not mean a simultaneous process of tearing up the roots of an archaic, non-egalitarian society, of establishing, positively speaking, a base of economics and social democracy, without which political democracy becomes an engine of oppression," said Dr. B. N. Ganguli. He had further observed as under:

> *Where social conscience is dead, there is a peculiar kind of indifference to social evils like Untouchability and the inhumanity of caste prejudices and disabilities. This indifference, according to Ambedkar, is the greatest inhumanity of which man is capable, as the result of which social legislation becomes a dead letter. Any individual's right implies an obligation on his part to respect the similar right of others. As Ambedkar used to argue, there can be, therefore, no democracy in a society in which there are only privileges for some and disability for vast majority of others and no equal rights and obligations for all.*

The Critic

A big, brusque fellow with a most belligerent manner, he delighted me by his utter difference from any other Hindu of my acquaintance. It is a form of genius to be so individual, and it is not much use explaining it by Untouchability. I have known a fir number of other untouchables, but nobody at all like Ambedkar. He enjoyed attacking me for what he considered my undue affection for India. These were the remarks of Vincent Sheen, about Dr. Ambedkar. Sheen had the following to say about the educational qualifications of Dr. Ambedkar:

> *"He was prodigiously educated. He had degrees from Columbia University and the University of London, had studied at Sorbonne and was a barrister of Grey's Inn. His degrees were MA, Ph.D., D.Sc. and LL. D. Degrees do not mean so much, perhaps, but in the torrential flood of his talk there came up great chunks and whirling avataras of learning."*

He continued, but Ambedkar is no more and critics of his calibre, so brilliant and merciless, are not to be found in public life today. Few politicians can possibly harp on the evils of the caste system as he did, because the sobre fact is that an overwhelming proportion of them belongs to higher castes. Many are indeed Brahmins...If the caste system is the chief hindrance to progress, as Ambedkar believed, it badly needs another inveterate enemy of low castes or untouchable origin who can fight it with all the unquenchable bitterness of personal experience. According to him, Dr. Ambedkar could never see any resemblance or connection between Gandhi and Buddha, at least in prolonged conversations.

The Dreamer

Madhu Dandvate in his Article titled *The Dreamer* had observed that Dr. B. R. Ambedkar was undoubtedly one of the chief architects of

India's democratic Constitution. But more than that he was a social rebel who raised the banner of revolt against the iniquitous caste ridden society. As a rationalist, he never encouraged any personality cult. On the other hand, he demolished the clay-feeted idols that were built on the unstable foundations of blind worship and superstition. Dandavate had further said about the impact of the work of Dr. Ambedkar on the Untouchables that:

> *Dr. Ambedkar roused their frozen conscience and brought new consciousness among them. He told them to forget all about the so-called sins of their ancestors and strongly pleaded with them not to wait for their fictitious rebirth or the amelioration of their sufferings. He urged them that their social liberation must be ensured in this very life and that too as their legitimate right as free citizens.*

Dandavate had also taken note of those who were irked by the bitterness of Dr. Ambedkar about certain issues and ideas. He had said that "those who complained against the bitterness exuberated by Dr. Ambedkar's Writings and Speeches hardly realise what humiliations Dr. Ambedkar had to experience in his own life only because he happened to belong to the Scheduled Caste.

Arun Shourie has tried to lend great force to Dr. Ambedkar's role as the member of the Viceroy's Executive Council. But look at the fate of the worth of Dr. Ambedkar before the Hindu orthodoxy [which had throughout been championed by the Mahatma] and the lack of effectiveness of Dr. Ambedkar even in the presence of the Viceroy himself:

> The Climax of humiliation came when Dr. Ambedkar was a member of the Viceroy's Executive Council in the pre-Independence days. At the request of the Viceroy and his wife, Dr. Ambedkar went to see the ancient architecture of a prominent temple in Eastern India. As Dr. Ambedkar put his foot on the very first step of the temple, the priest of the Hindu temple came down running and allowed the Viceroy and his wife, coming from thousands of miles beyond the seas, to enter the temple, but prevented entry to Dr. Ambedkar on the plea that he was an untouchable. If this was the humiliation suffered by a Member of the Viceroy's Executive Council. One could only imagine as to what must have been the plight of ordinary members of the Scheduled caste community at the lowest village level.

Dr. Ambedkar's greatest contribution to our social and political life has been that he made the socially-oppressed sections like the Scheduled Castes to challenge the social orthodoxy, with the piercing question which Abraham Lincoln had asked, "It might be in your interest to be our masters, but how is it in our interest to be your slaves?" To the extent this question finds its echoes in the remotest corners of India with the requisite follow-up action, Dr. Ambedkar's life-long dream of ensuring social liberation of the oppressed and the downtrodden will be translated into reality.

The Logician

It goes to the credit of the Congress leadership that, in the moment of liberation, Dr. Ambedkar could be harnessed to steer the framing of the Constitution. The generous offer found a responsive chord in Dr. Ambedkar. He saw in it his own redemption. From his redemption he hoped for the redemption of the depressed classes. He forgot his differences with the Congress, soared above his personal prejudices, played a major role in shaping free India's Constitution. He was elected as the chairman of the Steering Committee. He Logically negated the criticism, made by some members of the Constituent Assembly, that since the Assembly was not elected on adult suffrage, it could not be considered to be representative body. In his rebuttal, Ambedkar pointed out: "If the representative of the 13 States, assembled in a conference in Philadelphia could pass a constitution and say that what they did was in the name of the people, on their authority, basing it on their sovereignty, I personally myself do understand unless the man was an absolute pedant, that a body of people, 292 in number, representing this vast continent in their representative capacity, could not say that they are acting in the name of the country". This is what R. K. Murthi had felt about Dr. Ambedkar. He further remarked that:

> *The time found the man. The framing of the Constitution demanded the services of a man who could bring to his cause the full measure of logic without ambiguity. Occasionally, he came up with pithy statements, which revealed the flash of the genius. "In no country," "does the government of the day represent the whole body of people. Every where it represents only a majority."*

Other statements which indicate his word power include : "Men do not become a society in physical proximity any more than a man ceases to be a member of his society by living so many miles away from other men." and "Mahatmas have come and Mahatmas have gone, but the untouchables have remained untouchables."

31

Ambedkar in Hindu Mythological Context

Ambedkar's study abroad and experience had made it evident to him that there could not be any problem without a solution. His own ill-treatment in India at the hands of the Hindus and others that had come to be influenced by them had also taught him the lesson that the Upper Caste people were mainly led by their selfish objectives. Such selfishness, according to him, had left much to be desired in the background of considerations of morality or ethics, either at social or individual level. He had been greatly influenced by Christian philosophy and practices. He had come to know that the Christian behavior and practices were different from those of Hindus simply because the teachings of Christianity were different and more humane.

Accordingly, he decided to study the Hindu scheme of things with the help of Hindu scriptures. Hindu social organisation, is in fact *varna vyavastha* that had taken its roots from *Manu-Smriti.* He found that all the social, economic, religious and political problems of the Depressed Classes, as he liked to refer to the then untouchables, the *asprisyas*, *baahyas* or *panchamas* of the Hindu scriptures, arose from the caste and that the problem could be remedied if the root cause was removed. It was under these circumstances that he wrote *Annihilation of Caste.*

Arbitrariness of Caste Rules

That the caste rules were arbitrary was confirmed by the voluntary intervention of Mahatma Gandhi, who wrote some articles criticising Dr. Ambedkar and in defence of caste. Dr. Ambedkar accordingly wrote rejoinders to those articles and sent them to the Mahatma with a request that they (the rejoinders) might also be published in his paper. The Mahatma obliged him and his act of that obligation sent the name of Dr. Ambedkar in all those nooks and corners of India, where the organs of the Mahatma, namely, *Harijan* and *Young India*, went. He felt that he had never come across more unjust system than the Hindu caste system, which was being defended even by the Mahatmas and *Swamies.*

Caste Made to Suffer Both Caste Hindus and Untochables

His further study made it evident to him that not only the so-called untouchables suffered under the Hindu Scheme of things but also every caste had been bearing the brunt of the adverse effects of the system, which was simply oppressive and patently exploitative. The more deeply he went into the scriptures, more intrigued he became. He particularly found that there had been a long drawn cold war that had been going between Brahmins and Kshatriyas, for ages, which had got converted into hot wars.

Hindu Defensive Measures Suffer Superstition

Not only that he came across quite a few defensive measures that had been taken by the Brahmins, which were basically meant to spread superstition and blind faith. He also found that though the Vedas were being projected by the traditionalists as eternal and *swatah pramaana*, which term implied that the V*edic* statements need not be put to the test of logic, yet they were being disregarded by other scriptures like the Gita and in practice by the Brahmins themselves. He discovered many unsolved riddles, which had never been highlighted by anyone in history. In due course of time, he published a book titled *Riddles in Hinduism.*

Religious Terms Mere Symbols

Dr. Ambedkar found that most of the religious terms were mere symbols, which concealed hidden meanings that could be taken advantage of only by one who was well-versed in the scriptures. But then he discovered that the scriptures could be approached in any manner only by the Brahmins and others could be told only about their duties, since there was no concept of rights in the Hindu scheme of things.

Ambedkar found that the fight between *Brahmanas* and non-*Brahmanas*, or between *Suras* and *Asuras* or between gods and demons, is perennial, that there is no end to war, that it has to continue eternally. It was disclosed that gods are comparable to the *Brahmanas*, who have become immortal by snatching the *amrita* [ambrosia], from the *Asuras*, the non-Gods, or non-*Brahmanas* and that mythological Sukracharya, the preceptor of the *Asuras*, the non-gods or the non-*Brahmanas*, restores the dead Non-*Brahmanas* or non-Gods to life.

Analogy of Sukracharyas

Dr. Ambdkar rose to be the modern Sukracharya, who brought the non-Gods or Asuras, who stood condemned as demons and rakshasa, and enabled the latter to snatch the nectar of political power from the gods, who stood represented by the *Brahmanas*, in the shape of Bhu-Suras, or gods-on-earth. The first instalment of the political nectar came to the Dalits in a diluted form, in the shape of Poona Pact in 1932. Thus, he had brought the dead Dalits, the dead *Sudras* and the dead women to life. In the Constitution of India, he had got incorporated certain provisions aimed at the development of the OBCs (Other Backward Classes), who had been condemned in Hindu Scriptures as Sudras, devoid of any kind of rights like the Dalits, with the difference that the former were regarded as touchables.

Subsequently, Mandal Commission recommendations extended the principle of reservations in the legislatures and services etc. to the OBCs, on the pattern of Dalits. In an effort to take political advantage of the said provisions and the recommendations of Mandal Commission, the then Prime Minister, V P Singh, took another *avatara* (re-incarnation) of Sukracharya and announced 27 per cent reservation for the OBCs around 1990. The women also had been equated by the Scriptures with the Sudras. By now, they also have been granted extensive reservations.

Loss of Power and Samudra Manthana

According to Hindu mythology, whenever the dead people come to life, they snatch the heaven from the living people, the gods, the *Suras* as per the *Brahmanical* philosophy. Once the power slips out of their hands, the gods go to *Brahma* (their ideological guru) for help, then they go to *Vishnu* (the top strategist), their own creation, along with *Brahma* with a petition that their lost heaven may be got restored to them. Consequently, Vishnu advises them to "befriend" their *Asura* masters, and produce *amrita* or the political power, after churning the ocean (of public mind).

The ocean can be churned always with the help of the opposition or the oppressed people themselves who are always condmend as *Asuras*, the leader of the masses. When *amrita* is produced, or in modern democratic terminology, elections are over, Vishnu "dishonestly" engages the *Asuras* in merry-making, so that the gods get away with and consume the *amrita*. Bhajan Lal of Haryana provided the most interesting example of the type, quite a few years ago. At that time, he had converted majority of members of Haryana Legislative Assembly that was with Devilal, into one in his own favour, by organising whole sale defection of 45 MLAs in his own favour. Consequently, he himself became Chief Minister or immortal and continued to enjoy that enviable position for many years, with the blessing of the then Prime Minister, Mrs. Indira Gandhi, and through the agency of the then Governor of Haryana, G D Tapase.

Analogy of Rahu

Hindu mythology has a character known as Rahu, an *asura*, who is able to sneak into the queue of the gods, or among the leaders of a crafty minority, and become immortal. He is ultimately noticed and cut into two. Since he had become immortal, both the pieces remained alive. The original demon is *Raahu* and the other is *Ketu.* He alone is enough to occasionally frighten the leaders of gods, the Sun and the Moon. And all the gods cannot do just anything to him. This process has been going on and it will continue to go on like this forever.

Raahu always remains present among the gods. Sometimes he emerges as Jagjiwan Rams, sometimes as Kamrajes, sometimes he emerges as B. P. Mauryas, sometimes as Kanshi Rams or Ms. Mayawatis. And, at times he repeats performance in the shape of Ram Bilas Paswans. Since his original appearance, many have ruled over the *Indraloka* or the sphere of Indra, the king of gods or Suras or Brahmanas. Although *Indraloka* is headed by Indra yet Rahu continues to be a necessary adjunct to the former's brother, Surya, and, therefore, that of the ever-changing *Indras*.

***Indralok* Versus New Delhi**

Today, *Indralok* can be compared with New Delhi, which becomes out of bound for those who go out of power. More than anyone else, the *Brahmanas* are always in the know of these realities. Just like the Biblical Adam and Eve, the Hindu *Brahmanas* have tasted the fruit of true knowledge. Therefore, it is they who remain ever conscious of having been thrown on earth from heaven. And, it is they who feel the pangs of punishment. Others may enjoy the bliss of ignorance, but the crafty leaders have invariably to suffer the hell of their knowledge.

But Brahminism, on account of being a parasite of the Hindu masses, has nothing but leisure to lament over its own misdeeds and the possible adverse consequences. It has been a perpetual source of 'inspiration' for imagining the ways to take adequate protective measures for itself.

Analogy of Hiranyaaksha and Prahlad

The Brahminism also treats all *Loknayakas* and *Ambedkars* as mythological *Hiranyaakshas*. The latter can, of course, be killed, but by going to the Netherlands, *Paataala* or modern hells like J. J. colonies. Stooping to animal level can also kill them. Hiranyaaksha can be killed by his enemies masquerading as his son, Prahlaad.

Finding no way out to defeat a *Hrinyaaksha* with its own might, the Brahminism has devised the method of creating a Prahlaada, an anti-body of Hiranyaaksha, in the form of the 'offspring' of Hrinyaaksha, who is secretly trained to be the worshipper of its own God, Vishnu. On being adopted by the gods on earth and on being properly trained in the art of their own secret guerrilla warfare, with the help of Prahlaada, it makes an entry in the palace of Hrinyaaksha, and has him killed through someone wearing the mask of lion, who is then named Narasimha, man in the guise of lion or animal, and a re-incarnation of Lord Vishnu.

Loknayakas and Ambedkars Leave No Political Heirs

It is through such like machinations that the Loknayakas and Ambedkars do not leave their heirs, who may be capable of finishing their unfinished work or of following the footsteps of their saviours. Today, Prakash Ambedkar may be compared with Prahlaada, or the devotee of the modern day Vishnu in the form of Atal Behari Vajpayee. Therefore, when the Caste Hindus attacked Dr. B R Ambedkar, at a time, when I K Gujral was the Prime Minister, the grandson of Dr. B R Ambedkar does not feel too hurt to show equal reaction in any conceivable sense.

The same example can be applied to the time when VP Singh was politically killed through a childlike and helpless Chandra Shekhar, adopted by Rajiv Gandhi on behalf of the *Bhu-suras*. The gods had ultimately come to be restored to their lost glory through the agency of

Prahlaada, working through Chandra Shekhar. The modern *Bhu-suras*, or *Brahmin-Bania* combine, came to be restored to their heaven of political power [lost by them as Congressmen], under a new *avataara*, BJP, under a new banner of Lotus, in a new garb dyed in saffron, under a new *avatara*, Atal Behari Vajpayee.

Non-Brahmin Ganesha Takes Precedence Over Gods

Ganesha also suffers from an official disability on account of his unnatural birth. Although he enjoys precedence over all other deities, in the matter of worship, yet he is always reminded of being without a [known] father by being addressed as *Vinayaka* [literally, without a father]. As per mythology, he is a non-Aryan, non-*Brahma*na, non-Kshatriya and also non-Vaisya. Another important fact to be taken note of here is that in order to placate the non-Aryans and in order to teach a lesson to the *Kshatriyas* indirectly, the *Brahmanas* relegated Kshatriya God, *Vishnu* to a lesser position since it was made incumbent to remember or invoke Lord Ganesha, a non-Brahmana, a non-Kshatriya, a non-Vaisya before worshipping any other God, as already pointed out.

Granting of such a big concession like Lord Ganesha by *Brahmanas* to the non-Aryans, the fore-fathers of the present day Dalits and *Sudras*, might feel intrigued. But in the face of the need for securing precious gains and for humiliating their one time chief adversaries, we need not be surprised over such an action. Rather, one important fact comes on the surface. The *Brahmanas* do not appear to be the ardent believers in the Almighty in the ordinary sense. They have been experimenting with the idea of God and have been using the said idea as a tradable and dispensable item. In this sense, the ancient *Brahmanas* were as pragmatic as the modern ones and quite free from dogma, when faced with the question of satisfying their specific selfish ends, in a pragmatic manner.

Vyasa : Dalit As *Vipravara* [Good *Brahmana*]

Interestingly, in the *Ramayana* even *Brahma*na Ravana is described as *Asura.* Kauravas and Pandavas, the parties to the Mahabharata war have a common ancestor in sage Vyasa. *Rishi* [sage] is a universally known epithet of the senior *Brahmanas.* Vyasa was born as a result of a unapproved and illegitimate sexual union of the *Rishi* Parashara with a *Nishada* [one of the present day Scheduled Castes] girl, Satyavati, who could be only an untouchable according to the rules of *Smritis*. And, still, Vyasa is described in all the *Puranas* as *Vipravara* or [literally, the best of the *Brahma*na].

Kauravas and Asuras

In the *Mahabharata*, again the Kauravas and their associates, [the other rulers siding with the Kauravas], are also described as *Asuras*. But their cousins, the Pandavas, are spared of such an ignominy, disgrace and scorn. The latter, are regarded not only as *Kshatriyas* but the middle Pandava, Arjuna, has been shown as the best friend of Vishnu Incarnate, Lord Krishna. A legitimate question can be raised about a fact which is not directly relevant to the present context. Therefore, let us only raise it here to be taken up for analysis later on, but which deservés to be kept at the back of our mind.

The mother of the elder three, Yudhishthira, Bhima and Arjuna, had also given birth to another son, who was the eldest of them all, whose name was Karna, in the same unusual manner, through the questionable contact with a god [cf. *Bhu-sura*, the god on earth], like the above said three. He was, however, never regarded as one of them. As such, Yudhishthira was arbitrarily considered as the eldest of the Pandavas, and as such entitled to the throne at every relevant stage.

Younger brother cannot deputise for him automatically, nor he can take major decisions like waging of a war, and yet in the *Gita*, the prime importance has been given to the middle (so-called) son of Pandu almost to the exclusion of "the king" Yuddhisthira, by Lord Krishna and also by the authors of the *Gita* and those of the Mahabharata Epic. Here the catch seems to lie in Arjuna's being a more pliable tool of Krishna.

The fact of Arjuna being the middle son might remind us of the middle path of the Buddha. Lord Buddha had adopted the middle of the road policy in demolishing the Vedic religion. Can it suggest the Hindu's imitating the same idea to beat the Buddhists back with their own stick, by directly adopting only the middle of the Pandavas to play the most crucial role in staging a comeback? The scholars might remember that *The Gita* is post Buddha philosophy.

Dissident *Brahmanas* and *Kshatriyas* as *Asuras*

If the *Brahmanas* and *Kshatriyas* can be considered as being deserving to be killed at the hands of other *Kshatriyas* in the scriptures, created by a particular group, how and why the killers should be considered as being the God-Incarnates? The only sensible conclusion can be that even the dissident *Brahmanas* and the dissident *Kshatriyas* could be dubbed as *Asuras* and, thus, declared fit to be, repeatedly massacred or slaughtered like animals by the establishment, constituted by certain particular sections of the same Varnas of *Brahmanas* and *Kshatriyas*, who happened to usurp power.

There can be another possibility. After a long drawn war between the *Brahmanas* and the *Kshatriyas* continuing over scores of generations which fact is proved by the *Puranas* themselves through the story of continued extermination of *Kshatriyas* by Parasurama, a *Brahmana*, who is strangely regarded as the 6th *avatara* of Lord Vishnu, there had to be a lasting truce between the warring parties at some stage or the other on the basis of agreed terms.

The present day Indian society unfortunately continues to be divided into various castes, which are, on the whole, the tiny fragments of different *Varnas,* and into different tribes, various religions and their sects and sub-sects. And yet, at present, the country is being governed on democratic principles, under the above-said Constitution, which guarantees equality, social justice and fraternity to all citizens and which also prohibits all kinds of prejudices based on caste, creed or social status.

If Hindu religious leaders can persuade themselves to face the facts which have evolved into present shape after centuries of trials and tribulations, the society can be speedily cured of all kinds of social strife as also the religious and political irritants. But unfortunately such leaders are patently desirous of creating in the society the maximum possible confusion and illusion so that they are in a position to take the country to the previous near primitive stage, when there was almost none to remind them of their duty towards the deprived sections of vast humanity in the Indian sub-continent, in the name of human considerations.

Lord Krishna and Untouchables

We shall note yet another example of the type already mentioned above. Lord Krishna, though generally accepted as Kshatriya, is particularly regarded as a Yadava. And, Yadava is a title monopolised by *Ahirs* or *Aabheeras*. These *Aabheeras* represent one of the foreign invading groups as per *Manu-smriti.*

But, whatever may be the origin of *Aabheeras*, Manusmriti is clear on the status of the *Aabheeras*. They are neither *Brahmanas*, nor

Kshatriyas, nor *Vaisyas*, nor the *Sudras*. They are one of the middle castes and, therefore, according to the *smritis*, they are to be placed below the *Sudras*.

The only known position lower than that of the *Sudras*, is that of the *Antyajas*, the erstwhile Untouchables or modern Scheduled Castes or Dalits. Interestingly, the bulk of the *Aabheeras* and *Yadavas*, are officially counted today among the Other Backward Classes, which is only the modern title of the *Sudras*. This means that analytically speaking, the *Yadavas* are Untouchables and officially speaking, they are the Other Backward Classes or the traditional *Sudras*.

In view of this, Lord Krishna deserves to be placed among the *Antyjas* or erstwhile Untouchables, according to the *Vedic Dharma*, whose legal basis is the *Manusmriti*, and for whose restoration, Lord Krishna had to visit this earth as a Vishnu Incarnate. What does this means? This means that the leadership of the crafty minority always trip to prop up someone from the majority in order to grind its own axe. But such role is reserved always for more pliable individuals from amongst those who are to be suppressed or who are to be used as tools to suppress the enemy among the crafty minority itself.

Brahmana Wasistha Versus Kshatriya Visvamitra

The Brahminism has devised another method of finishing one who happens to challenge them on their own terms, like Kshatriya Visvamitra had challenged Brahmin Wasishtha. Here we may again refer to the Washishtha-Visvamitra strife. According to the analysis of Hindu mythology, Kshatriya Visvamitra had humbled *Brahma*na Wasishtha by removing Kshatriya Rama from the latter's charge as family priest of the Ayodhya Kings. Then Visvamitra had made Wasishtha irrelevant in the matter of Rama's marriage with the 'adopted' daughter of Kshatriya Janaka, King of Mithila.

This Kshatriya Janaka had already shown *Brahmanas* their place, by making them sit as ordinary persons among the audience, while he was lecturing on *dharma*, as if he was a *Brahma*na preacher. Preaching is the traditional prerogative of the *Brahmanas*. Viswamitra had, in the meantime, trained Rama and his brother Lakshmana in the art of dealing with the *Brahmanas*.

BJP's Attempt to Snatch Ideal of Ram Rajya from Gandhi

Ram Rajya ideal was taken by the Mahatma and the BJP or its predecessors from the Ramayana Epic, which had incorporated all the basic teachings of The Hindu Scriptures. The orthodox Hindus had started organising themselves as Hindu Mahasabha. Even the Mahatma took pride in referring to himself as an orthodox Hindu or one as following the Sanatana Dharma, the orthodox wing of the Hindus. The Sabha had come into being basically to fight out the Muslims through a non-political platform. The Sabha had raised a body of Hindu militant volunteers, known as Rashtriya Svayam Sevak Sangh [RSS]. The members of both, the Sabha and the RSS, had been working as direct associates of the Congress, almost up to 1942. But their direct association was a certainty till 1934. Pandit Madan Mohan Malaviya, the President of the Hindu Mahasabha had been simultaneously the President of the Congress in or around 1919. He had also been nominated by Gandhi as the representative of all the Hindus, for the purpose of signing the Poona Pact, the other signatory being Dr. Ambedkar himself. This means that RSS and Congress had been sharing the same platform for a long period of 9 years between 1925 and 1934. The founder of the RSS, Hedgewar had been an active Congressman and associate of Mahatma Gandhi up to 1934.

Congress Endeavour To Exploit Ambedkar's Name

After that the Congress used Dr. Ambedkar's name only ceremoniously. After the fall of the Congress under Smt. Indira Gandhi, the other emerging political parties started wooing the Dalits by speaking in laudatory terms about Dr. Ambedkar. Thus, Dr. Ambedkar was revived as the unquestioned leader of the Dalits by a section of the Hindus themselves. With the rise of V P Singh as Prime Minister, Ambedkar became really resurrected through the official celebration of the Centenary of Dr. Ambedkar. As already pointed out, VP Singh government conferred the title of Bharat Ratna on Dr. Ambedkar posthumously and made the latter confirmed as Babasaheb. Many other things had followed creating a halo around Dr. Ambedkar.

Hindu Political Party Wanted Foothold

V P Singh government had in a way tried to make the Hindu fundamentalists irrelevant in Indian politics. They were kept at the bay for quite some time. The fundamentalists in Indian politics have been changing the names of their party like chameleon in a bid for survival. They came to the firm conclusion that so long as Dr. Ambedkar continued to be a hero of the Dalits and to be recognised to be so by their political opponents, their own existence would remain in danger. Their fears came true, when the Dalits started clamouring for the highest office of the President of India in 1997 and when K R Narayanan, elected as the President of India, became a compromise candidate for the office of the Vice President of India. They feared that unless Dr. Ambedkar was demolished as a national leader and as the dignified symbol of Dalit identity, it was impossible for them to re-emerge as a party, and a possible contender for power.

It appears that all other political parties had decided to stall the rise of BSP in importance, which started gathering the support of Other Backward Classes, and the Minorities. All such parties had realised that the BSP and its followers had started using Dr. Ambedkar and his philosophy, which is now referred to Ambedkarism, as the ultimate source of inspiration. The significant factor behind that had been that Dr. Ambedkar had been the first person after the Buddha who had challenged the so-called Hinduism, (which has started taking shelter behind Vedic religion, discarded by the Hindus themselves centuries ago) through thread bare analysis of its scriptures.

The spectacular return of Ms. Mayawati of BSP and the fact of her becoming the Chief Minister of U.P., tor the fourth time, with the active help of Brahmanas, Kshatriyas and Vaisyas, is a sure indication of the fact that at political level, Hinduism stands already finished. What remains to be seen is whether its end is to be experienced on the religious level also, and if so, when? Ms. Mayawati has declared (or prophesied ?) that she would turn a Buddhist on the day she becomes the Prime Minister of India. If that happens, the history of total annihilation of modern Vedic religion or Hinduism, by the neo-Buddhism or Ambedkarism will be repeated in the 2600th year of rise of original Buddhism. Again, if so, Dr. B R Ambedkar would automatically get confirmed as the Man of the Millennium for Social Justice, and get established as the only and real Bharat Ratna.

32

Dr. B R Ambedkar : Man of Millennium for Social Justice

We know that the Poona Pact of 1932 is the very basis of emancipation of Dalits in India.We also know that the parties to the said pact were Madan Mohan Malviya on behalf of the Hindus and Dr. Ambedkar on behalf of the then Untouchables or modern Dalits. The question about the Pact had arisen out of Communal Award announced by the then British Government. Mahatma Gandhi had put himself on probation for doing some thing for the uplift of the Dalits in 1934 in pursuance of the Poona Pact. Subsequently, Dr. Ambedkar alone had been finding fault with the progress of the success of Gandhi's programmes aimed at uplift of the Dalits. Then, the Dalits themselves voluntarily accepted Dr. Ambedkar as their Messiah. In the face of all this, it was entirely unnecessary to raise the question mark on Dr. Ambedkar being the unquestioned leader of the Dalits

Shourie has found fault with the fact of Dr. Ambedkar's being the undisputed leader of Dalits, who are tauntingly referred to by Shourie as his followers in the following words:

> *Two other points should be borne in mind. It is glibly assumed that the Babasaheb was the sole and undisputed leader of the Dalits. As a matter of fact his influence was confined to Mahars of Maharashtra. His Scheduled Caste Federation counted for very little. It failed to make a dent on the electorate and he himself had to be elected to the Constituent Assembly from*

Bengal with the support of the Muslim League, Europeans and Anglo-Indians. And when that constituency was abolished, it was the Congress Party and the influence of men like Babu Rajendra Prasad and Sardar Patel which helped him to be re-elected as a member of the Indian Constituent Assembly.

Mr. 'S' commits a grave mistake here also. The mere fact of Dr. Ambedkar having been placed at a very high pedestal by the history, which has caused the pangs of jealousy to the self-proclaimed "objective writer", Mr. 'S', provides certain answer to the charge that Dr. Ambedkar was not the undisputed leader of the Dalits. If not Dr. Ambedkar, who else was there to claim their leadership?

Ambedkar as Sukracharya of Non-Brahmanas

The fight between Brahmanas and non-Brahmanas, or between Suras and Asuras or between gods and demons, is perennial. There is no end to war between them. It has to continue eternally. Gods, according to Manu-Smriti, are comparable to the Brahmanas, who have become immortal by snatching the *amrita* [ambrosia] or political power, from the Asuras, the non-Gods, or non-Brahmanas. Mythological Sukracharya, the preceptor of the Asuras, the Non-Gods or the Non-Brahmanas, restores the dead Non-Brahmanas or non-Gods to life.

In independent India, Loknayak Jai Prakash Narayan rose to be one of the modern Sukracharyas, who brought the non-Gods or non-Brahmans to life by being responsible for giving political supremacy to Kshatriya castes over the Brahmanas. Earlier Dr. Ambedkar had risen to the level of Sukracharya. He had brought the dead Dalits, the dead Sudras and the dead women to life. Whenever the dead people come to life, they snatch the heaven from the so-called living people, the gods, the Suras or the Brahmanas, as per the brahmanical philosophy. Once the power slips out of their hands, the gods go to Brahma for help. From there, they go to Vishnu along with Brahma with a petition that their lost heaven may be restored to them. Consequently, Vishnu advises them to befriend (dishonestly?) their Asura masters, and produce *amrita* after churning the ocean.

The ocean can be churned always with the help of the Asuras or the lay masses. When *amrita* is produced, Vishnu dishonestly engages the Asuras in merry-making, so that the Suras (gods) consume the amrita. But invariably there is always an Asura, who is able to sneak into the queue of the gods and become immortal. He is ultimately noticed and cut into two. Since he had become immortal, both the pieces remain alive. The original demon is Rahu and the other is Ketu. He alone is enough to occasionally frighten the gods. And all the gods cannot do just anything to him. This process has been going on and it will continue to go on like this.

Ambedkar Not Proved as Gandhi-Hater

Mr. 'S' himself is not aware of the fallacy of his own argument that Dr. Ambedkar deserves to be condemned by anyone on account of his being the Gandhi-hater. He has mentioned that Babu Rajendra Prasad and Sardar Patel had helped Dr. Ambedkar in election. Incidentally, both of them are known to be among the best Gandhians and the best of the Congressmen. And, if they had helped Dr. Ambedkar, surely, they must not have regarded Dr. Ambedkar as being the Gandhi-hater, or even as being someone, who had been a tool in the hands of the British rulers to stall the fight for freedom of the country. If Mr. 'S' has decided to paint Dr. Ambedkar in poor light, he is trying to be more interested in Mahatma Gandhi than the Mahatma himself was interested in himself. Mr. 'S' perhaps tries to excel the Mahatma's devotees like Babu Rajendra Prasad, the first President of Independent India, and Sardar Patel, the first home minister of Independent India, in the matter of loyalty to the Mahatma.

Inviting Attention to Sad Plight of Dalits: No Fault of Dr. Ambedkar

Dr. Ambedkar was the most important individual among the Dalits, who was able to draw the specific attention of the parties to the negotiations, to the unenviable plight of the Dalits and to the moral obligation of all concerned. Main parties concerned in this behalf were both, the rulers and those who were aspiring to succeed such rulers. Ambedkar's appeal was so direct that it touched the hearts of all concerned, excepting of course the hearts of Hindu fundamnetalists and their freinds.

The British had been ruling the country, by virtue of their being in conspicuous racial minority, through a more 'humane' policy, of course, without impairing in any way their empirical objectives. They were exploiting this human concern at a time when they were faced with a situation of being in threat of ouster from the country. Their distracters were also using the human arguments against the British, which were, in turn, aimed at perpetrating their regime in India. Both the parties, ostensibly set against each other, had to try to outwit each other at least for the consumption of their respective camps. In such a situation, the voice of Dr. Ambedkar had to be heard by all concerned with due sense of concern and sympathy and also some sense of helplessness.

Question of Providing Special Safeguards

Special safeguards for the religious minorities had already been on the agenda of the British and the Congress Party for decades. The British had been ruling, by giving unequal weightage to some of the minority communities, in the matter of recruitment to government services and in that of providing share to different communities in legislatures and municipal bodies. Dr. Ambedkar was able to successfully raise the question of share of governance for the Dalits, who were being called as Untouchables but who were being referred to as Depressed Classes in official records.

Ambedkar's Conscious Stand of Not Siding with Gandhi

Apparently Dr. Ambedkar had good reasons for taking a conscious stand of opposing the Mahatma. Dr. Ambedkar had never been against the fight for freedom but he was aspiring for the proper freedom for all sections of population, particularly for such sections of population, which had been the subjected to an organised exploitation of every kind. Dr. Ambedkar had differed with Gandhi over the manner of fighting for freedom and with that of the objectives of the intended freedom. He had been regularly articulating his ideas from the platform and through his writings, which had always been in the notice of all concerned. His ideas now stand incorporated, inter alia, in his Writings and Speeches, which have been published by Maharashtra Government, which are being sold on subsidised rates and are by now available in quite a few government and public libraries.

Dr. Ambedkar's Right to Differ

Dr. Ambedkar had been articulating his stand and his philosophy, throughout his life. As such, one does not have taken the help of imagination in order to understand his mind. He had duly explained every intention of his, which has been in print for decades. Why he had not sided with the Congress or why he had been criticising Mahatma Gandhi, in the matter of the latter's fight for freedom or in that of the latter's concern for the Untouchables, had been duly explained by Dr. Ambedkar, in the relevant contexts.

Every one has a right to differ with anyone else's opinions or views. Mr 'S' can also be said to have a right to criticise Dr. Ambedkar or for that matter any other individual. But the criticism must be balanced and free from personal or group prejudices. It is here that Mr. 'S' has failed, and failed miserably.

Arun Shourie has laboured hard to unsuccessfully prove that Dr. Ambedkar had been hankering after the offices and posts. He needs to be informed about the sacrifice of the office of Law Minister by Dr. Ambedkar when the latter found that it was no more possible for him to play the role of being the real emancipator of all the exploited sections of Hindu population, including the women, and thereby to reform the Indian society by reforming the Hinduism. Murthi points out:

> *After serving for a short term as Law Minister, Dr. Ambedkar quit. His differences with the Congress centred on the Hindu Code Bill. Pandit Nehru, who initially supported the case, had to bow to the militant section of the Party. It left Dr. Ambedkar bitter. He lashed out at the regime, became an important Opposition leader. The nation benefited by his logic, by his refusal to compromise his principles to serve his personal cause."*

He [Dr. Ambedkar] was a rebel with immense funds of logic. Dr. Ambedkar once noted, 'the world owes much to rebels who would dare to argue in the face of the pontiff and insist that he is not infallible', He lived up to his definition of a rebel.

Mahatma Gandhi was great admirer of the ancient Indian village republics. But "Ambedkar was sceptical, rather contemptuous of the much-eulogised village republics of India. In a modern democracy, moreover, the individual is considered everywhere as the primary unit. Looking at the corrupt and inefficient functioning of the various village panchayats in India, it is to see the foresight of our Constitution-makers in accepting the human individual as the primary unit."

Shourie Knows Little, So He Knows Accurately

Arun Shourie seems to be very emphatic in the matter of condemnation of Dr. Ambedkar. Perhaps he needs to be reminded of the words of Goethe that we know accurately when we know little. We wish Arun Shourie had known enough to be able to appreciate the real worth of Dr. Ambedkar and the weakness of character of those by measuring with whose yardstick Dr. Ambedkar has been shown to be a pigmy.

G S Thind on P. 275 of his book titled *Our Indian Sub-continent Heritage*; Crosstown Press Ltd., 6992 Russel Avenue, Burnaby, BC, Canada – V5J 4R9; 2000 says the following about the loyalties of Dr. Ambedkar:

"But I will also leave no doubt in the minds of the people of this country that I have another loyalty to which I am bound and which I can never forsake. That loyalty is the community of Untouchable, in which I am born, to which I belong and which I hope I shall never desert. And I say this to the House as strongly as I possibly can, that whenever there is any conflict of interests between the country and the Untouchables, so far as I am concerned, the Untouchables' interests will take precedence over the interests of the country. I am not going to support a tyrannizing majority simply because it happens to speak in the name of the country. I am not going to support a party because it happens to speak in the name of the country. I shall not do that. Let everybody here and everywhere understand that —-"That Is My Position". As between the country and myself, the country will have precedence, as between the country and the Depressed Classes, the Depressed Classes will have precedence———the country will have no precedence. That is all that I wanted to say with regard to these two amendments of mine.

Religion is for Man, not Man for Religion

G S Thind also reproduces the views of Dr. Ambedkar on religion in the following words:

- I tell you, religion is for man and not man of religion. If you want to organize, consolidate and be successful in this world, change this religion;
- The religion that does not recognize you as human beings, or give you water to drink, or allow you to enter the temple is not worthy to be called a religion;
- The religion that forbids you to receive education and comes in the way of your material advancement is not worthy of the appellation 'religion';
- The religion that does not teach its followers to show humility in dealing with its co-religionists nothing but a display of force;
- The religion that asks its adherents to suffer the touch of animals but not the touch of human beings some classes from education, forbids them to accumulate wealth and to bear arms, is not religion but a mockery; and
- The religion that compels the ignorant to be ignorant and the poor, is not religion but a visitation!

Only Subhas and Ambedkar Engaged in Freedom Struggle

As per the assessment of G S Thind, Dr. Ambedkar was the only one of the two persons engaged in the freedom struggle. The other being Netaji Subhash Chandra Bose, who refused to be brow beaten by a Mahatma, or a Dictator of a mighty political party or by a Prime Minister of the state. He goes on to say that Ambedkar was the only minister of Jawaharlal Nehru, who never compromised his principles and his position for material gains or selfish motives.

Who was respecting invited by the rulling party to shape the future of the national, more or less in his own discretion.

He was the only ohe who did not develop issustible love for a chair or a high political office, or who did not be tray his own bithran for the sake of selfish ends or material gains.

He was the only scholar of Hindu religion, who acquired the mastery over the scriptures, inspite of heavy odds and institutional disabilities and shcdfully challenged the best of its adherments followings and leaders miclding Mahatma Gandhi on the question of its in trmistic wealth.

Only Ambedkar Provides Insight Into Gandhi

But for Ambedkar's thought and action the world at large would have failed to gauge reality about the fight for India's freedom and good peep into the mind of Gandhi as a saint. It is only Ambedkar's sharp intelllect that has provided us an insight into Gandhi. The conflictimg characters of theirs have been acting as scales to measure the truth about correct relation of things in the context of the Mahabharata between conflicting philosophies, which continued to confuse the Indian political scene from the day Gandhi emerged therein through his *Indian Home Rule* published in 1908, while in South Africa, butwhose author, Gandhi came back to India only in 1915, only to receive the *Kaiser-I Hind Gold Medal* from the then Viceroy of India, in exchange for the most outstandig services to the then British Empire. This gesture of the British Empire had become instrumental in the matter of making Gandhi shoot into international prominence since the limits of the Empire did not allow even the Sun-god to take rest by setting for a while.

There is book titled *Verdict on India* (New York: Harcourt, Brace and Company, 1944) by Beverley Nichols, a famous novelist, musician, playwright, essayist, reporter, and a journalist visited British India. According to a website, during his visit to British India, he met Dr.

Ambedkar, who told him: "Gandhi is the greatest enemy the untouchables have ever had in India." So what did Ambedkar mean? Mr. Nichols explained it as follows:

> "We can best explain it by a parallel. Take Ambedkar's remark, and for the word "untouchable" substitute the word "peace." Now imagine that a great champion of peace, like Lord Cecil, said of Gandhi. "Gandhi is the greatest enemy of peace the world has ever had." What would he mean, using these words of the most spectacular pacifist of modern times? He would mean that passive resistance—which is Gandhi's form of pacifism—could only lead to chaos and the eventual triumph of brute force; that to lie down and let people trample on you (which was Gandhi's recipe for dealing with the Japanese) is a temptation to the aggressor rather than an example to the aggressed; and that **in order to have peace you must organise, you must be strong, and that you must be prepared to use force.** Mutatis mutandis, that is precisely what Ambedkar meant about the untouchables. He wanted them to be recognised and he wanted them to be strong.

He rightly considered that the best way of gaining his object was by granting them separate electorates; a solid block of 60 million would be in a position to dictate terms to its oppressors. Gandhi fiercely opposed this scheme. "Give the untouchables separate electorates," he cried, "and you only perpetuate their status for all time." It was a queer argument, and those who were not bemused by the Mahatma's charm considered it a phoney one. They suspected that Gandhi was a little afraid that 60 million untouchables might join up with the 100 s million Muslims— (as they nearly did)—and challenge the dictatorship of the 180 million orthodox Hindus.

Part X

Conclusion

Bibliography

Index

Conclusion

Among some non-Dalits, Ambedkar is an object of great resentment, chiefly for his alleged decision to carve out a political career independent of and sometimes in opposition to Gandhi's Congress. That is of course the burden of Shourie's critique but curiously, Guha stands up in defence of Ambedkar in an unprecedented manner:

> *I think, however, that for Ambedkar to stand up to the uncrowned king and anointed Mahatma of the Indian people required extraordinary courage and will-power. Gandhi thought so too. Speaking at a meeting in Oxford in October 1931, Gandhi said he had "the highest regard for Dr. Ambedkar. He has every right to be bitter. That he does not break our heads is an act of self- restraint on his part."*

Guha further refers to another occasion when Gandhi observed while writing to an English friend two years later and said that he found "nothing unnatural" in Ambedkar's hostility to the Congress and its supporters. At that time, Gandhi justified the agony of Ambedkar in the following words:

> *"He has not only witnessed the inhuman wrongs done to the social pariahs of Hinduism, but in spite of all his culture, all the honours that he has received, he has, when he is in India, still to suffer many insults to which untouchables are exposed."*

Guha goes on to disclose that in June 1936 Gandhi pointed out once again that Dr. Ambedkar "has had to suffer humiliations and insults which should make any one of us bitter and resentful." "Had I been in his place," he remarked, "I would have been as angry." But one may ask whether Gandhi had felt any anger against the British, who had thrown him out of the railway train in South Africa.

Guha discloses that the Mahatma had no suspicions about Ambedkar's patriotism and probity, since he told a bunch of Karachi students in June 1934 as under;

> *The magnitude of (Dr. Ambedkar's) sacrifice is great. He is absorbed in his own work. He leads a simple life. He is capable of earning one to two thousand rupees a month. He is also in a position to settle down in Europe if he so desires. But he does not want to stay there. He is only concerned about the welfare of the Harijians.*

To Gandhi, Ambedkar's protest held out a lesson to the upper castes. This is proved by his observations made in March 1936 on the question of possibility of Ambedkar's and his followers were embracing another religion. His observation was as under:

> *"We deserve such treatment and our task (now) is to wake up to the situation and purify ourselves."*

This warning of Gandhi went unheeded so that towards the end of his life Gandhi spoke with some bitterness about the indifference to Harijan work among his fellow Hindus:

> *"The tragedy is that those who should have especially devoted themselves to the work of (caste) reform did not put their hearts into it. What wonder that Harijan brethren feel suspicious, and show opposition and bitterness."*

For the facility of researchers, he maintains that the words quoted in the preceding paragraphs have been taken from that reliable and easily accessible source: the Collected Works of Mahatma Gandhi. While referring to Arun Shourie's book of vilification against Ambedkar, he laments that perhaps the most perverse aspect of an altogether perverse book is that Shourie does not once tell us what Gandhi said or wrote about his great adversary. Had Shourie done so, the need for writing the said book of vilification would have entirely vanished or at least boomeranged. Guha's indictment of Shourie becomes almost complete with the following observations of his:

> *One of the few Gandhians who understood the cogency of the Dalit critique of the Congress was C. Rajagopalachari. In the second half of 1932, Rajaji became involved in the campaign to allow the so-called untouchables to enter the Guruvayoor temple in Kerala. The campaign was led by that doughty fighter for the rights of the dispossessed, K. Kelappan Nair. In a speech at Guruvayoor on December 20, 1932, Rajaji told the high castes that it would certainly help us in the fight for Swaraj if we open the*

doors of the temple (to Harijans). One of the many causes that keeps Swaraj away from us is that we are divided among ourselves. Mahatmaji received many wounds in London (during the Second Round Table Conference of 1931). But Dr. Ambedkar's darts were the worst. Mahatmaji did not quake before the Churchills of England. But as representing the nation he had to plead guilty to Dr. Ambedkar's charges.

As it was, the managers of temples across the land could count upon the support of many among their clientele, the *suvarna* Hindus who agreed with the Shankaracharyas that the Gandhians were dangerous revolutionaries who had to be kept out at the gate, maintains Guha.Further, he makes an interesting and yet a correct disclosure that unhappily, while upper-caste Hindus thought that Gandhi moved too fast, Dalits today feel he was much too slow. He went on to stress:

... the Dalit politician Mayawati has, more than once, spoken of the Mahatma as a shallow paternalist who sought only to smooth the path for more effective long-term domination by the suvarna. Likewise, in his book Why I am Not a Hindu Kancha Illiah writes of Gandhi as wanting to "build a modern consent system for the continued maintenance of brahminical hegemony" - a judgment as unfair as Shourie's on Ambedkar.

Guha is of the opinion that whereas in their lifetime Gandhi and Ambedkar were political rivals, now, decades after their death, it should be possible to see their contributions as complementing one another's. He quotes the Kannada critic D. R. Nagaraj who once noted that in the narratives of Indian nationalism the "heroic stature of the caste-Hindu reformer", Gandhi, "further dwarfed the Harijan personality" of Ambedkar. Nagaraj maintains:

In the Ramayana, there is only one hero but, as Nagaraj points out, Ambedkar was too proud, intelligent and self-respecting a man to settle for the role of Hanuman or Sugreeva. By the same token, Dalit hagiographers and pamphleteers generally seek to elevate Ambedkar by diminishing Gandhi. For the scriptwriter and the mythmaker there can only be one hero. But the historian is bound by no such constraint. The history of Dalit emancipation is unfinished, and for the most part unwritten. It should, and will, find space for many heroes. Ambedkar and Gandhi will do nicely for a start.

The entire discussion in all the parts of the book in hand, read in the background of the disclosures made in this chapter must lead to the irresistible conclusion that for the advent of Ambedkar on the political, social, religious, sociological and economic field in India, the freedom would have continued to mean only that of the upper castes and that the weaker sections or the masses, comprising the Sudras and Ati-Sudras, constituting about 90 per cent of Hindu population would have continued to suffer all kinds of indignities including the social injustice.

In this sense, Ambedkar is definitely proved to be India's Man of Millennium, not only for the millennium ending the year 2000, but also for all the past millennia, since the revolution he was able to usher in has been unprecedented not only in the entire recorded history of India, but also in prehistory, in so far as it can be deduced from the Hindu religious literature, philosophy and mythology, all taken together.

Reappraisal of Dr. Ambedkar

In fact the efforts to slur Dr. Ambedkar had started immediately after the Mandal-Mandir controversy which began with the ordering of reservations for the OBCs, by V P Singh Government at the Centre. The Babri Masjid demolition was itself an action taken as a preparation in that direction. The trend to slur Dr. Ambedkar had been taken note of by V R Krishna Iyer, in an article appearing in the Hindustan Times dated 22 February 1995, under the title Why Slur Ambedkar. He wrote in connection with the publication of 20 Volumes biography of Babu Rajendra Prasad, the first Rashtrapati of India. In the said Biography the editor of the Biography, who had also been the private secretary of Dr. Rajendra Prasad, namely, Valmiki Choudhary, had tried to denigrate Dr. Ambedkar. In that connection V R Krishna Iyer had began his article as follows:

> Dr. Ambedkar whom the country remembers as the foremost architect of the Constitution of India, has been slighted and disparaged without foundation or provocation by Valmiky Choudhary who has produced a comprehensive work of 20 volumes on Dr. Rajendra Prasad's correspondence and Selected Documents but added barbed words against Ambedkar. Undoubtedly the volumes are a tribute to Rajen Babu, as great patriot, but there was no need whatever for Choudhary to try to enhance the value of his work by denigrating Dr. Ambedkar not unwittingly but deliberately. Small minds and great works sometimes mismatch.

Strangely, Hinduism has never produced a man like Ambedkar. He took birth in a family of untouchables, for whom all doors of education, riches and power were closed, yet he rose to be one who came not only to possess all the things denied to him by tradition, in good measure. He also developed an intellect the like of which is not to be found elsewhere, even in the best of the topmost upper caste intellectuals. In spite of becoming better qualified than the best of the upper caste men, he could not study Sanskrit as a subject in a college or a university.

Ambedkar was born with series of serious disabilities, and his inability to study Sanskrit was no less serious a disability. Still, he was able to study all the scriptures of Hinduism with such thoroughness that he came to have a confidence to analyse all of them threadbare and present the result of his analysis in the form of mind-boggling books, none of which has been challenged so far by any of the scholars of Hindu religion, philosophy and culture. As such, Dr. B R Ambedkar literally stands on the highest pedestal, symbolized by his statues depicting him standing high holding in one hand a copy the book of liberation of masses, the Constitution of India, and pointing the finger of the other hand towards the sky, telling the humanity that only sky is the limit for putting its dreams into reality.

Bibliography

Ambedkar, Dr. B.R., 1945. Mr.Gandhi and the emancipation of the untouchables, Thacker Co., Bombay; (Dr Babasaheb Ambedkar Writings and Speeches, Volume 9, Education Department, Government of Maharashtra, Bombay.

Ambedkar, Dr. B.R., 1989, Dr. BabasahebAmbedkar Writings and Speeches, Vol.5, Education Department, Government of Maharashtra, Bombay.

Ambedkar, Dr. Br, 1989, *Dr. Babasaheb Ambedkar Writings and Speeches;* Education Department, Government of Maharashtra, Bombay, Volumes 5 and 9.

Arun Shourie; *Worshipping False Gods, Ambedkar and the facts which have been erased;* SAS Publications, Noida, 1997.

B. L. Basham (The Wonder That was India; Fontana-Books is association with Rupa & Company, India 1947.

B.N. Luniya: *Evolution of Indian Culture*; Lakshmi Narain Agrawal; Education Publishers, Agra-3, 1970.

B.G. Tilak; *Vedic Chronology and Vedanga Jyotisha*; Messers Tilak Bros; Gaikwar-Wada, Poona City, 1925.

Chandrakant Gajanan Raje; *Biography And History In Sanskrit Literature*; University of Bombay, Fort, Bombay, 1958.

Das, N.G., 1988, *Was Gandhi A Mahatma?* Dipali Book House, Calcutta.

Dharmalingam, Prof. A.M., 1985; *Dr. Ambedkar and Secularism*, Dalit Sahitya Akademy, Bangalore.

Dev Raj Chanana; Slavery In Ancient India; People's Publishing Huse Pvt. Ltd; Rani Jhansi Road, New Delhi, 1960.

Edwards, Michael, 1986; *The Myth of The Mahatma*; Constable And Company Limited, London.

F.E. Pargiter; *Ancient Indian Historical Tradition*; Moti Lal Banarsi Das, Delhi, 1962.

Gandhi, M.K., 1954; *Untouchability,* Navajivan Press, Ahmedabad, Edited By Bharatan Kumarappa.

Gopal. S: *The Viceroyalty of Lord Irwin;* London, 1953.

Grenier, Richard, 1983; *The Gandhi Nobody Knows,* Commentary.

Huq, F., 1990; *Gandhi - Saint Or Sinner?* Dalit Sahitya Akademy, Bangalore.

Iyengar, A.S.: *All Through The Gandhian Era;* Bombay, 1950.

Keer, Dhananjay, 1971; *Dr. Ambedkar: Life and Mission,* Popular Prakashan, Bombay, Third Edition.

Kuber, W.N., 1979; *Ambedkar, A Critical Study,* People's Publishing House, New Delhi.

Lobo, C.H.J., 1984; *Dr. Br Ambedkar, The Champion of Social Democracy in India*; Hilerina Publications, Bangalore.

Masani, RP: *Dadabhai Naoroji;* London, 1939.

Mayo, Katherine, 1927; *Mother India,* Greenwood Press Publishers, New York.

Mayo, Katherine, 1929; *Slaves of The Gods,* Harcourt, Brace and Company, New York.

Nanda, BR: *Mahatma Gandhi*; London, 1958.

Natarajan, S.: *A Century of Social Reforms in India;* Bombay, 1959.

Nichols, Beverley, 1944, Verdict on India, Harcourt, Brace and Company, New York.

Payne, Robert. 1969; *The Life and Death of Mahatma Gandhi*, Konecky & Konecky, New York.

Rajshekar, V.T; 1985; *A Recipe for Revolution,* Dalit Sahitya Akademy, Bangalore.

Rajshekar, V.T; 1986; *Why Godse Killed Gandhi?*, Dalit Sahitya Akademy, Bangalore.

Rajshekar,V.T; 1988; *Karl Marx And Dr. Babasaheb Ambedkar,* Dalit Sahitya Akademy, Bangalore.

Rajshekar, V. T; 1989; *Mahatma Gandhi and Babasaheb Ambedkar;* Dalit Sahitya Akademy, Bangalore.

Rajshekar,V.T; 1985, A Recipe for Revolution, Dalit Sahitya Akademy, Bangalore.

Rajshekar, V.T; 1986, Why Godse Killed Gandhi?, Dalit Sahitya Akademy, Bangalore.

Rajshekar,V.T; 1988, Karl Marx and Dr.Babasaheb Ambedkar, Dalit Sahitya Akademy, Bangalore.

Rajshekar, V. T; 1989, Mahatma Gandhi and Babasaheb Ambedkar, Dalit Sahitya Akademy, Bangalore.

Sunder, Shyam, 1987; *They Burn,* Dalit Sahitya Akademy; Bangalore.

Sitaramayya, P; *History of the Indian National Congress;* Vol. I, Bombay, 1946.

S L Dhani; *1984; Politics of Gods: Churning of the Ocean;* D D Books, Panchkula, Haryana (India).

S L Dhani; *1987; Hindu Scheme of Things: Socio-Political Analysis of Manu-Smriti;* D D Books, Panchkula, Haryana (India).

S L Dhani; 1987; Philosophy of Administration: Mythological Interpretation; D D Books, Panchkula, Haryana (India).

S L Dhani; *1992; Dharma aur Rajniti ko Dalit Chunauti* (Dalit Challenge to Religion and Politics) (Hindi); D D Books, Panchkula, Haryana (India).

S L Dhani; *1990; Bhagwan Siva: Daliton ke Mitra athvaa Satru* (Lord Siva: Friend or Foe of Dalits?) (Hindi); D D Books, Panchkula, Haryana (India).

S L Dhani; *Worshipping False Gods: Arun Shourie Exposed on Facts and Sense of Objectivity*; *Web site* www.sldhani.com on the Internet, Operative from mid-2001).

S L Dhani, Indian Freedom Struggle : Now Insight, 2003, Tipome Offset Press, Okhla Industrial Estate, New Nelhi.

Sunder, Shyam, 1987, They Burn, Dalit Sahitya Akademy, Bangalore.

Thangaraj, P., 1977; *Selected Thoughts of Dr. Ambedkar*, Puratchikkanal Publication, Madras.

Zakaria, Rafiq (Ed.) *A Study of Nehru;* Bombay, 1960.

Sources of Indian Tradition; Published By Sundar Lal Jain, Moti Lal Banarsidass, Bungalow Road, Jawahar Nagar Delhi-6; 1963; Compiled by Win. Theodore de Bary, Stephen Hay, Royal Weiter, Andrew Yarrow etc.

Index